THE WINGED GOSPEL

THE
WINGED GOSPEL

America's Romance with Aviation, 1900-1950

Joseph J. Corn

New York
OXFORD UNIVERSITY PRESS
1983

Library of Congress Cataloging in Publication Data

Corn, Joseph J.
The winged gospel.

Includes index.
1. Aeronautics—Social aspects—United States—
History.   I. Title.
TL521.C643   1983   629.13'0973   83-11418
ISBN 0-19-503356-6

Two chapters of this book in a somewhat different form
have been published previously: "Making Flying 'Thinkable': Women Pilots and the Selling of Aviation, 1927-
1940," *American Quarterly*, XXXI, No. 4 (Fall 1979),
556-71; and "An Airplane in Every Garage—The Rise and
Fall of a Most American Dream," *American Heritage*, 32,
no. 5 (Aug/Sept. 1981), 48-55.

Printing (last digit):   9 8 7 6 5 4 3 2 1

Printed in the United States of America

In memory of my mother and my father

Preface

This is the history of a love affair. It documents the extraordinary affection millions of American men, women, and children felt for the flying machine during the half century after its invention in 1903. During this period Americans were, to use a contemporary expression, "airminded." They avidly followed and promoted aeronautics. The mere sound of an engine overhead caused them to pause in their work and raise their eyes to the heavens. Crowds assembled at the smallest airfield to watch planes take off and land, while the public voraciously consumed the many stories about aviation in newspapers and magazines. It was an era when pilots were popular heroes. So central was the airplane in the American imagination, in fact, that many people expected that they would soon take to the sky, flying their own family plane or helicopter. But more than anything, the airplane symbolized the promise of the future. Americans in this period viewed mechanical flight as portending a wondrous era of peace and harmony, of culture and prosperity. This was the promise of the "winged gospel."

Although there has been a great deal of attention paid to the history of the airplane, most writers have been interested in the technical, military and, to a lesser degree, the commercial aspects of aeronautics. The largest portion of this literature has been written by aviation buffs, who have given us detailed accounts of particular types of aircraft, such as the seaplane or airliner, and complete histories of specific planes, like the Ford trimotor, the Monocoupe, or the B-17. I have used a number of these studies, and they are invaluable. Yet not surprisingly their authors, writing from within the tradition of aviation enthusiasm, have not documented or analyzed the feelings, attitudes, and behavior which characterize the phenomenon. Nor have any academic historians of aeronautics explored this dimension of the airplane's impact on our culture. Indeed, to the detriment of our understanding of the relationship of technology to society, scholars have largely ignored the emotional aspects of our historical response to machines like the airplane. Yet as Eugene S. Ferguson, one of the founders of the history of technology, warned in 1974, "if we fail to note the importance of [the] enthusiasm that is evoked by technology, we will have missed a central motivating influence in technological development."* *The Winged Gospel* represents my effort to illuminate one such instance of technological enthusiasm in American history.

My book's title comes from a phrase used by airminded individuals in the twenties. Long before the airplane was even a dream, human beings had associated flying with spiritual matters. This was particularly true of Christianity, where angels flew and the heavens constituted the divine sanctuary of God. As Americans searched for language appropriate to the excitement they felt for the airplane, they inevitably borrowed from this Christian tradition. They often spoke of themselves as "disciples," "apostles," and "prophets," and thought of aviation as a "winged gospel" or "holy cause," one that would literally transform the conditions of life. Their rhetoric suggests that aviation enthusiasm was a kind of secular religion, an interpretation I have developed in the pages that follow. In examining this airplane-based faith, I delineate the messianic expectations aviation enthusiasts held for flying; treat the various activities through which the faithful worshipped the flying machine and sought to promote the aeronautical cause; and evaluate the consequences of their thought and action, both for the development of aeronautics and for American culture generally. The winged gospel, we discover, not only reflected attitudes and habits deeply rooted in the American past but also influenced the course of history.

My study has benefited from the work of a number of scholars who have studied the historical relationship between technology and society. From writings by Leo Marx, Daniel J. Boorstin, and John Kasson, I have gained a fuller understanding of the attitudes and values which Americans historically have displayed toward the machine and of the symbolic force that technology has had on the

* Eugene S. Ferguson, "Toward a Discipline of the History of Technology," *Technology and Culture*, 15 (Jan. 1974), 21.

popular imagination. These scholars have provided me with suggestive leads for thinking about the winged gospel in American life and thought. From books and articles by Elting E. Morison, Merritt Roe Smith, and Thomas P. Hughes, I have been sensitized to how the ideas, values, and behavioral styles of different groups can influence technological change. The studies by these scholars of steel makers, armorers, and entrepreneurs in the early electric power industry showed me ways of thinking about how my aviation enthusiasts might have influenced aeronautical development. All of these historians have been pioneers in the creation of a social history of technology, and for their leadership and inspiration, I am indeed grateful.

In research and writing, I accumulated a number of specific debts which it is a pleasure to acknowledge. I am particularly appreciative of support from the University of California, Berkeley, which provided me with the time and funds while a doctoral student to research and write the dissertation on which this book is based; the Smithsonian Institution, which sponsored my research at the National Air and Space Museum as a Smithsonian Postdoctoral Fellow and as a Daniel and Francis Guggenheim Fellow; and Stanford University, which subsidized the final typing of the manuscript. In my research I have been helped greatly by the staffs of numerous libraries and archives, including the Manuscript Division of the Library of Congress, the New York Public Library, the Oral History Archives of Columbia University, the Henry Ford Archives, and the libraries of Stanford University, Yale University, the University of Wyoming, and the University of California at Berkeley and at Los Angeles. I especially want to thank the staff of the National Air and Space Museum library, where Dominic Pisano, now the museum's Department of Aeronautics, and Pete Suthard and Phil Edwards greatly facilitated my access to materials. Other NASM and Smithsonian personnel who provided me with information, sharpened my understanding of aeronautics, or helpfully criticized my manuscript include Paul A. Hanle, Robert C. Mikesh, Arthur P. Mollela, Claudia M. Oakes, Frank H. Winter, and Howard S. Wolko. My official mentors while at the National Air and Space Museum were Richard P. Hallion, now Center Historian at Edwards Air Force Base, and Tom D. Crouch; for their continuing support and assistance, I am very grateful.

A number of other friends, teachers, and scholars have also earned my thanks. While at the University of California, Berkeley,

I benefited greatly from the advice and thoughtful criticisms of Professor Richard M. Abrams and Professor Gunther Barth. In the role of my dissertation advisor, Professor Barth exercised a Job-like patience and an editorial precision that were truly wonderful. Others who have read and constructively commented upon my work en route to publication include Lonnie Bunch, Susan Ciriclio, Rolf Diamant, Richard Hirsh, Moira Roth, W. J. Rorabaugh, and J. William Youngs; to all of them a hearty thanks. The book is stronger for their help. For his expert and patient work at a new word processor, I owe thanks to Curt Philips, my typist. And finally, I want to acknowledge my co-pilot on this scholarly flight. Although the destination was often unknown and the going rough, Wanda Corn kept faith in my eventual arrival and often relieved me at the controls; that I landed safely is in no small part thanks to her.

Contents

I   "The Moment of Miracle":
Americans Greet the Airplane   3

II   "A New Sign in the Heavens":
The Prophetic Creed of Flight   29

III   "Let Your Airmindedness Be Shown Forth Among Men":
Evangelizing for Aviation   51

IV   Making Flying "Thinkable":
Women Pilots and the Selling of Aviation   71

V   "An Airplane in Every Garage?" The Gospel's Most
Pervasive Promise   91

VI   Adults and the "Winged Superchildren
of Tomorrow"   113

VII   Epilogue   135

Notes   149

Index   171

THE WINGED GOSPEL

I

"The Moment of Miracle": Americans Greet the Airplane

Through the heat and humidity of late summer, 1908, tens of thousands of people converged on Ft. Myer, Virginia, not far from the nation's capital. Arriving by horse and buggy, streetcar, automobile, and on foot, the crowds represented a kind of pilgrimage, responding to most amazing reports. The daily papers were reporting that an inventor named Orville Wright had built a machine that could fly, and that he was demonstrating his Flyer or airship at the U.S. Army base. Many of those who went out to Ft. Myer were probably skeptical, doubting that a machine, carrying a man, could leave the ground unless lifted by gas bags, like an ordinary balloon. Some of the pilgrims believed such a heavier-than-air flying machine an impossibility, a fanciful chimera, the delusion of addled minds. All of them required more than mere words to believe that man could now fly. As one of them told a reporter, "Those Wrights may be doing it, but seeing's believing."[1] If anybody was really flying, he just had to see for himself, and most of his contemporaries felt similarly.

It was true. Beginning on September 3, 1908, and continuing day after day for two weeks, interrupted only by bad weather, Orville Wright was publicly demonstrating the airplane he and his brother Wilbur had invented almost five years earlier. The Army Signal Corps had organized the flight trials to determine whether an airplane could serve military purposes. And along with the military observers many dignitaries, government workers, and curious citizens gathered to witness a device, constructed of wood and metal, leave the ground with a human being at its helm. As the news spread and Orville set one duration record after another, the daily crowds grew, reaching over 5,000 on Labor Day, September 7th. As people watched Orville put the machine through its paces, as they saw him turn and bank in the sky and listened to his clattering engine over their heads, disbelief and shock mingled with excitement and elation. It was hard to believe what they were seeing; it contradicted good sense and all previous experience. The "seeing's believing" man wandered around the parade grounds as if in a daze, stammering over and over again, "My God!" The entire crowd that day uttered "a sound of complete surprise" as the Wright Flyer left the ground, recalled Theodore Roosevelt, Jr., son of the President and one of the many celebrities in attendance. It was a sound he would "never forget."[2]

And so it was at the first demonstration of each airplane. The event was both unexplainable and unbelievable. Unlike most other phenomena encountered in daily life, there seemed to be no words to describe an airplane flight except ones borrowed from the supernatural and mystical realms. Airplane flight was "miraculous," "inhuman," "occult," or most commonly a "miracle."[3] The reaction of a witness in Los Angeles, in January 1910, present at the first air meet ever held on the Pacific coast, was typical: "Thirty thousand eyes are on those rubber-tired wheels," he wrote, describing the airplane poised for takeoff,

> waiting for the miraculous moment—historical for him who has not experienced it. Suddenly something happens to those whirling wheels—they slacken their speed, yet the vehicle advances more rapidly. It is the moment of miracle.[4]

Later that same year, a plane first flew over Chicago, attracting a throng estimated at over a million people. A minister was among the crowd and recorded his impressions of the persons assembled in the streets. "Never," he wrote, "have I seen such a look of wonder in the faces of a multitude. From the gray-haired man to the child, everyone seemed to feel that it was a new day in their lives."[5]

The popular perception that airplanes augured a new day in human affairs, that they were something wondrous and miraculous, erupted first in 1908 in response to the public flight trials held at Ft. Myer by the Army. Yet by then Wilbur and Orville Wright had been flying airplanes for almost five years. As early as 1897, in fact, after reading about the accidental death of German aeronautical pioneer Otto Lilienthal while he had been flying a glider, the Wrights became interested in heavier-than-air flight. They mastered the existing literature on aeronautics and studied the experiments of prior aeronautical investigators like Lilienthal and American engineer Octave Chanute, who in the 1890s also built man-carrying gliders. Those men also had wanted to build a machine that would rise from the ground under its own power, not merely be lifted into the air by gas as a balloon, which had been known since the late eighteenth century. Toward that same end the Wrights worked, systematically studying the problem and then experimenting first with kites, then with small unmanned gliders, and finally in gliders which they flew themselves. This work led them to Kitty Hawk, North Carolina, a coastal site blessed with strong and steady breezes. After acquiring hours of flight experience piloting the gliders, Wilbur and Orville perfected an innovative control system that gave them mastery over their aircraft's attitude in the air. By 1903 they were ready to add an engine and attempt powered flight.

On the morning of December 17, 1903, at Kitty Hawk, they prepared their new powered Flyer for a test. Men from the nearby coastal lifesaving station were summoned as witnesses while Wilbur and Orville completed preparations for the flight, even giving one of the witnesses a camera to record the event for posterity. The machine was a delicate-looking craft dominated by two large wings, one atop the other. Forward of the wings was a smaller horizontal surface, an elevator, which the pilot could move to control ascent and descent. Behind the wings was a rudder with which to turn the aircraft. A home-built gasoline engine, turning two large propellers, provided power. With all in readiness, Orville assumed a face down, prone position on the lower wing of the aircraft and grasped the controls with his hands. The propellers were spun, starting the engine. Orville signaled for release of the machine, which now began to move along a track installed on the soft sand to facilitate takeoff. Slowly at first, and then with gathering speed, the Flyer advanced into a twenty-seven-mile-an-hour headwind, while Wilbur ran alongside steadying the wing. Then, at precisely 10:35 a.m., the machine lifted from the ground under its own power. After centuries of earthbound dreaming, the impossible had happened. Man at last could really fly!

That first flight lasted twelve seconds and covered 120 feet. The brothers made three more flights, the longest covering almost half a mile, before a gust of wind damaged the Flyer and ended their work for the season. Although the day was an historic one, it

afforded little clue to the popular enthusiasm the airplane soon
would generate. Indeed, only one of the witnesses at Kitty Hawk
experienced the kind of emotion that shortly would characterize
the public response to airplanes. Seeing the Flyer rise from the
sand, a husky sort from the lifesaving station later remembered
that he had felt "kind o' meek and prayerful" as the machine rose
into the air.[6] The two inventors themselves displayed no awe or
euphoria and no "Eureka"—like surprise at having unlocked the
secret of flight. They so expected success that they showed little
excitement. "We had faith in our calculations and felt so sure we
were going to fly," Orville later wrote of the day, "that when we
succeeded we were not surprised. In fact I had got more kick out
of flying before I had ever been in the air—while lying in bed
thinking of how exciting it would be."[7] The brothers did, however, realize the historic importance of their achievement and kept
the Kitty Hawk plane intact.

When people heard of the Kitty Hawk flights, most simply rejected the news as but another wildly exaggerated story. Over the
years many mechanics and inventors had made the claim that they
had solved the "riddle" of aerial navigation and knew how to
build a successful flying machine, but all turned out to be cranks.
There was no reason to assume the Wrights were any different,
and indeed U.S. Army officials first treated the Wrights' inquiries
regarding the military's interest in their airplane as crank letters,
assuming the brothers possessed nothing more than an idea. After
all, experts such as Simon Newcomb, a Johns Hopkins University
scientist, had said that flying machines were impossible and had
published articles to that effect. It seemed most unlikely that two
unknown bicycle mechanics could have succeeded in flying when
so many previous aeronautical experimenters, many with greater
resources, had failed. Given the ubiquity of this attitude, the press
understandably ignored the Kitty Hawk story. The Wrights had
notified major newspapers of their first day of flights, but only
one news account appeared at the time. This was in a Norfolk,
Virginia, paper and was itself a piece of crank fantasy. Its author
had not seen the flights but had overheard the Wrights sending a
telegram reporting their success to their father in Dayton, Ohio.
Knowing only that the brothers claimed to have made some kind
of flight, the reporter fabricated the rest of his story from imagination. His account had Wilbur at the controls of the "big box,"
sixty feet off the ground, "first tacking to port, then to starboard,

and then driving straight ahead," as if he were flying a sailboat. The writer imagined Orville on the ground, watching his brother and shouting, "Eureka," like "the alchemist of old," as if the airplane's invention were lucky happenstance.[8]

During the summers of 1904 and 1905, when the Wrights continued their experiments, making numerous flights, many of half an hour and more in duration, the press missed further opportunities to report the story. The brothers made no secret of what they were doing. They flew from Huffman's Prairie, just outside of Dayton, in full view of the interurban line which ran along one edge of the flying field. Some passengers on the trains saw the airplane in the air and excitedly telephoned the local newspaper. Only after many such calls did a reporter come out to take a look. The brothers were not flying that day, however, and after asking a few questions the reporter decided there was no story and left.[9]

The indifference and skepticism greeting the airplane's invention derived in part from the fact that people did not realize what exactly the Wrights had built. They had invented, of course, an airplane, a motor-powered, heavier-than-air flying machine, but many people thought they had flown just another gas-filled "airship." It was the word "airship" that caused confusion in that it referred both to what we call an airplane and to a gas-filled flying machine with engine and propeller which could be steered and maneuvered in the air. This latter type of aircraft, also called a "dirigible," had been invented in the late 1880s and was widely known when the Wrights first flew their airplane at Kitty Hawk. In 1901, for instance, the Brazilian aeronautical pioneer Santos-Dumont flew a lighter-than-air craft over Paris, and photographs of him circling the Eiffel Tower appeared in magazines and papers everywhere. In France as early as 1903, the Lebaudy brothers made a thirty-eight-mile flight in their airship or dirigible. So when the American press finally began to notice the Wrights, on the eve of public trials in 1908, it usually referred to their airplane as an "airship." Late summer headlines that year saying, "Wrights To Test Airship" or "First Description of Wright Airship" understandably created little stir among people to whom "airship" meant "dirigible."[10]

In the final analysis, however, people just had to see an airplane to understand it was different from any airship buoyed aloft by gas. And it was not until Orville Wright flew at Ft. Myer in September 1908 that Americans began to understand that the airplane was something totally new and very special. Unlike the large and cumbersome dirigible, here was a machine that was compact and fully maneuverable. The pilot of an airplane semingly possessed the freedom and control of a bird. At the controls of the new invention he not only rose into the heavens but mastered them, moving at will in three dimensions. At last the earthly shackles that for millennia seemed so restricting had been broken. In an airplane one now could fly anywhere, perhaps, thought some, even to heaven! No wonder the flying machine struck people as a miracle.

Orville's flights at Ft. Myer in 1908, unlike those at Kitty Hawk five years earlier, *were* widely reported. The press now published detailed and accurate descriptions of the Flyer and of its performance, along with photographs of the machine in flight. Millions read about this dramatic new invention and studied the pictures intently. But at a fundamental level the news still lacked credibility. The airplane was not like, say, the Panama Canal, the U.S. Navy's latest unsinkable dreadnought, or a device that projected moving photographs on a screen. Americans read about such technical feats in their newspapers and believed what they read. But a machine that could fly sounded too incredible to be true. In city after city where airplanes first appeared in the years after 1908, therefore, people gathered to see for themselves.

New Yorkers got the first chance to see an airplane after the Army trials. In 1909, while Orville toured Europe demonstrating one of their airplanes, Wilbur visited New York and made a series of flights. Crowds estimated at over a million people watched him fly along Manhattan, out over New York Harbor, and around the Statue of Liberty. The local papers rapturously praised his flying. The silence and skepticism earlier shown the Wrights was over. Every time the brothers now flew, the public gave them an enthusiastic reception. The same response greeted other pioneer airplane builders such as Glenn H. Curtiss, a mechanic and former motorcycle racer from Hammondsport, New York, who became one of the Wrights' early competitors. In 1910 Curtiss flew his *Albany Flyer* from Albany to New York City, winning a $10,000 prize put up by the New York *World*. He set out from the New York capital and, after brief stops in Poughkeepsie and Yonkers, landed two and a half hours later on Governors Island in New York Harbor. The number of spectators watching Curtiss's flight exceeded the crowd observing Wilbur Wright's the previous year, and the New York *Times* devoted six full pages to the achievement.

Curtiss was one of a growing flock of self-taught "birdmen"—there were also "birdwomen"—who carried forth the message, through actual flight performances, that the air had been conquered. Soon both Curtiss and the Wrights were taking on students and thereby increasing the number of fliers. In 1910 the Wrights established the Wright Exhibition Company to promote their airplanes, and Wright-trained pilots such as Arch Hoxsey and Ralph Johnstone flew at country fairs, racetracks, aero meets, and almost any kind of affair where a promoter would guarantee the Company's exhibition fee of $5,000 per plane. Although the Wrights did not accept women into their flight school, a handful of female pilots also participated in the exhibition game. Blanche Scott, Mathilda Moisant, Harriet Quimby, and others learned to fly and became, like the birdmen, heroes to awed earthbound observers. These exhibition fliers earned considerable money—fifty dollars on every day they flew, and twenty a day otherwise, in the case of Wright Exhibition Company pilots. But the work was dangerous in the extreme. The men and women vied with one another to perform ever more difficult and dangerous aerial stunts, knowing that such flying—and even the prospect of crashes—lured the paying crowds. Indeed, "the savage desire to look upon mangled bodies and hear the sob of expiring life" animated too many spectators, claimed a critic of the rising death toll in the air.[11] Not only stunt flying and competition increased the risks of flight, so did the primitive state of aeronautical design. Wings collapsed under the stress of acrobatics, and planes fell apart in the sky. For a variety of reasons, then, few exhibition fliers lived long enough to retire. By 1915 Arch Hoxsey, Ralph Johnstone, and Harriet Quimby were but three of many martyrs to the cause of aerial conquest.

As exhibition fliers convinced Americans that flight was a reality, all resistance to printed stories about flying machines disappeared. A new branch of journalism, specializing in aeronautics, grew out of public fascination with airplanes. As early as 1910 the New York *World* employed a full-time reporter to cover the aerial beat, and soon major dailies everywhere inaugurated regular columns devoted to aviation. Magazines simultaneously met the demand for articles and stories about flying. Whereas technical periodicals, such as *Scientific American,* had followed aeronautical experiments closely throughout the nineteenth century, lay magazines now began to do the same. One of the first to do so was

Town and Country, which in 1910 engaged Elizabeth Hiatt Gregory as its flight writer. In that year she covered the large international aviation meet at Belmont Park, Long Island, and began a long and distinguished career in aviation journalism. She and her colleagues busily reported the parade of developments in the sky. Aviation's rapid development, bringing forth a stream of firsts and new records, provided unending news. Just in the 1910s alone, some of the aviation "firsts" given big play in the press included the first use of planes to commute from home to office (1913); the first flights by a scheduled airline (1914); and the inauguration of government air mail service (1918).[12]

To the aviation-loving public, each "first" or record confirmed the seeming miraculousness of flight and inspired greater awe and wonder. One of the more spectacular was Calbraith P. Rodgers's 1911 flight from New York to California. Rodgers sought to win the $50,000 prize, put up by publisher William Randolph Hearst, for the first person to fly across the country in under thirty days. Flying a Wright machine named the *Vin Fiz* after a soft drink manufactured by his sponsor, Rodgers cut a dashing figure. A husky six-foot-four college football star, he never flew without an unlit cigar clenched between his teeth as he sat, bare-headed, in a seat on the lower wing of his airplane. In this pose he took off from Sheepshead Bay, New York, on September 17, 1911, cheered by thousands of well-wishers. As he fought his way across the continent in his open craft, exposed to the crisp fall weather, a special train followed him on the ground, carrying his wife and mother-in-law, food, and spare parts for his airplane. Progress was arduous in the face of accidents, mechanical problems, and bad weather. On November 5th, forty-nine days after he left New York, Rodgers landed in Pasadena to a "hearty and tumultuous" welcome from 20,000 people who, according to the newspaper, "simply went mad" with excitement. Because he failed to meet the thirty-day time limit, Rodgers did not win the Hearst prize. But he succeeded in being the first to cross the continent by air—"I made it, didn't I?"—he retorted to friends who thought only of the lost prize money. His feat was indeed staggering. He was airborne 103 hours and averaged 51.59 miles an hour for 4,321 zigzagging miles, dictated mainly by the rail lines he followed. He survived a dozen crashes and many injuries, including a wrenched knee, a broken leg and collarbone, and an arm incapacitated by steel splinters from an exploding engine, to list just the worst of them. The next year Rodgers's luck ran out. Flying low over the beach at Long Beach, California, his hands off the controls to demonstrate the stability of his airplane, he died when the machine suddenly dove into a few feet of water.[13]

Writers decried the carnage attending aerial conquest but did not let that diminish their enthusiasm for airplanes. Even the deliberate use of planes to kill people, demonstrated first in the Balkan War of 1912 and developed to a high art in the European conflagration of 1914-18, worked no such result. Quite to the contrary. Americans expressed revulsion at the introduction of new weapons such as machine guns, tanks, poison gas, and submarines—but not at airplanes. Even though men died in the sky, often incinerated in their flaming planes, and even though civilians died on the ground in aerial bombardment, somehow the public perceived air war as purer than ground war. The aviators were "freed from much of the ruck and reek of war by their easy poise above it," explained one commentator, and could "take time and pains to be gentlemen-warriors."[14] Their behavior recalled days when battle was valorous and chivalric. Pilots fought each other individually, in dramatic dogfights or duels, man against man. If one fell in battle, his vanquisher often flew over the site the next day and dropped a wreath. "The man aloft is a popular hero whose adventures thrill the bosoms of countless thousands," remarked a writer in 1918.[15] The most heroized were the so-called "Aces," pilots who registered five or more kills of enemy planes. The leading Allied aces— Edward Mannock of England, Billy Bishop of Canada, and René Fonck of France—along with German aces like Max Immelman and the feared "Red Baron," Manfred von Richthofen, were respected and their exploits closely followed by the American press. Once the United States entered the war in 1917, Americans soon had their own aces to revere, the best-known being Eddie Rickenbacker. By ignoring his mother's advice to "fly slow and stay close to the ground," the former automobile racer scored twenty-six victories over enemy planes, most of them in the final two months of the war.[16]

After the Armistice, military expenditures on aeronautics fell to prewar levels, and few officers showed any inclination to develop an air force. But public interest in aerial war continued to thrive. This was primarily through the efforts of Hollywood, which, in the twenties, discovered aviation. Flying became a popular sport among members of the film community, with stars such as Col-

leen Moore and producers such as Cecil B. deMille, learning to fly
and buying personal planes. More importantly, studios turned out
dozens of aviation films, many about the World War. *Air Circus,
Cloud Rider, Flight, Sky Skidder, Won on the Clouds,* and *Phantom
Flyer* were just some of the productions thrilling audiences with
aerial dogfights and flaming crashes. A few of Hollywood's aerial
epics—*Dawn Patrol, Lilac Time,* and *Hell's Angels*—were great
feats cinematically and have become classics. The last-mentioned
film, released in 1930 by millionaire pilot and movie producer
Howard Hughes, set a new standard for magnificent aerial foot-
age and action. Hughes spent more money on the production—
allegedly more than $4 million—than had been spent on any
previous film, much of it to acquire his own private air force
of some eighty World-War-vintage aircraft. *Hell's Angels* depicted the lives of English fighter pilots assigned to defending
London against the terrifying German Zeppelin raids. Excellent
in its combat scenes but somewhat wooden in its dialogue and
acting, the film managed a mild anti-war spirit while extolling
flight.[17]

The popularity of aviation films after the war was but one indicator of the public's growing "airmindedness." To be "airminded,"
as contemporaries used the word, meant having enthusiasm for airplanes, believing in their potential to better human life, and sup-
porting aviation development.[18] Perhaps no group did more to
foster and spread airmindedness in the twenties than the barnstormers. These aerial gypsies, often ex-military aviators, flew about the
country taking people for airplane rides at a few dollars a head
and staging aerial circuses, featuring acrobatics, wing-walking, and
other stunts. Unlike pre-war exhibition fliers, who tended to perform where large audiences could be gathered—in towns and cities
or at country fairs—barnstormers flew for any audience anywhere.
In inexpensive war surplus aircraft which they bought from the
government, barnstormers operated on a shoestring budget and
plied their trade from farmers' pastures, country roads, and any
other location where they could sideslip down to a bumpy landing
and attract a few potential customers. Claude Ryan, a barnstormer,
described how he and his colleagues had an "evangelical dedication" to the flying cause. Ryan, soon to be famous as the builder
of the airplane in which Charles A. Lindbergh flew the Atlantic,
believed "that if he could talk anyone into his first flight, he would
change that person's life for the better."[19] By decade's end, Ryan

and other flying missionaries had exposed nearly every hamlet and crossroads in the land to the airplane.

Lindbergh himself began his aviation career as a barnstormer, and his experiences in Mississippi in the early twenties were typical. One day he was on his way to Texas, flying from Meriden, Mississippi, when he got lost, not an unusual incident in that era of few navigational instruments and no ground markings. A storm was developing, so Lindbergh made an emergency landing on a rough field, which damaged his propeller. He found himself stranded in the vicinity of the small town of Maben, miles from any substantial city. Local residents eagerly helped him and soon Lindbergh had replaced his propeller and was taking folks for rides. He later reported that both whites and blacks were fascinated by the airplane, and that many traveled fifteen miles by oxcart just to see it fly. He ended up staying in the area two weeks, just to satisfy people's demand for his flying.[20]

Barnstormers regularly encountered such enthusiasm. While in Mississippi, however, Lindbergh observed one instance of interest in his airplane that impressed him as unusually noteworthy. An elderly black woman came up to him and, in total seriousness, asked him how much he would charge to fly her to heaven and leave her there.[21] The woman no doubt believed in heaven as a tangible place, above the earth, inhabited by her personal God. Knowing nothing about airplanes or about the physical laws governing their performance, heaven seemed a plausible destination for an airplane flight. Her linking of the spiritual heaven with mechanical flight, however, was not unique. In 1928 a Troy, New York, man wrote Orville Wright a long, rambling, and ungrammatical letter praising airplanes as divine. "The Flying-Machines come now out and proclaim the Eternal Truth of God to all Mankind," he announced, and established convincingly "that the earth stands still" and other "statements made in the Bible."[22] Another literal believer in heavenly destinations for flying machines, apparently an inventor, in a letter written somewhat earlier to Thomas A. Edison, hinted that he "knew of a machine to go to heaven." He hesitated to share the secret with Edison or other "capitalist parties" because, as he told Edison, "you would make the machine ready by yourself and took a patent upon it . . . or organize a company to carry some people up to heaven with your new machine but I would be left behind in my struggle on earth."[23]

One did not have to believe in the possibility of flying to heaven to be excited about aviation in the 1920s. The aerial frontier was fast succumbing to conquest. Airplanes had come a long way since 1911 when Calbraith Rodgers conquered a continent hop by hop. By the twenties, spurred in part by the demands of the recent war, planes had become faster and more reliable. They now flew higher, carried far bigger loads, and had considerably greater range. Inaugurating what proved to be the golden era of distance flights, in May 1919, three U.S. Navy flying boats departed on a mission across the Atlantic. The large three-engined seaplanes took off from Long Island, bound via Nova Scotia, Newfoundland, and the Azores, for Portugal. Two of the planes lost their way in fog and were forced down in the ocean. Heavy seas prevented them from taking off, and eventually one foundered and sank, its crew being rescued by a nearby Navy ship. The other downed plane battled the waves and motored, under its own power, the more than two hundred miles to Ponta Delgada in the Azores. But the third plane remained airborn and completed its flight as planned, landing in Lisbon Harbor on May 29, 1919. It had tamed the Atlantic, prompting great celebrations in Lisbon and, on the return home of the NC-4's six-man crew, in the United States as well. The Navy plane became the first of a veritable procession of planes that would cross the Atlantic in the ensuing years.[24]

Americans watched excitedly as the airplane shrank not only oceans but also continents. The first non-stop cross-country flight occurred in May 1923. Lieutenants John A. Macready and Oakley G. Kelly of the U.S. Army, flying a large and lumbering single-engined monoplane, a Fokker T-2, covered the 2,250 miles between the two coasts in just under twenty-seven hours. The flight elicited great interest. All along the plane's route, people listened intently for the sound of its engine, hoping to glimpse the historic machine. On arriving in San Diego, the fliers triggered wild celebrations. A "great throng" assembled at the airfield to greet them, while all over San Diego residents honked car horns and blew factory whistles. "The impossible has happened," former World War pilot Major Henry H. Arnold told reporters, while President Harding telegraphed similar sentiments to the two pilots. It was an editorial writer for the San Diego *Union*, however, who best expressed the awe and optimism generated by the flight. Macready and Kelley were "prophets of a dream," the editor claimed, and in the light of their accomplishment "imagination itself must pause." Indeed, "the word impossible has been erased from the lexicon of air history," he concluded. "We of San Diego who actually saw the great monoplane heading to its final goal have seen history with our own eyes—a new thing, almost incredible, an achievement that will give rise to new miracles."[25]

The regularity with which miracles seemed to occur in the sky thrilled contemporaries. Hardly a year passed that men and women, mounted on their newly invented wings, did not leap some new continent, span another ocean, or penetrate some heretofore inaccessible corner of the globe. Whole new concepts of time and distance were being wrought through aerial conquest. In 1926 Lt. Commander Richard E. Byrd, U.S.N. Ret., became the first to fly over the North Pole, bringing one of the most hostile parts of the planet that much closer. The public followed Byrd's assault on the Pole with eagerness. For almost a century Arctic expeditions had possessed great charisma, in part because of the sublime desolation of the area, in part because of the monumental challenge nature presented there to human survival, and in part because international rivalries flavored these Arctic adventures. Byrd himself vied with Norwegian Roald Amundsen to be the first to fly over the Pole and just beat his rival's dirigible to the goal by three days. On returning to the United States, Byrd and his pilot, Floyd Bennett, became instant heroes, widely honored and feted. Byrd went on to attempt other long-distance flights and wrote and spoke widely about the progress of aviation and its future potential. Even his airplane became famous. Named the *Josephine Ford*, after the daughter of his sponsor, Henry Ford, the machine went on display in the window of Wanamaker's department store in Philadelphia and in New York, where thousands came to see it.[26]

Shattering the isolation of the Arctic represented one kind of thrilling aerial achievement, but not one that appeared to have direct implications for the future of ordinary Americans. Few people, after all, could imagine themselves going to that land of perpetual ice and subzero temperature. The first direct trans-Pacific flight to China by a commercial airliner, however, symbolized a quite different order of potential. Americans long had considered that vast and populous country an untapped market. When Pan American Airways' giant, four-engined flying boat or "Clipper" lifted off the waters of San Francisco Bay on November 22, 1935, bound for China, that far-off land suddenly seemed a neighbor, and the dream of a China market almost a reality. More than 20,000 people lined the approach to San Francisco Bay Bridge, then under construction, to watch the historic departure, and the crowd cheered and "gasped" as the plane took off. All over the Bay Area, in fact, throngs assembled to try and catch sight of the China Clipper as it winged through the Golden Gate. The enthusiastic send-off capped almost twenty-four hours of continuous celebrations and ceremonies. One of these, held at the plane's dock in Alameda, directly to the east across the Bay from San Francisco, illustrated the place accorded flight in the popular imagination. The occasion was the loading of mail sacks into the China Clipper. The first sack of mail fell into the plane's cargo bay automatically, when a switch was triggered by an electrical impulse transmitted to the Alameda facility from Mt. Wilson Observatory. The impulse itself was derived from the distant star, Betelguese, in the constellation Orion. To underline the progressive orientation of aviation, the organizers then had the last mailbags arrive at the plane in a nineteenth-century stagecoach, "a relic of the fleet of Wells Fargo road rockers of the sixties," the New York *Times* reported. The contrast between the airplane, pointing toward the stars and the future, and the wheeled vehicle, stuck on earth and mired in the past, struck a responsive chord among airminded Americans everywhere. When President Roosevelt cabled the China Clipper's crew "the heartfelt congratulations of an air-minded sailor," adding, "I thrill to the wonder of it all," he spoke for millions.[27]

The thrill and wonder that Americans felt over the flight of the China Clipper in 1935 was of a piece with the response to aviation generally. People distinguished little between one airplane and another, or between one flight and another. All flying seemed wondrous; all planes miraculous. The barnstormer's dilapidated biplane generated rapt attention and seemed to portend further miracles no less than Pan American's new Clipper or the Army's T-2. The dramatic flights across continents and over oceans seemed to herald a marvelous new day in people's lives no more or less than other forms of aeronautical endeavor. Air racing, recreational flying, and even the flying of model planes by youngsters—all were aviation. And to an airminded nation, all possessed interest and fascination. The press lavished coverage on events, such as the Pulitzer Trophy and the Schneider Cup races of the twenties, dominated by military aircraft racing around closed courses, or the Bendix Trophy races of the thirties, in which civilians sped across the continent. Almost equal in popular appeal were matters concerning private flying. When the Roosevelt administration subsidized small plane development in the early thirties, this "New Deal of the Air" heralded for many Americans the imminent arrival of wings for the masses, and the media covered these developments closely. Even at the ubiquitous model airplane meets of the period, large crowds of adults, 25,000 or more in the larger cities, would turn out to watch youngsters fly miniature rubber-band or gasoline-engine-powered airplanes. Airmindedness, in short, was a very catholic, all-embracing enthusiasm.[28]

One flight, however, represented a high-water mark for aviation enthusiasm and was itself a major stimulus to airmindedness in the period. This was the 1927 New York to Paris flight by Charles A. Lindbergh.[29] Lindbergh's solo, nonstop performance catalyzed a celebration unlike anything ever witnessed in American public life. Literally overnight his name became synonymous with aviation. Even today, if one recalls any personage from the aeronautical past, it is likely to be Lindbergh. He emerged the victor in what by the mid-twenties had become a veritable race to fly from America to Europe. Fliers had already crossed the Atlantic, of course; in 1919 the Navy's NC-4 had done it via the Azores, and in the same year two English pilots crossed nonstop in the high northern latitudes, between Newfoundland and Ireland. But nobody had spanned the ocean at its full girth, from New York to France. This dream, dating from the birth of flying, had eluded aviators. In 1919 Raymond Orteig, a New York restaurant owner, in a gesture commemorating Franco-American friendship and cooperation during the late war, offered a $25,000 prize to the first person to make such a flight. Good for five years, his prize attracted no takers. No one dared the crossing. Aircraft still lacked the reliability and range to have a chance. Orteig then renewed his offer for five more years, and by 1926 a number of pilots were readying for the challenge. Polar flier Richard E. Byrd, veteran pilot and aviation promoter Clarence Chamberlin, and Commander Noel Davis of the U.S. Navy were the Americans favored in the Atlantic sweepstakes. And from France, two former war aces, René Fonck and Charles Nungesser, headed flight teams preparing for an assault on the Atlantic and the Orteig prize.

Then there was Lindbergh, the dark horse of the field. He was not well-known and had relatively modest financing. But he was hardly inexperienced as a pilot. Indeed, for all of his twenty-four years he had been acquiring experience that would aid him in getting to Paris. Raised in Little Falls, Minnesota, the young Lindbergh became an adept outdoorsman and naturalist, honing powers of concentration and observation that would later make him an exceptional pilot. He also loved machinery and tinkering with it. But Lindbergh hated school and gladly left high school to work on a farm when World War I produced an agricultural labor shortage. The farm machinery interested him but little else, and with the Armistice he left farming forever. On his parents' urging, he briefly attended the University of Wisconsin, where his primary accomplishments appear to have been performing daring stunts on his motorcycle—and catching the flying bug. He decided to become a pilot and in 1922 enrolled as a flying student at the Nebraska Aircraft Company in Lincoln. A natural flier, he quickly soloed. Buying a used biplane, he then joined the ranks of the barnstormers, working the Midwest and South, where he experienced his Mississippi adventures. A stint with the United States airmail service further increased his flying hours and also acquainted him with the parachute, which twice saved his life when he had to jump from crippled planes. Although hardly a neophyte in the air when he set his sights on the Atlantic and the Orteig prize in 1926, Lindbergh nevertheless was known to very few people.

With the extensive media attention being given the Atlantic preparations, however, Lindbergh soon became a celebrity. On May 10-11, 1927, after taking delivery in San Diego of the plane he intended to fly to Paris, Lindbergh dramatically flew into the public's gaze. He piloted his plane from California nonstop to St. Louis in fourteen hours, a record. He paused in that city only briefly before flying on to New York, arriving only twenty-one hours flying time after he left the west coast. The flight put the name of "Lindy," or "Slim" as he was sometimes called, on the lips of millions.

Everybody liked the flier's boyish reserve and modest confidence (Lindbergh's notorious hostility to journalists emerged only after the New York to Paris flight). But many people also thought him crazy, a "Flying Fool," because he intended to fly the Atlantic alone, in a single-engined plane, without even a radio or a life raft for emergency use. This struck many knowledgeable observers as suicidal. Lindbergh's rivals carried such equipment, and some of them flew three-engined planes, so that if one engine failed the plane could continue on two. Most significantly, all flew with one or more crew members to relieve them at the controls during the long, grueling hours the crossing would require. Lindbergh rejected these choices, not because he was a fool or wanted to die, but because he had carefully calculated the costs and benefits of each of them—and arrived at a different view of how best to beat the Atlantic. The key to success, he believed, lay in minimizing the weight of his plane. To that end he wanted no extra crew and but one engine, so as to reduce drag and increase speed and fuel efficiency. He also rejected the extra weight of life rafts or radios, reasoning that if he were to survive an ocean landing, his chances of rescue would be slim at best. Better to carry a few gallons more gasoline than the weight of even a raft or primitive radio, he thought, as every extra minute he could stay in the air would extend his range and better ensure his survival.

No amount of calculating or precaution could reduce the risks entirely, as was evident from events prior to Lindbergh's own departure. In September 1926, taking off on a practice flight, René Fonck's fuel-laden plane, the *America*, crashed and burned. Fonck escaped unhurt, but two of the four-man crew died in the conflagration. The next April, in a final test flight before hopping off for Paris, another of Lindbergh's rivals, Noel Davis, along with his co-pilot, perished in a crash. Then in Paris on May 8, 1927, Charles Nungesser took off in his *White Bird* and headed west across the Atlantic. He and his co-pilot, François Coli, were attempting the more difficult east-to-west crossing, permitted under the terms of the Orteig prize. Twelve days later, when Lindbergh himself took off from Long Island, Nungesser and Coli had not been seen or heard from. Neither the plane nor their bodies were ever found.

Their disappearance only dramatized the hazards Lindbergh was courting. That he departed in poor weather conditions seemed, once again, the act of a fool. A large bank of fog had blanketed the eastern seaboard for days, delaying his departure and that of his one remaining rival, Clarence Chamberlin. Weather reports on the evening of the 19th, the day before his take-off, however, called for clearing to the east, out over the Atlantic. Lindbergh took a chance on this, although it was hardly a wild roll of the dice; like all his decisions, he reached it only after considering all aspects of the question.

Once Lindbergh was airborne over the fogbound seas, alone and out of reach of help, his countrymen suspended the question of his foolhardiness. All controversy over life rafts and radios, or over the number of engines and crewmen, evaporated. Lindbergh might not conquer the Atlantic, but by just daring to try he captured his country's collective heart and spirit. Not a person who knew of the young pilot's departure did not hope for his success. Americans thrilled to the bold decisiveness of his action and relished the fact that a dark horse and underdog, a "Flying Fool" even, might beat better qualified and subsidized competitors. All around the country on the evening of May 20th, at gatherings ranging from the local Rotary Club meeting to a nationally important prizefight at Madison Square Garden in New York, people prayed for Lindbergh. They intently followed the hourly radio bulletins and watched for the special editions appearing on the newsstands, although nobody besides Lindbergh had any reliable information about the progress of the flight.

For his own part, Lindbergh knew nothing of the emotions heating up back home. He was not the kind of person to think about the social implications of the flight or to muse about fame and fortune; furthermore, the business of flying totally occupied him. Fighting ice and fatigue, headwinds and storms, he bore on eastwards, the steady roar of his engine providing a numbing counterpoint, deafening even through his earplugs, to the silent blackness outside the cockpit. His flying so busied him, in fact, that although he became very hungry, he forgot for a day that he had stowed sandwiches aboard before leaving New York. As the hours passed, sleep pursued him; once he dozed off and only the plane's natural instability, its tendency to fall into a spin if not controlled every instant, jolted him to consciousness and saved him. Dawn soon appeared in the east, and shortly thereafter Lindbergh sighted a small fishing boat, the first intimation he had of nearing land—and success. Now he was flying over the lush green and the tidy hamlets of Ireland, excitedly observing that people on the ground were waving at him. He savored this first sight of human beings after the eternity of solitude. As he flew over Cornwall and headed toward the English Channel and France, the sun set for the second time on the flight. This time nightfall brought no fatigue. Although he had slept little the two nights before taking off, and not at all for the twenty-four hours in the cockpit, excitement drove all traces of tiredness from his body. Spotting the well-lit Eiffel Tower, he quickly found Le Bourget airport and lined up the plane for a landing. As he touched ground, thirty-three and a half enervating hours of flying were over—and all he felt was euphoria!

So, too, did Parisians, and as fast as telegraphy could convey the news, so did his fellow Americans. In Paris thousands of citizens had been alerted to Lindbergh's imminent arrival and descended upon Le Bourget to await his landing. At the first glimpse of the *Spirit of St. Louis* the crowd overwhelmed police control and swarmed toward the plane, forcing Lindbergh to quickly cut his engine before the whirling propeller injured somebody. He barely got out of the cockpit before the cheering mob was upon him, grabbing at his clothing. In the melee, a man captured Lindbergh's helmet and goggles, held them up triumphantly to the crowd, and was promptly mistaken for the flier and carried off on excited shoulders. The diversion permitted the real Lindbergh to escape, and only the prompt arrival of police kept enthusiastic souvenir hunters from dismantling the now historic aircraft.

The wild scene at Le Bourget previewed Lindbergh's more polished but equally exuberant reception at the hands of European monarchs and heads of state. He received medals and decorations, gifts, and fetes at every turn. The French Assembly and the English Parliament prevailed upon the reticent flier to address the two bodies, and everywhere the flying emissary stirred a wave of pro-American feeling such as had not been seen since the arrival of United States troops on European soil back in 1917.

Back home, Americans impatiently awaited their hero's return. President Calvin Coolidge dispatched a Navy ship to bring Lindbergh and his plane home, while the American ambassador to France, Myron T. Herrick, dissuaded the flier from the idea of continuing his flight into eastern Europe and perhaps around the world. So on June 10, 1927, the "Lone Eagle" arrived back in the United States, as a passenger on the deck of the *U.S.S. Memphis* rather than as pilot of his own plane. A flotilla of warships fired their guns in salute, and military planes wheeled overhead as the *Memphis* steamed into Chesapeake Bay. The welcome then moved to the capital, where President and Mrs. Coolidge hosted Lindbergh at a small dinner, the first of many Washington events in the flier's honor. Congress honored him next by inviting him to address a joint session. At a ceremony on the Washington Mall, the President then awarded the pilot the Distinguished Flying Cross in front of thousands, some of whom had witnessed Orville Wright's demonstration flights at Ft. Myer twenty years earlier.

It was not the feelings Lindbergh elicited that were novel. Previous aeronautical achievements had prompted similar ones. What

distinguished the response to Lindbergh was its scope and intensity—and its persistence. Other fliers became heroes for a day so to
speak but then faded from popular memory. But not Lindbergh.
Years after his flight, for his entire life, in fact, he remained a figure whose every action fascinated, if it did not always thrill—as
was the case with his empathy for the Nazi regime in Germany—
the American public. In 1927 the sheer number of people who
wanted to see him, to glimpse his plane, or otherwise to pay homage to him and his achievement, was extraordinary. When Lindbergh visited New York City after the official Washington welcome, an estimated four million people, a number nearly equal to
the city's entire population, lined the streets of Manhattan to see
his auto cavalcade. New York tickertape parades functioned as the
nation's informal welcoming committee in the twenties, led by
New York's flamboyant mayor, James "Jimmy" Walker. They
also provided a measure of the fame and importance of any hero,
celebrity, or dignitary so honored. By any measure, Lindbergh
broke all records. The unprecedented avalanche of confetti and
paper that descended upon him as he was driven through the city's
streets showed the place he had carved in people's hearts and
minds. When Mayor Walker presented him with the key to the
city—also a traditional part of the welcoming ritual—and said,
"New York is yours. You have won it," he did not exaggerate.

As the summer cooled into fall, Lindbergh "won" other towns
and cities. Thanks to radio and film he became the best-known
American of the day; some thought him the best-known personage in world history. And thanks to his own favorite medium of
air travel, an unprecedented number of people saw and heard him
in person. This was the result of an aerial tour he made under the
auspices of the Guggenheim Fund for the Promotion of Aeronautics, a philanthropic effort launched in 1926 by airminded mining
millionaire, Daniel C. Guggenheim, and his son Harry. Funded by
the Guggenheims, Lindbergh in three months flew the *Spirit of
St. Louis* 22,350 miles and logged 260 hours in the air. He visited
each of the 48 states, stopped in 82 towns and cities, attended 69
official dinners, and delivered 147 speeches extolling the coming
era of mass air transport and urging airport building, according to
figures from the Guggenheim Fund's final report. To mollify the
hundreds of communities he disappointed by not stopping, Lindbergh dropped from the air 192 messages of regret, expressing

hope that people would understand and that they would still work for the development of aviation.[30]

The celebration of Lindbergh and his flight extended beyond parades, speeches, and public gatherings. Americans named babies, schools, and streets after the flier. Artists and crafts workers found subjects in the hero and his airplane. With paint on canvas or ink on paper; out of soap, wood, bronze, and gold; or with thread and beads on quilts, pillows, slippers, and clothing, these men and women painted, carved, and stitched homages to Lindbergh. Some sent their creations to the flier as gifts, but many desired simply to make some material symbol of the flight, an icon as it were, to honor the feat. In somewhat the same vein, applications poured into the United States Patent Office for design patents covering lamps, clocks, radios, mailboxes, jewelry cases, food containers, condiment holders, and even buildings and automobiles, all resembling the *Spirit of St. Louis*.[31]

It was in words, however, that Americans most fully celebrated the flight. Letters, poetry, essays, sermons, and speeches streamed forth in praise of Lindbergh and his accomplishment. A few writers presumed intimacy with the hero and demanded money, proposed marriage, or requested business or technical advice. Most simply wanted to pay homage. So, too, did the nation's clergy. The day after Lindbergh landed in Paris was a Sunday, and in New York City alone, ministers at Grace Episcopal, Fifth Avenue Presbyterian, the Cathedral of St. John the Divine, and the Church of St. Mary the Virgin, all took Lindbergh's flight as the text for their sermons. The flight illustrated, the clerics claimed, the rewards of courage, persistence, and modesty. And Lindbergh also exemplified the self-control needed "to discipline the flesh" so as to lead the "heroic adventure of Christian life."[32] Another divine suggested that the flight offered "a practical lesson in mystical religion," for only the "true mystic" sets off into the unknown, "trusting to God."[33]

The most extravagant response to Lindbergh's flight came not from preachers but from poets. An outpouring of rhyme and couplet, unmatched in quantity and hyperbole, greeted the flier. More poems were written about Lindbergh and his flight, a recent study claims, than about any other personage or event in Western history.[34] Thousands were sent to him by their authors, while others appeared in newspapers and magazines. Some 4,000 poems alone were entered in a contest held during the summer of 1927 to select the best Lindbergh poem. Contest entries included "very little of the facile rubbish that has been flooding many provincial papers," asserted a critic close to the competition.[35] Whether facile or artful, however, most of the poems enunciated a common message: flight is divine and the pilot (or his plane) is a god. A typical example of this deification is this stanza from "A Chantey for Celestial Vikings," one of the contest poems:

> I cannot die,
> Who have flown as eagles fly
> Into the blue unknown.
> I have throttled oblivion.
> I have fathomed the myths of space and time.[36]

In other poems the aviator—Lindbergh is seldom mentioned by name—became "Son of the Sky," "Lord of the Air," "Master of the Empyrean," or a "god from a golden isle."[37] Some of the Lindbergh-prompted poems suggested the flying machine itself was divine, a "steel miracle" as one put it, or that flying was associated with spiritual matters, as in this couplet from another of the contest entries:

> Our gaze drew upward—from the skies you taught,
> "Man is divine, and meant by God to soar!"[38]

With considerably less hyperbole than the poets or preachers, the press had the most to say about the Lindbergh phenomenon. It was through the newspapers, after all, that most Americans followed the flight and its aftermath. On receiving confirmation that Lindbergh had landed safely in Paris, many papers rushed into print with special editions, thereby jumping their circulations by as much as half. Sensationalist tabloids quite naturally capitalized on the flight, but even conservative dailies like the New York *Times,* aloof from the era's tendency to ballyhoo and excess, dropped all restraints when faced with Lindbergh. The May 22, 1927, edition of the *Times* gave over the first five pages entirely to Lindbergh, and for days afterwards let news of his activities dominate the front page. The public absorbed virtually anything written on the subject: minute accounts of the flight, the weather encountered, the plane's instruments and how they worked, Lindbergh's youth and family background, his personal plans, and his vision of aviation's future.

The extent of the Lindbergh celebration has intrigued and puzzled students ever since 1927. In seeking to understand the unprecedented fervor prompted by the man and his act, most writers agree that the mere fact of his flying the Atlantic Ocean explains little. After all, by the time he made his flight in 1927, dozens of men, including the crew of a British dirigible that made a round-trip in 1919, had already crossed the ocean by air. To be sure, Lindbergh flew farther than any of his predecessors, directly vaulting the long distance from the United States to France; and he did it without stopping. But it was the fact that he flew alone that people responded to and which scholars believe is the essential key to his impact. They point out that for millions of Americans in the twenties, Lindbergh's flight appeared as a confrontation of man and nature and thus recalled the country's wilderness beginnings. Contemporaries hailed him as a "pioneer" and as the conqueror of a "new frontier." The "Lone Eagle" was compared to Daniel Boone, Davy Crockett, and other individualists who, with knife and axe, wit and muscle, tamed a virgin land and built a civilization. By fitting Lindbergh to an already mythologized vision of their frontier past, argues a leading historian, Americans reassured themselves of their continuing vitality as a people and a nation. Although mechanization and industrialization had wrought dislocations and anxieties and dwarfed the individual amidst corporate expressions, Americans nonetheless took Lindbergh's flight as affirming the continued strength of pioneer instincts and virtues.[39]

Had Lindbergh not been who *he* was, such associations would have been harder to draw and sustain. Myth-makers made much, for instance, of Lindbergh's being descended from Swedish-American pioneer stock and his "Viking" ancestry. But they also found his character and temperament easy to aggrandize. Lindbergh appeared polite, modest, honest, and without moral faults. He neither drank nor smoked and was anything but a womanizer. By spurning all the get-rich-quick schemes proferred him and by dedicating himself to the promotion of aviation, Lindbergh also showed himself to be an idealist. These qualities, particularly in the twenties when many Americans anguished over corruption, gangsterism, intemperance, and immorality, made Lindbergh seem like a saint, standing out "in a grubby world as an inspiration," as one journalist put it.[40] Another observer, writing in the New York *Herald Tribune* in 1929, marveled that "five centuries have been required to make a saint of Joan of Arc, but in two years Col. Charles A. Lindbergh has become a demigod."[41] Deemed a pioneer, a saint, and even a demigod, Lindbergh was the irresistible hero.[42]

Lindbergh's importance in the history of aviation and in twentieth-century culture is indisputable. Yet all of the attention given him by historians tends to obscure the fact that the American public had been tremendously enthusiastic over airplanes and flight long before they had heard of the Lone Eagle. Lindbergh's flight did not create airmindedness, nor did it significantly alter the way Americans thought about flying. Many other fliers had been characterized as gods; other flying machines had been viewed as miraculous; and other flights had been thought to portend divine possibilities for humanity's future. Indeed, Americans from the first days of the airplane era commonly borrowed words from their religious lexicons—words like "god," "miracle," "saint," "heaven," "evangelist"—to describe aeronautical activities. From the first "moment of miracle" when they first saw an airplane leave the ground through Lindbergh and down to the mid-twentieth century, many people perceived the conquest of the skies as a profoundly spiritual activity, somehow linked with the divine and the supernatural. Contemporaries of the Wright brothers responded to Kitty Hawk as if it were somehow a divine happening. Straining to explain the otherwise inexplicable, one man characterized Wilbur and Orville as "an instrument in the holy hands of God" for the introduction of "His gift of wings," as if the brothers were passive aeronautical virgins and God the airplane's father.[43] And more than twenty years after Lindbergh, ex-World War I ace turned airline executive, Eddie Rickenbacker, similarly invoked the divine in characterizing aviation. In the preface to a book on the history of flight, written by his friend Major Roger Q. Williams, U.S. Air Force, and published in 1949, Rickenbacker claimed pilots "have always felt inwardly that what they were doing was all part of some mysterious Universal Plan," and that they "were just chosen pawns of the Creator." The same notion informed Williams's entire history. "Long before earthbound souls broke the steel shackles binding their feet of clay to the breast of Mother Earth," Williams wrote, "the Creator had completed His Universal Plans for the airplane and carefully selected His truest leaders to carry out that mission."[44]

Faith in that mission, in flight as a veritable religious cause, energized not only fliers but also millions of other Americans during the first half of this century. Airminded men and women embraced what was often called the "gospel of aviation" or the "winged gospel."[45] Like the Christian gospels, the gospel of aviation held out a glorious promise, that of a great new day in human affairs once airplanes brought about a true air age. Lindbergh offered one version of this gospel, prophesying a future in which air travel would be commonplace and large transport planes shuttle from city to city, unhampered by the weather. Other enthusiasts voiced even grander prophecies, looking to aircraft as a means of achieving perfection on earth or even immortality, promises usually identified with more traditional religions. Together the various prophecies made regarding the airplane were both an expression of and a cause of the great popular enthusiasm shown for aviation. Prophecy comprised a kind of creed for the winged gospel and provided the motivation for those who practiced this secular religion of technology. The content of that creed, and the prophets and apostles who preached it, are the subject of the next chapter.

II

"A New Sign in the Heavens"
The Prophetic Creed of Flight

Enthusiasm for flight went hand in hand with glorious expectations. Much of the excitement displayed toward, say, Calbraith Rodgers's odyssey across the United States in 1911 or Pan American's leap across the Pacific Ocean in 1935 flowed from the idealistic and often utopian expectations which Americans held regarding the airplane's future. Ideas regarding aviation's future prospects, in fact, often excited contemporaries more than present aeronautical accomplishments. From the moment the public learned of the Wright brothers' invention, of the fact that a flying machine had successfully left the ground, speculation regarding the airplane's future became a popular activity.

Men and women from many different occupations and backgrounds, including architects, artists, business leaders, clergy, editors, educators, engineers, soldiers, and writers, all addressed the shape of things to come. In articles with titles such as "The Present and Future of Aerial Navigation" (1908), "The Aeroplane—A Retrospect and a Forecast" (1909), "Aircraft and the Future" (1913), "The Future of the Airplane" (1918), "The Coming Age in Aviation" (1927), "Air Flivvers and the Future" (1929), "Flying in the Future" (1938), "Will You Fly Your Own Plane After the War?" (1945), they attempted to describe the air age that allegedly lay just around the corner.[1] Their efforts to imagine the future encountered all the usual pitfalls of prediction, not the least of which was that aeronautics was a new and rapidly changing field. Accordingly, few prophets anticipated the rapid obsolescence of lighter-than-air craft and of seaplanes for long over-the-water flights or the invention of the turbojet which facilitated a tremendous increase in the speed of airplanes. Where prophets erred most consistently, however, was not in the technical but rather in the social and moral realms. They consistently overestimated the airplane's capacity to effect social change, yet this was what really interested most observers about the conquest of the skies, particularly those outside the aeronautical field.

In this regard, listen to Mary M. Parker, writing in 1910 of the first airplane to fly over Chicago. "Toward what were they gazing," she rhetorically asked, alluding to the vast throng which had gathered to witness the historic occasion. "Was there a new sign in the heavens that told of a future scarcely dreamed of?" Yes, she answered, asserting that:

> Not a man but felt that this was the beginning of such a mighty era that no tongue could tell its import, and those who gazed felt awestruck, as though they had torn aside the veil of the future and looked into the very Holy of Holies. . . . We bowed our heads before the mystery of it and then lifted our eyes with a new feeling in our souls that seemed to link us with the great dome of heaven, stretching above and over all, and hope sprang eternal for the great new future of the world.[2]

Parker published her account in a religious weekly and presumably well understood the Christian symbolism she used to describe the frail biplane that flew over Chicago. By calling it a sign in the heavens, she recalled the Star of Bethlehem which two millennia earlier signaled the birth of Jesus. Thus she linked the airplane with the Saviour, aggrandizing it into a mechanical messiah whose coming would wondrously transform life and society.

Americans widely shared Parker's notion of the airplane as a messiah. They never considered the flying machine simply as a way of moving people or things from one spot on the earth to another. Rather, it seemed an instrument of reform, regeneration, and salvation, a substitute for politics, revolution, or even religion. This messianic view of aviation emerged immediately after the airplane's public debut in 1908 and continued through the Second World War, although prophecy was at his boldest during the first twenty or so years of the air age. In those years, as men and women gazed into their crystal balls and tried to read the aerial future, many did so in widespread ignorance of the potential and operation of aircraft. Not knowing the physical forces or the principles governing airplane operation, they more easily voiced expectations and prophecies that were extravagant and utopian; even expertise in aeronautics by no means immunized one from making extravagant predictions. Furthermore, because the first generation to face the airplane had often grown up associating flying with angels in heaven or with other spiritual matters, individuals like Mary Parker more easily viewed it as God-given and divine, a device of unlimited power and promise.

The various predictions made regarding the airplane's social impact made up a kind of creed for aviation enthusiasts. Contemporaries do not appear to have used the term, but it is congruent with the phrase, "winged gospel," and with other terms they borrowed from religion will be useful here. The aviation creed, like that of various Christian faiths, spoke to questions of ultimate meaning and purpose and to the underpinnings of one's faith in god. It described the wondrous transformations which would occur if people only believed in and accepted the airplane. Prophecy then, provided justification for the most fervent and exuberant embrace of the new technology and for the devoted prosyletizing which airminded individuals undertook on the airplane's behalf.

No individual accepted each and every tenet of this creed. A person might embrace some prophecies, reject others, and still keep faith with the gospel of aviation. Only one tenet seemed universal: the idea that the airplane's coming portended a fundamental and marvelous change in human affairs. This notion, evident in Mary Parker's predictions of a "mighty era" and a "great new future of the world," also lay behind prophets' frequent allusions to the dawn of a "new epoch" or the imminent arrival of a "true" or "real" air age. Such references reflected the widespread conviction, again paralleling Christian doctrine, that the airplane had irrevocably cleaved history into two epochs and pointed prophetically toward a third. Kitty Hawk began what prophets usually termed the "air age" or "aerial age" and thus ended humanity's long and frustrating earthbound existence. Enthusiasts rejoiced that they lived in this air age, yet they looked forward nonetheless to an epoch more glorious still, the mighty era when the airplane's promise had been wholly fulfilled. This *real* air age, they predicted, would be an era not only of free and untrammelled movement for everyone in three dimensions but also of peace and harmony, of culture and humanity. The airplane, it seemed, would bring about a virtual millennium, an era beyond history when everything would be perfect, as in a utopia. Prophets seldom provided any timetable for the arrival of this millennium, and as the years passed it elusively kept receding further into the future. It was always scheduled for "tomorrow," and remained just around the corner. Yet the vision of flying machines bringing about perfection and making human society like heaven proved remarkably resilient and enduring.[3]

Of all the predictions Americans made about the airplane, the most oft expressed was that soon everybody would fly. Indeed, the expectation that democracy would prevail in the sky and that flying would become as common as riding or even walking was the cornerstone of the winged gospel. Without universal flight, prophets could not imagine a transformed society. In the coming air age, therefore, people would take to the air, it was predicted, not merely as a means of travel but for their health, for recreation, and even to perform their jobs. As for basic transportation, enthusiasts embraced either a vision of private aerial mobility along the lines of an automobile or what might be called a vision of aerial mass transit, modeled after a train or bus. When Alexander Graham Bell predicted in 1909 that the "aerial motor car" was just around the corner, the inventor of the telephone and a scientific authority identified himself with the more popular of the two images.[4] Indeed, the expectation that Americans would soon trade in their cars for aircraft so powerfully engaged the American imagination that it warrants more extended discussion, which is provided in Chapter five. The other vision of aerial mobility, extrapolating from experience with trains and even ocean liners, animated far fewer prophets. To predict, however, as a journalist did in 1911, that "within a few years there will be regularly scheduled passenger lines of airplanes carrying about a hundred passengers each, between the big cities of the Eastern Coast," was bold indeed.[5] Today such prophecies seem prosaic, so thoroughly has aeronautical development surpassed them. Yet at a time when aircraft struggled to lift two or three passengers, when experts claimed planes would never carry more than a handful of people, those who envisioned aerial mass transit probably sounded more visionary than those who anticipated a sky filled with small aerial limousines.

Moving beyond mere transportation, other seers described how Americans in the near future would go to work in the air. Air-age explorers, it was predicted, would make discoveries more easily and quickly; real estate agents would sell more readily after showing potential clients a property from aloft; and traveling salesmen would fly around the country using their planes as mobile show-rooms for their wares. Hunters would take to the air in open-cockpit planes and pit their "airmanship" against birds on the wing and animals on the run, asserted one prophet, while another expected the jockeys of tomorrow to ride winged mechanical steeds, thereby tolling the end of horse-racing. A collegian, writing in the Yale *News* in 1911, anticipated the day when the Harvard-Yale air races would draw large crowds and become a social occasion, just like football games and regattas.[6]

Such prophecies gained credibility from the fact that somebody, somewhere, had taken off from or landed in a football stadium or tried hunting from an airplane cockpit, and they in turn deepened the popular faith that tomorrow everyone would fly for every possible reason. Even "prophecies" mocking or satirizing that vision helped inculcate an ethos of we-all-shall-fly and publicize the possibilities of the new technology. A cartoon appearing in a December 1912 magazine, for instance, depicted an airminded, flying Santa Claus. It was Christmas night, and Santa was flying over a sleeping town. He stood in the sleigh-shaped cockpit of his airship and tossed Christmas greetings over the side. To underscore the revolution portended by flying machines, the cartoonist in a small inset showed Santa's reindeer and sleigh over the caption, "Abandoned."[7] A less sanguine spoof on the expected era of universal flying appeared about the same time in *Century* magazine. The author, Charles B. Loomis, decried the imminent demise of "the age of public safety," because criminals, incompetent operators, and other "reckless devils" would all be flying. "Think of the minor vexations that are sure to come," he wrote:

> droppings of oil on afternoon and evening gowns, the spilling of German aeronauts into Irish parades, the demolishing of chimneys and plate glass windows by fellows learning to fly, the obscuring of light by vast crowds collected over ball-grounds in order to see the national game for nothing.

But this was not all. Loomis described a flying machine, "in appearance much like a swallow," swooping down over the carriage of a "plutocrat" driving with his infant daughter on New York's Fifth Avenue. The pilot of the "trim" machine drove lower and lower and just as the craft was ready to collide with the carriage, his accomplice grabbed the baby from her father's arms. The kidnappers then headed for the heavens and freedom, exulting over their prospective ransom money.[8]

Although Loomis's jesting account suggested that undesirable consequences might result from the aerial revolution, most prophets imagined nothing but good as flowing from the widespread adoption of airplanes. This was the messianic thrust of the winged gospel. Americans widely expected the airplane to foster democracy, equality, and freedom; to improve public taste and spread culture; to purge the world of war and violence; and even to give rise to a new kind of human being. Before 1920, in fact, the airplane's future usefulness was usually discussed in the context of its social or moral impact. The man who predicted that planes would make horse-racing obsolete was typical. He cared little, really, about the use of aircraft or whether jockeys rode horses or piloted planes; what he loved was racing. But he resented having to pay for his pleasures. Airplanes would change this, eliminating the aristocratic pomp associated with the sport. Once jockeys took to the air, everyone for miles around could watch for free, and horse-racing would become "a democratic spectacle."[9]

Although relatively few people would have shared his devotion to horse-racing, many possessed a similar interest in making American institutions more democratic. It was a period of broad support for political reform, and Presidents Theodore Roosevelt, William Howard Taft, and Woodrow Wilson all thought of themselves as progressives and lined up on behalf of measures to ameliorate the social problems stemming from unchecked industrialization. The airplane, according to various prophets, would deliver the country from these conditions, among them the so-called railroad problem. Even before the Civil War, railroads had become giant corporations and appeared to pose a great threat to democratic values and practices in the United States. Railroads monopolized control over transportation in many parts of the nation, favoring some shippers by the granting of rebates while discriminating against others and in general charging what the traffic would bear. Furthermore, in legislatures around the country railroad lobbyists flaunted the democratic process and through bribes and favors demonstrated that corporate money easily prevailed over the people's desires. By the time the airplane flew into popular awareness, considerable legislation had been directed at the railroad problem, but discontent remained. Not surprisingly, the new invention seemed a panacea. "When man flies," predicted one enthusiast, "goodbye to the railroad for long distance traveling and—happy thought—to the rebate controversy." Another anticipated that the flying machine would eliminate "railroad rebates, overcharges, discriminations and the evils which our capitalistic system of distribution has brought upon us." Still another extolled the prospect "of transportation through the free air." For him the sky represented "the realm of absolute liberty; no tracks, no franchises, no need of thousands of employees to add to the cost."[10] The allusion to franchises reflected his generation's experience with street railways, which required municipal permission for their rights of way and constituted a tempting source of corruption in local politics. But it was the fact that airplanes rose above such messiness, above earthly corruption and avarice, that mesmerized observers. "Even Rockefeller with all his power," observed aeronautical publisher Alfred W. Lawson, in 1908, invoking the era's pre-eminent symbol of what Roosevelt called the malefactors of great wealth, "has not been able to control the air."[11] Enthusiasts could make no more telling point on behalf of the might of the winged gospel than this.

While some prophets interpreted the new sign in the heavens as ending corporate exploitation and promoting democracy, others read it as auguring the expansion of freedom and an end to discrimination. Such was the case with many of the women and blacks, mostly pilots, who worshiped the airplane. In 1911, shortly after learning to fly, New York journalist Harriet Quimby, soon to become the first woman to pilot a plane across the English Channel, confidently predicted that aviation would become a "fruitful occupation" for women. For Quimby, who died in an airplane crash the following year, the prophecy proved poignant indeed. Yet the notion of aerial liberation through flight found other proponents, especially in the twenties, as more women took up flying. Louise Thaden, a prominent air racer and pilot in that period, claimed that "sex distinction in the region of the air" was impossible and therefore predicted a great future for women fliers. Margery Brown, another pilot, offered a less mechanical vision of how sexual equality would come about. In "Flying Is Changing Women," she argued that flying was making them into confident, aggressive, and independent individuals who would soon demand and receive equal treatment.[12] Similar claims came from some of the small group of black pilots who were beginning to fly in the late twenties. Despite the prejudice and hardship they encountered learning to fly, procuring aircraft, and functioning as pilots, these fliers still predicted wonderful "opportunity," "increased prestige," and a "great future" for their race in the sky.[13] The most sanguine was William Powell, a college-trained engineer and World War I veteran from Chicago. He became airminded immediately after Lindbergh's flight and, after a long struggle to find a flying school that would admit him, around 1930 acquired his license, becoming one of the first of his race to do so.

Not much is known about Powell's subsequent career, but he preached a number of variants of a black gospel of wings. In a preface to *Black Wings*, his 1934 autobiography, Powell set forth one vision of the black aerial future: Well-to-do white people would soon be replacing their automobiles with airplanes, and black chauffeurs, therefore, would have a splendid opportunity to get in on the ground floor of aviation if they learned how to fly. This servile prophecy, wherein blacks chauffeured whites around in the sky rather than on the ground, gave way a few years later to a new vision of future black wings. In 1938 Powell envisioned a "gigantic industry" of black-owned and constructed airplanes, all operating under black control. His dream echoed earlier schemes by black leaders, such as the black owned and operated steamship line begun in 1919 by the charismatic Marcus Garvey. But Powell's vision was also pure, winged gospel in that his all black aviation enterprise would not only allow blacks to travel by air in the South, where other airlines barred them, but also it would convince whites of black abilities and thus lead to interracial harmony.[14]

Airplanes would also alter aesthetic values and taste, according to various prophets. Flying "fires the imagination of poet, sculptor, and painter," claimed an early writer, but not simply because planes possessed such "great beauty and interest that artists will hereafter seize upon" them as subjects.[15] Rather, as Stanton Macdonald-Wright put it, "the artist's inherent outlook" would change as a result of flight. Macdonald-Wright, a pilot, writer, and member of the avant-garde, developed his ideas in an article titled "Influence of Aviation on Art," published in an aeronautical magazine in 1919. Modern painting, he argued, was "a statement that the possibilities of realistic depiction of nature has been exhausted and that the details of faces, figures, landscape or still-life are no longer of any value," an insight confirmed by looking at the world from an airplane. Through flying, he predicted, would come a transformation in people's thinking that would make inevitable the triumph of abstract art.[16] Indeed, access to the same bird's-eye view would also cause city planners, landscapers, and architects to reassess their work, suggested other prophets. "The architect of the future may be obliged to lavish the same care upon the roof as he now bestows upon the façade of a public building," predicted science writer, Waldemar Kaempffert, while an architectural authority claimed that "country and certainly city architecture will be modified in style," simply because roofs will of necessity have to become flat to handle aircraft landings.[17]

Yet another widely anticipated change in attitude would have the result of curbing violence and bringing about the end of war. Airplanes, prophets thought, would usher in an era of perpetual peace, deterring aggressors and even eliminating the conditions that cause war. This was perhaps the most enticing promise of the winged gospel. To a 1909 commentator, the age of aviation would be the "age of peace" because only "fools" would dare fight when armies employed flying machines. Assuming that anybody could inexpensively manufacture airplanes, he expected small countries to possess as many machines as the largest nations, thereby preventing the latter from bullying the former. The mightiest nation in the air age would thus fear the smallest and weakest country, guaranteeing the deterrence of war.[18] Fear also would spread broadly through society, helping to assure perpetual peace. As Major G. O. Squire of the U.S. Army's Aeronautical Board explained in 1908, "the men who provoked wars have been pretty sure in the knowledge that their own skins were safe, and that others would have to do the fighting, now they will be in the thick of it and inclined to think twice before launching a war." He concluded that planes would therefore "lessen the number of wars." A contemporary of Squire's, drawing his metaphor from the realm of labor strife, envisioned a future in which soldiers, if attacked by aircraft, would "lay down their weapons" and simply walk off the job.[19]

Other prophets glimpsed a prospect far brighter than terror-induced deterrence. This was the elimination of the very cause of human conflict. Airplanes, claimed Philander C. Knox, prominent Republican and Secretary of State under President William Howard Taft, would "bring the nations much closer together" and in that way eliminate war. In more ornate prose, a contemporary wrote that the airplane "creates propinquity, and propinquity be-

gets love rather than hate."[20] Rhoda Hero Dunn, in a poem published in the *Atlantic* in 1909, caught some of the euphoria generated by the vision of peace: "Hearts leaped to meet a future
wherein unfenced realms of air have mingled all earth's peoples
into one and banished war forever from the world." This idea,
more than any other tenet of the winged gospel, spawned considerable poetry, a typical expression of which was "Wings," by
Charlton L. Edhold, also published in 1909.

> What narrow space holds man today apart from brother
>   man,
> A range of rock, a river or a span of Channel?
> Our wings shall overleap
> These dwarfish landmarks. *Then* what king shall keep
> His folks from merging with humanity
> As waters intermingle in the sea?
> Sail forth, winged Argonauts of trackless air
> And as upon your homeward course you fare
> Bring heavenly treasure. Neither gold nor steel,
> Nor gross and earthly wealth weight your light keel;
> Man's Brotherhood, bring *that* as Golden Fleece
> On sun-blessed wings, bright harbingers of peace.[21]

Even the flying machine's debut in combat, during the Balkan
War of 1912, hardly ruffled American faith in the airplane as a
harbinger of peace. Writing in 1915, shortly after the outbreak
of World War I, the editor of the magazine *Flying*, Henry Woodhouse, claimed the European war had to be "the last great war in
history" because, if it "had not taken place at this time," it could
never have occurred. "In less than another decade," Woodhouse
confidently argued, the airplane would have eliminated the factors
responsible for wars. Despite the raging conflict abroad, made
worse by aerial attack and bombardment, Woodhouse believed
that in the near future the airplane would render meaningless all
physical barriers dividing the world's peoples—the mountains,
oceans, and vast distances—as well as political obstacles to global
unity, such as border fortifications, customs houses, and protective
tariffs. Overleaping all such impediments the airplane would usher
in a "new period in human relations." Whereas the peoples of the
world had formerly been divided and hostile, in the coming air
age they would share a common sky and participate in a "peaceful
social revolution," Woodhouse confidently concluded.[22]

This aviation-wrought revolution would not only be peaceful, if the prophets were correct, but also thorough. It would, we have seen, produce a society at once more democratic, egalitarian, and cultured. But there was even more. Some Americans read the new sign in the heavens as portending nothing less than a great leap forward in human evolution, leading to a species physically and even spiritually transformed as a result of flying. Flying would change what men "strive for," believed sportsman and pioneer aviator Clifford Harmon. "All that is sordid and ugly and discordant [on the ground] seems remote and impossible" in the air, Harmon noted, and he was convinced the new angle of vision would alter people's earthly behavior. Charlotte Perkins Gilman, writer and radical theorist of the turn-of-the-century women's movement, even posited the emergence of an "aerial" person. In an article in *Harper's* titled "When We Fly," she predicted that the new type would possess a wholly different value system. Unlike inferior "earthy" man, the new "aerial" man "cannot think of himself further as a worm of the dust, but [only] as butterfly, psyche, the risen soul." The new attitude would bring about human "intercourse on a new plane," she buoyantly predicted.[23]

Pointing in that direction were claims that flying would create a healthier and sturdier race. Pilots reported that flying improved their eyesight, and journalists commented on the intensity of gaze and penetrating vision of the aviators; from such unscientific assertions, it was but an easy step to believe that human beings would eventually evolve into some kind of "air type." That people who had flown were reporting seemingly miraculous cures of ear and throat maladies further supported the idea that the heavens were a most powerful therapeutic environment. One publicized case was that of Grace Ford, a singer whose vocal cords had collapsed while entertaining troops during the late war. Thirty months after the accident, still unable to sing, she went up with friends in a plane. At about 8,000 feet, she later reported, "there came an unusual sensation in my throat and nose, just as if something had given way." At 10,000 feet her throat and nose felt "surprisingly clear. I instantly thought of my voice—the thing always uppermost in my mind—and there high in the sky softly tried a few notes. They were clear and surprisingly audible above the whirr of the propeller." Such testimonials just encouraged enthusiasts who, like the author of a 1921 article "The Therapeutic Value of Flying," anticipated that "the aerial sanitorium and the aerial therapist will yet have their day."[24] Patients would soon go aloft to partake, in the words of another prophet, of the "healthfulness of the upper regions of air" and return to earth cured of their various maladies. "Up, up into the pure microbeless air," chorused yet another believer, "the sick and suffering will be carried and nursed back to health in private air sanitoria and state and municipal air hospi-. tals."[25]

Alfred W. Lawson also believed in aerial healing, but his vision of the aerial future included not simply healthier people but a species reborn in the heavens. We have met Lawson in the capacity of aeronautical publisher, but he was a man of extraordinary versatility and energy whose career path moved erratically. In the 1890s he had played professional baseball and lectured on the Chautauqua circuit. He then drifted into writing and publishing, authoring in 1901 a utopian novel titled *Born Again* which, in its sanguine, Christian-focused enthusiasms, revealed the direction of his later aviation prophecy. It was in 1907, as he later explained, that God called him to the cause of flight and showed him his life's work.[26] First Lawson simply turned his literary talents to the new field and became the publisher of two aviation magazines. But soon he learned to fly, bought an airplane, and used it to travel to and from his office. By the time of World War I Lawson was designing airplanes, the most innovative being his 1919 "Airliner," a plane capable of carrying a then remarkable twenty-six passengers. After a widely publicized tour of the Northeast, including a stopover in Washington, D.C., where he made headlines by giving various congressmen a ride, Lawson retired from aviation. In the thirties he heard another call and once again was in the news, this time as the founder, prophet, and self-proclaimed messiah of "Lawsonomy," one of the many quasi-religious political movements that flourished on the margins of the Great Depression.[27]

In 1916, however, Lawson published one of the most extraordinary articles about the future of flying. Called "Natural Prophecies," the piece appeared in *Aircraft*, an aviation periodical published by Lawson. In the article he peered more than 8,000 years into the aerial future, stopping in the year 10,000 A.D. only because he doubted that his readers could follow him were he to prophesy further. Lawson began his "Natural Prophecies" with the near future, "prior to the year 1930." By that time airplanes would fly non-stop across the Atlantic, fly faster than 180 miles per hour, and carry passengers over regular routes. Moving ahead in time, he predicted that "prior to the year 1970 traffic rules of the air" would become necessary due to heavy airplane traffic.

It was not operations or even performance that interested Lawson, however, but rather the airplane's moral and spiritual implications, its ultimate consequences. The technical and utilitarian predictions that took him down to 1970 occupied but one page of "Natural Prophecies." The next four pages probed the distant future wherein he glimpsed the true promise of wings. The first point in this chronology, beyond 1970, was the year 3,000 A.D., by which time he posited the emergence of a "superhuman" among the pilots who spent a great deal of time in the upper atmosphere. This superhuman would "live in the upper stratas of the atmosphere and never come down to earth at all." Indeed, he would be incapable of descending beneath a certain altitude, having been "reconstructed physically and anatomically by long sojourning in the upper air." This creature, however, was but an intermediate form along the evolutionary flightway to what Lawson termed "Alti-man," one of "two distinctive types of human beings" that would appear "prior to the year 10,000 A.D." Alti-man would "be born and live his whole life" in the heavens, while "at the bottom of the atmospheric sea like a crab or an oyster" would exist "ground-man," presumably the descendants of those contemporaries of Lawson's who failed to accept the aviation gospel. Alti-man would be "ethereal," without body or substance, and he would "swim" in the air just at old-fashioned human beings swam in water. Obviously, Alti-man would have transcended any need for a flying machine. Having learned to control the weather, Alti-man would grow whatever food he needed in the sky. He would also be all knowing, as "great truths" would be revealed to him. Finally, Lawson stated that Alti-man on high would rule over ground-man on the earth below.[28]

Residing permanently in the heavens and possessed of superhuman power and intelligence, Alti-man was nothing if not a god. He epitomized the winged gospel's greatest hope: mere mortals, mounted on self-made mechanical wings, might fly free of all earthly constraints and become angelic and divine. With the airplane, Lawson suggests, human beings quite literally could move to the heavens and, given sufficient time, acquire the power of gods. Lawson deemed this evolution so inevitable that he called his prophecies "natural" and spoke of the distant future with a confidence unique among aviation enthusiasts, themselves a confident lot. This gained him a reputation for eccentricity, and indeed Lawson was a bit of a crank, "the craziest man I ever knew," recalled a leading aircraft designer and friend of his.[29] With over 8,000 years to run before the accuracy of his prophecies can be fairly assessed, however, perhaps history will vindicate him. Time already has shown his 1916 predictions regarding the short-term aviation future to have been remarkably prescient. He missed Lindbergh by only three years and of his generation was almost alone in sensing that air traffic control might someday be required. What is important here, however, is not the degree to which Lawson was a crank or whether Alti-man will or will not exist in the year 10,000. What is significant is that a major figure in the aviation field in 1916 could invest such potential in the airplane.

Lawson's natural prophecies, in fact, differed only in degree from the others we have been considering. The prophecies that together comprised the creed of the winged gospel may be arrayed on a spectrum, but all of them tended to promise something beyond the capacity of mere machines to deliver, something unattainable and utopian. At the most utopian end of this spectrum of belief stood Lawson, who more than any other prophet explicitly linked the airplane to man's becoming god-like and omnipotent. At the least utopian end would be those prophets who believed the airplane was simply the paramount catalyst working for beneficial social change. In the middle of the spectrum we can place individuals who expected airplanes to expand democracy, to foster equality, or to improve us in other ways. Yet what linked Lawson at one end of the spectrum with, say, the practical Lindbergh on the other, was the belief, as Mary B. Parker had written, that the airplane portended a "great new future of the world."

Remarkably few Americans opposed this view, that is, fell off our spectrum altogether. Virtually no American in the period appears to have attacked the flying machine as evil or undesirable. Unlike earlier transportation innovations, such as the railroad or the bicycle, which from their first use attracted passionate opposition, the airplane elicited virtually no negative comment. Nobody denounced the flying machine for imperiling the beauty of the natural landscape, say, as Hudson River residents had the railroad in the 1850s, or warned that the use of airplanes by young men and women would lead to immorality, as clergy had during the bicycling craze of the 1890s. The seemingly miraculous performance of flying machines, the fact that they in fact had little observable impact on the ground, guaranteed that almost anyone could love them, even the strictest moralists. What people disagreed on was not whether airplanes would be bad or good—most Americans assumed the latter—but rather what would be the shape of tomorrow's air age.[30]

A minority of commentators sounded a note of caution and skepticism amidst the din of unrestrained prophecy greeting the airplane. They criticized the "flights of fancy" and "extravagant claims" greeting the new invention. "Aerial transportation," one journalist critically observed, "puts a greater strain upon the average imagination than any other kind ever undertaken."[31] It was a subject, wrote another, that "unfortunately lends itself with peculiar facility to the fantastic dreams of the visionary." Such voices, it must be emphasized, were not anti-airplane or even negative toward the invention's impact. Often such critics accepted the general promise of the winged gospel while ridiculing particular extravagant prophecies. A background in science or some technical field, particularly aeronautics, characterized many of those who took a more skeptical stance. Most doctors, for instance, dismissed out of hand predictions about aerial sanitaria or about flying as therapy. Claims that flight would cure deafness, fulminated Dr. Wendell C. Phillips, founder of the American Federation of Organizations for the Hard of Hearing, was "intellectually on a par with the old faith in the curative qualities of the left hind foot of a rabbit shot in a graveyard on the dark of the moon by the seventh son of a seventh son."[32]

Similarly, men involved with the designing and building of aircraft, with some notable exceptions such as Alfred Lawson, escaped some of the strains which aerial navigation imposed on the popular imagination. In 1909, Glenn Curtiss, a pioneer airplane builder and pilot, warned that "we can hardly expect to see railroads, steamboats, and motor cars entirely displaced by flying machines as has been expected by some." The eminent civil engineer Octave Chanute, who had built railroads for a living and then in retirement experimented with gliders and became a mentor to the Wrights, ridiculed the popular writers who were claiming the airplane would "remodel civilization." Orville Wright usually resisted extravagant prophecies, displaying at times what appears to have been excessive caution, just to counter popular fantasies. One on occasion he categorically denied that airplanes will ever "compete with railroads or automobiles," while on another he said planes were never likely to fly faster than their present forty-five or so miles an hour. And Wright often refused to make any predictions. When asked in 1909 what aviation would be like in ten years, he replied: "I am not a prophet. I can't say. I don't know."[33] Some years later he explained "the difficulty" with prophecy:

> The moment you picture the future, the reader or the listener at once draws the conclusion that that period of flying has arrived. Such an impression invariably is followed by disappointment when it is realized that we are still short of what we believe to be easily attainable.[34]

Yet Orville Wright, like others participating in the conquest of the sky, was ultimately a believer in the airplane and an enthusiast. At times he did not not heed his own prescription against prophecy, like in 1917 when he predicted that the airplane soon would make wars impossible. That one as reticent and prudent could at times abandon his customary realism and embrace the airplane as a messiah demonstrated, better than anything else, the hold which the winged gospel had on Americans.[35]

It was only in the United States that enthusiasm over the airplane gave rise to anything like the winged gospel. The English, for example, did not imagine the airplane as creating utopia, quite to the contrary. They took a far more realistic view of what flight would accomplish. Indeed, in that country anxiety rather than anticipation characterized most public reaction to the dawn of flying. As early as 1908, the year before Frenchman Louis Bleriot first piloted a plane across the English Channel and threw into doubt England's insular security, London papers were already talking about possible aerial invasions. An American journalist thought the papers' "desperate prophecies" and "gravest apprehensions" silly, for he believed air attack "improbable" and not "worthy of serious discussion."[36] But Englishmen did discuss the matter. In 1908 H. G. Wells published *The War in the Air*, and at the same time the English popular press abounded with articles such as "The Command of the Air," "The Wings of War," "The Aerial Peril," and "The Airship Menace," all portraying the flying machine as a most ominous intrusion into human affairs and a dire threat to national security.[37]

Harold F. Wyatt, author of the article "Wings of War," typified this darker, more pessimistic response to the airplane, a response that in retrospect appears prophetic indeed. Englishmen, Wyatt wrote in 1909, would in the air age be "doomed helplessly to gaze into the skies while fleets which they are powerless to reach pass over their heads." English homes would suffer tremendous and crushing attacks. Furthermore, "a new set of elaborately trained warriors" would be needed to operate the new machines, posing "a great peril" to a democratic nation accustomed to defense by "mases of briefly-trained men." Wyatt's prescient glimpse of some of the institutional changes likely to flow from the widespread adoption of aircraft technology had little parallel in the United States, where prophets often equated the future air age with the elimination of specialists, large organizations, and even the transportation industry itself. Paradoxically, English prophets glimpsed the future with great accuracy, while Americans, who had developed the techniques of mass production and large-scale organization to the most advanced level in the world, still often believed in a future of airplanes built by individuals in backyards and barns. Yet it was not the emergence of a military technocracy which seemed to Wyatt the worst augury of the impending air age. Rather, he worried most about the airplane's impact "upon the British Empire." "We shall be torn from our pedestal of insularity and flung into the same arena in the dust of which our fellow-nations strive," he predicted. Distances "will shrivel into insignificance," and England and Canada would become exposed to attack from the Orient. "Signs of coming danger" were everywhere, Wyatt concluded, and it would be folly not "to recognize the gigantic shadow cast by the wings of war."[38]

Geography, of course, helps explain why Englishmen looked aloft and saw shadows while Americans saw bright harbingers of peace and a new sign in the heavens. If one lived 3,000 miles from potential enemies, if one were protected by broad oceans, it was much easier to believe that "propinquity begets love rather than hate" and that airplanes were doves of peace. But the English and American reactions to the airplane diverged on more than simply the issue of war and peace. English commentators rarely spoke of the airplane as if it would transform values, behavior, taste, or the human race. In fact they often faulted Americans for entertaining such romantic and utopian expectations. All the discussion of the "purpose" of airplanes in the United States was ridiculous, charged one English critic, and "to talk about their changing the conditions of life and the face of the world is a poetic exaggeration."[39]

Poetic exaggeration regarding the promise of technology was an old habit in the United States, running back to the second quarter of the nineteenth century. At that time Americans already were investing their machines with messianic powers. In an 1832 article about the "moral effects" to be expected from the recently invented railroad, Charles Caldwell, a physician, typified a newly emerging attitude. Railways would weld the nation into one "mighty city," Caldwell predicted, but not the corrupt and decadent kind of city Americans associated with Europe and so detested. Railroad-generated cities in the United States would have "the knowledge, refinement and polish" of traditional urban centers but also possess "the virtue and purity of the country," he confidently asserted. Furthermore, railroads would "grapple" the feuding sections of the country together and halt the deepening rift over slavery. Railroads would also provide "a sort of guarantee against the commission of crimes," because they would eliminate the deprivation which nourished such anti-social actions. Finally, railroads would lead to more travel by women, whose moral example on the trains would prompt imitation and thus improve the "personal cleanliness, dress, manners, taste, knowledge, and morals" of the less refined classes! All told, Caldwell expected the railroad innovation to be one of "the leading causes of the country's millennial perfection."[40] In concert with other mechanical inventions, the railroad was, as another nineteenth-century writer wrote, "ushering in the very dawn of the millennium." Machinery, in fact, in the words of yet another observer, was "a gospel worker" whose mission was "the same as that of the savior."[41]

This kind of response to technology, termed by recent scholars "technological messianism" or "technological utopianism," went beyond the traditional faith in progress inherited from the Enlightenment. Eighteenth-century thinkers had developed an equation holding that systematic application of reason to human affairs would inevitably bring about moral progress. They did not discredit science or mechanics in that formulation, and indeed their philosophy conduced to advances in those realms. Yet eighteenth-century observers seldom elevated mere devices to the primary agents of progress. Only in the nineteenth century did people begin to speak of the machine as if it alone, more than human reason, could effect beneficial social and moral changes in society. Then, for the first time, the machine became a messiah.[42]

In the United States, technological messianism grew out of religious and industrial developments. By the time Caldwell speculated in 1832 on the future moral impact of the railroad, Americans had experienced the beginnings of an industrial revolution. A middle-aged observer at the time would likely have seen in his own lifetime the advent, among other inventions, of steamboats, agricultural machinery, power-driven textile equipment and integrated mills, and finally railroads, all of which had not existed in his youth or at least in his parents' time. He would have witnessed, again within memory, dramatic changes in work and leisure, in transportation and commerce. And he could easily quantify these changes, reading in the hours saved traveling, say, from Boston to New York or in the time required to produce a given quantity of yardgoods the actual pace of progress. The giddy rate of recent technical innovation suggested further improvements in the future, and it was but a step to assume tomorrow's technical advances would further improve society and advance civilization. The machine became not only the symbol of social change but, in the eyes of many, the primary agent of change.

Simultaneously with the introduction of mechanized factories and steam-powered transport, religious developments contributed a second necessary ingredient for technological messianism. Evangelical Protestantism became more influential in American culture, and salvation, once limited by a sterner, more Calvinistic interpretation to the divinely elected, now was promised to all. Preachers extolled the prospects of replicating heavenly perfection right on earth, if only people had faith. Particularly during the 1820s, charismatic preachers had carried this new version of the gospel around the country, holding large outdoor revival meetings which attracted thousands. The combination of an optimistic, this-worldly religion with an industrial revolution encouraged many to view secular developments as evidence of religious progress. Machinery became a "gospel worker," and devices of iron and steel seemed pregnant with great moral and spiritual implications.[43]

The winged gospel, then, built upon an attitude toward technology that was three-quarters of a century old. But it also owed much to an even older tradition, one running back to earliest recorded history. This was the idea that flying was somehow divine. Since ancient times, virtually all of the world's religions had pos-

tulated some sort of heaven-dwelling or flying god. Long before
the airplane was even a dream, human beings had associated flight
with omnipotence and immortality, traits frustratingly absent in
themselves. It was the connecting of this tradition with the newly
invented flying machine which distinguished the gospel of aviation from responses to all other inventions. For the flying machine
possessed a unique and extraordinary intellectual prologue, a history of accumulated longings and projections which a scholar,
Berthold Laufer, once called the "prehistory of aviation." Laufer
was a well-known anthropologist with the Field Museum in Chicago when, in the year after Lindbergh's flight, he published a
book with that title. In the monograph he explored the myths,
legends, and religious beliefs incorporating flight motifs which existed in Far Eastern cultures. He argued that there was "no field of
human exertions in which imagination and romantic dreams have
played a greater role" than in aviation and believed that such
dreams underlay the age-long quest to build a machine that could
fly. He was right, though it was not Eastern religions which mo-
tivated Westerners to develop the airplane. Instead, it was Christianity which provided the relevant "prehistory of aviation." But
while we might easily document the influence of Christian faith
on the invention of the airplane, its influence is even clearer with
regard to the popular response to flying machines once they were
invented. Without the prehistory represented by Christianity, the
gospel of aviation would have been inconceivable.[44]

Christianity bequeathed a cargo of assumptions and rhetorical
patterns which Americans, even non-believers, were hard-pressed
not to load onto the newly invented flying machine. The various
Christian faiths, of course, in cosmology, doctrine, and iconogra-
phy richly manifested the ageless human fascination with flight.
The Christian God dwelt in heaven, above the earth, and His only
son, Jesus Christ, following his crucifixion, was resurrected from
the dead and then rose or ascended into heaven. This was the central miracle of Christianity, an article of faith for Christians for
over a thousand years. In nineteenth-century America, particularly during the generation preceding the invention of the airplane, however, religious rhetoric prepared people to greet the airplane as a heavenly gift in the twentieth century. In children's
primers, for instance, youngsters read rhymes such as the following, which appeared on the page alongside a picture of a balloon:

In joy and glory
We shall rise
To be with Christ
Above the skies.[45]

Their elders listened to sermons that similarly confused flight as a mode of transportation and as a spiritual accomplishment. In a typical "flight" sermon, later published, Phillips Brooks, a prominent Boston divine, characterized men and women as "poor wingless things who strut and grovel in their insignificance." He urged his audience, therefore, not to emulate their fellow human beings but rather the Seraphim who could fly. This ability made the Seraphim moral exemplars and sources of unlimited spiritual power, Brooks observed. Sometimes preachers, rather than setting up flight as an ideal urged a kind of imaginative or vicarious flying, as with a sermon by the famous New York cleric Henry Ward Beecher. "Begin if you will on the earth," Beecher instructed his parishioners, directing his remarks particularly to businessmen, who he felt were weighted down by anxieties over trade and other earthly matters. He told them to "rise" into the heavens and partake of the elevating influences available there. Finally, Beecher commanded his listeners to "come back again to earth from whence you ascended, bringing something more than you took on your flight."[46]

Such late ninetenth-century training inevitably influenced the response to the airplane in the twentieth century. Consider the words of Gill Robb Wilson, the son of a clergyman who became an ordained minister. Wilson learned to fly during the World War and went on to a career as a committed evangelist of the winged gospel, covering aviation as a correspondent for the New York *Herald Tribune*, writing flight poetry, and serving as New Jersey's Commissioner of Aeronautics. "I think the origin of my interest in aviation would probably go back to the place where I read that Heaven was upstairs and the angels flew," recalled Wilson later in his life. "It wasn't a technical interest in an airplane so much as it was an interest in what could be accomplished if the fundament was a highway of man's ambitions."[47] Wilson exemplified how enthusiasm for aviation and hope for the aerial future rested upon traditional Christian beliefs. Flight as a technical achievement blurred with deeply embedded associations of the heavens as a place of spiritual promise, even for pilots, who knew best what aircraft were and what they could and could not do. Indeed, pilots often described their aerial experiences in the language of religion. "Flying is something spiritual as well as practical," reported one flier, while another reported feeling "a power akin to Godliness" while flying alone in a plane.[48] It was the "freedom from the earth" that made flying seem so "supernatural," observed yet another who thought it would remain so "until the nature of the race has been changed by flying."[49] They all would have agreed with pilot Norman Hall, who, looking down on "the masterpiece of The Master Hand" in 1920, asserted that the flier "finds that his viewpoints concerning many of the vital issues of existence are undergoing a subtle change":

> The small, petty disturbances of life become lost in insignificance, as the great eternal truths become more and more evident. Who shall say that this new flying perspective, concerning old worlds and new, is not broadening mankind today?[50]

It was not just pilots who believed that the airplane was broadening mankind, that flying brought one closer to heavenly perfection. We have seen that many earthbound Americans, individuals like Mary M. Parker, also read the new sign in the heavens as auguring a marvelous new future. Historically accustomed to think of machines as engines of beneficial social change, conditioned by religion to confuse mechanical flight with spiritual transformation, the generations of Americans that responded to the airplane after 1908 accepted eagerly the promises of the winged gospel. Visions of future promise, in fact, underlay present enthusiasms. For many enthusiasts, however, it was not enough simply to believe in the prophetic creed of wings. Belief demanded action. Accordingly, airminded men and women sought ways to demonstrate their faith in the airplane, to convert others to that faith, and to promote aeronautics in whatever way possible. Through action they hoped to hasten that glorious day when the promise of wings would be fulfilled. Their evangelical efforts on behalf of the winged gospel are the subject of chapter 3.

III

"Let Your Airmindedness
Be Shown Forth Among Men":
Evangelizing for Aviation

In 1929 some St. Louis men took off in a plane with an unusual cargo, what the New York *Times* called "an airminded cow." At 2,000 feet in the air, the cow's handlers milked the animal and put the milk in pint-sized containers, attached each to a small parachute, and then dropped them over the city. A year later in Los Angeles, a group of people gathered as a tri-motored plane was hitched to a walking plow, the sort farmers had employed since the nineteenth century to prepare soil for planting. A man, dressed in flight suit and wearing goggles, grasped the plow's handles and held on tightly to avoid being blown over by the prop wash as the plane revved up its engines. The plane then started to move forward while the plowman walked behind the plow, guiding it through the soil. The activities were part of a very airminded ground-breaking ceremony for a new airport.[1]

At one level such behavior was of a piece with the zany exhibitionism of the Jazz Age. The aerial dairying over St. Louis and the airport ground-breaking in Los Angeles strongly recall the marathon dancing, goldfish swallowing, flagpole sitting, and numerous other fads or unusual competitions of the twenties and early thirties. In that period, many Americans went overboard, as it were, in a cultural climate that supported a new permissiveness regarding public and intimate behavior. The ballyhoo of the era also reflected new and more aggressive ways of merchandising and advertising products, including the use of public relations professionals and new forms of media, such as radio and billboards. The greatest billboard of all, of course, was the sky, and in a climate of sensation seeking, airminded journalism, taking a cow aloft to milk or virtually anything else one did with or in an airplane earned a story in the newspaper and became an easy way to boost ones product.

At another level, however, the St. Louis and Los Angeles actions were part of a pattern of behavior by which enthusiasts demonstrated their faith in the airplane and sought to recruit others to their vision of the aerial future. By employing airplanes in as many aspects of daily life as possible, by practicing what might be called an airminded lifestyle, enthusiasts believed they were advancing the cause of aviation. Such motives no doubt animated, at least in part, the actions of the flying dairymen in St. Louis and the airminded airport promoters in Los Angeles. When Angeleanos hitched a modern transport plane to a plow, for instance, they probably hoped their action would garner publicity for their airport. At the same time, however, they considered the ground-breaking a kind of ritualistic celebration of the winged gospel, an act of faith in the airplane's promise to transform the world and the human condition. Furthermore, the ground-breaking ceremony, and even behavior as blatantly commercial or exhibitionist as the St. Louis cow episode, represented a means of trying to inculcate airmindedness in the broader public. Indeed, one can view such behavior as emphatically evangelical, an effort to win converts to the prophetic vision of the aerial future.

Aviation enthusiasts tended to view flight as a "holy cause," one requiring not only total devotion but also dedicated prosyletizing or evangelizing. The idea was, as a World War pilot and engineer put it, addressing an aviation conference in Boston in 1927, to "let your airmindedness be shown forth before men," for the world would be better for it. His language followed closely the wording of the benediction traditionally given at the end of Christian worship, pointing up once again the strong influence of religion on the thought and behavior of aviation enthusiasts. Indeed, airminded men and women felt that everyone should worship the winged gospel. "The spirit would indeed be dead," wrote one partisan, "that would be unwilling to lay some little sacrifice on such an altar."[2] The sense of aviation being a holy cause for which one offered sacrifices prompted many kinds of behavior.

Perhaps the first act of airplane worship was by the Wright brothers. After making their epochal flights at Kitty Hawk in December 1903, the brothers returned to Dayton, Ohio, arriving home in time for Christmas. They decided at that time to preserve the

Kitty Hawk Flyer intact, as a "symbol of the beginning of an era." In this act they departed from the usual practice of inventors and mechanics who, without sentiment or concern for history, tinkered with a machine to make it work better or cannibalized it for parts to build another one. But the Wrights shared the conviction, the heart of the winged gospel, that the miracle at Kitty Hawk marked a new and wonderful age in history. Therefore they kept their plane for posterity, whole and unchanged.[3]

Their Flyer became the primary relic of that miracle, not simply a piece of the true cross but the cross itself. Over the years, the collecting of aviation relics became common, a form of airplane worship analogous to the reverence for relics shown by traditional religions. An early instance of the appeal of relics to the airminded occurred in 1906, when members of the New York Aero Club, comprised of balloonists and aeronautical experimenters, were organizing an aeronautical exhibition to promote interest in flight. Knowledge of the Wrights' Kitty Hawk flights was still limited, for they had not yet flown in public. Yet some men in the Aero Club had heard of the achievement and wrote asking to borrow their flying machine for the New York exhibition. The Wrights refused, explaining that they were trying to sell their patents on the machine and did not want to reveal its exact construction and workings. The Aero Club spokesman persisted, begging for the loan of "any relic" of the Kitty Hawk plane. Finally, the Wrights offered him a few parts from the Flyer's original engine, though they doubted that "it would be worth while" to display them. The Aero Club was delighted, however, and in New York grandly exhibited the fragments with the label: "crankshaft and flywheel of the motor which for the first time in the world's history carried human beings in long, birdlike flight, unsupported by gas and starting from the level."[4]

To the airminded even the tiniest remnants that could be linked to the miracle of Kitty Hawk, or to any important flight, took on symbolic importance. One of the largest collections of such relics was that of Mrs. C. A. Tusch of Berkeley, California. It's origins were somewhat accidental. In 1917 Mrs. Tusch lived near the campus of the University of California where an aviation ground school was being conducted. When the flu epidemic hit the area, a disaster that took the lives of many Americans that year, she volunteered as a nurse and got to know the young men training to become aviators. After the crisis passed, "Mother" Tusch, as she was called, became a kind of one-woman USO for the cadets, her home functioning as an informal canteen where they always found refreshments and hospitality. Soon her young friends were leaving Berkeley for flight school and then the front. They remembered "Mother" Tusch and began sending her aeronautical memorabilia, first from Europe and then, after the Armistice, from literally all over the world. By the 1920s, her home bulged with relics, including the propeller used on the first flight from San Francisco to Oakland, in 1912; a gasoline cap from the plane in which Canadian World War ace Major William Bishop achieved his final victory; a piece of fabric from the Navy's NC-4 which in 1919 became the first plane to cross the Atlantic; a spare hose carried by Lieut. Russell Maughan of the U.S. Army during the 1923 Dawn to Dusk transcontinental flight; and a drain plug from the 1926 Pan American Good Will Flight. These objects, and many, many more, jammed Mrs. Tusch's simple frame cottage, now known to pilots as "the Hangar." The relics filled bookcases and cabinets and covered the walls, where they competed with an even larger collection of photographs, also sent her by her "boys."[5]

The boys often dropped by to see "Mother" Tusch and to admire the collection. Although most people would have had difficulty identifying many of the objects had they not been labeled, to the aviators these prosaic objects resonated with great aerial accomplishments and could inspire wondrous aerial deeds in the future. It was this kind of perspective that turned aeronautical debris into treasured relics of the secular religion of flight. And it was this reverential stance toward the objects that explained why "Mother" Tusch could be called aviation's "Patron Saint" and her house dubbed the "Chapel of Aviation" and the "Shrine of the Air." For her house and its contents were sacred to many fliers in the years from the First World War through the Second. In 1947, in fact, when the University of California expanded its campus and planned to raze her house, a number of her former cadets campaigned to preserve it as a shrine. One proposal, never followed, even called for moving her cottage by ship to Washington and installing it intact as the centerpiece of an aviation museum and memorial.[6]

Other kinds of behavior displayed a similar faith in aviation's inspirational powers. One of these was the effort of Henry Woodhouse, beginning around 1926, to develop what he called "George Washington Air Junction." Woodhouse, a former aeronautical publisher and president of the Aerial League of America, hoped to build this facility on a mile-square portion of George Washington's ancestral homelands near Alexandria, Virginia. The Junction would in part be an airport, meeting the need of the capital which still lacked an adequate landing facility. But Woodhouse's vision encompassed something far grander than merely transportation. George Washington Air Junction really was a testament to his faith in the gospel, his belief in the airplane as a messianic instrument for change. The Junction, he announced, would be a "twentieth century, aeronautic, scientific and historic center." On its grounds would be an "artists' airpark," where painters would congregate to soak up inspiration from the airplanes landing and taking off, and a "junior airpark," where boys and girls would fly their model planes and learn about aeronautics. The Junction would also house Woodhouse's large collection of Washingtoniana and thus become as well an historic and patriotic "shrine." Tourists would come to see the collections, to ramble over the "gorgeous eighteenth century pastoral setting," or to take off on aerial sightseeing trips over the routes traveled in earlier times by George Washington himself. Although Woodhouse obtained options on land, secured some supporters in Congress, and generated considerable publicity for his plan—a two-page banner headline in a local paper prematurely announced that "Nation's Greatest Air Center Is Located Near Alexandria"—George Washington Air Junction never became an operating reality. When Congress a few years later finally chose a site for a capital airport, the location on the Potomac River that would in 1939 become National Airport, Woodhouse's dream collapsed. But in trying to build an institution that made the airplane central to cultural, artistic, and educational development, he showed himself to be truly airminded. George Washington Air Junction was a most worthy offering on the altar of the holy cause of flight.[7]

The easiest way to show one's airmindedness was to fly. Indeed, pilots frequently thought of themselves as missionaries, spreading the truth of airplanes by deed rather than by word. Such was the barnstormers' view of their work. In the 1920s and 1930s, enthusiasts perceived almost any kind of flight as advancing the aviation cause if only because it demonstrated the possibilities of the airplane. There were some flights, however, which demonstrated airmindedness more purely. These were usually flights that either took some normally earthbound activity and made it aerial, like milking a cow, or which, through some grand aerial gesture, aimed to change society by influencing popular opinion. The first type might be called flights of the mundane, while the second could be labeled flights of the ideal. The first type was quite common, the second rare, but both spoke to the same belief, almost universal among fliers, that *everyone* would fly tomorrow and that almost literally, society would take to the heavens.

Enthusiasts adopted all kinds of earthly rituals and actions to an aerial idiom, particularly in the post-Lindbergh years. One example occurred high over New Jersey in early 1930, when a man and woman took their wedding vows, solemnly repeating the ancient phrases as they were spoken by the clergyman who sat in the rear seat of their cabin monoplane. Only the fact that the groom was also the pilot, handling the plane with one hand as he slipped the wedding ring on his bride's finger with the other, made the ceremony newsworthy, so common had aerial nuptials become by that time. In one such wedding, the newlyweds had not only been married aloft but also departed for their honeymoon by parachute.[8] Far less common than weddings in the air were births, and predictably most of those were the result of poor planning. In Florida, however, a couple chose to have their child born in the heavens. When Mrs. T. W. Evans of Miami went into labor in October 1929, she and her doctor husband, along with Mrs. Evans's mother, another doctor, two nurses, and a pilot, all rushed to the local airfield. Twenty minutes later, as their large cabin plane circled steadily at 1200 feet, Mrs. Evans gave birth to "Aerogene," a baby daughter and member of what the New York *Times* could not resist calling "the rising generation."[9]

Even death received airminded treatment. When an aviator died in an airplane accident, his fellow pilots often flew over the spot of the crash and dropped wreaths or flowers. In the case of a natural death, or when a non-pilot died, scattering the ashes of the deceased from a plane became popular. In 1949 a man from Texas came up with an idea whereby a conventional burial might be adapted for the air age: he patented an airplane-shaped coffin. His patent drawing shows a coffin, rounded in shape like a fuselage, to which is attached the stabilizer, elevators, and stubby wings, each carrying two dummy engines. Like aircraft designed for use on carriers, the wings of the coffin fold to permit it to be lowered into a conventional-size grave. And on one side of the coffin, leaving no doubt as to its relation to the winged gospel, were inscribed the words, "Wings to Heaven."[10]

The rituals of birth, marriage, and death were not the only flights of the mundane, that is, earthly events performed in the air. One ritual that especially lent itself to the heavens was preaching. As early as 1922, Lt. Belvin M. Maynard, the "flying pastor" of the U.S. Army, delivered an Easter sermon from the cockpit of his airplane, beaming his message by radio to a large audience. Not a few ministers followed his example and found the heavens an attractive—and attention-getting—pulpit. On December 25, 1929, Harold McMahan adapted to the air age a ritual connected with Christ's birthday. As he took off from Mitchell Field, Long Island, with his family for Florida, the cabin of his plane held a fully decorated Christmas tree, "for the children."[11] Moving from the sacred to the profane, the rage for card playing that capitivated Americans in the twenties and thirties not surprisingly moved to the air. A group of Philadelphia matrons allegedly invented aerial bridge, claiming the game to be superior to the earthly variety, and many well-heeled individuals took up the fad. The most publicized aerial foursome was surely that hosted by Eleanor Roosevelt, shortly after her husband had been elected to the Presidency. Just as he had shown his airmindedness by flying to Chicago in the summer of 1932 to accept personally his party's nomination, pledging in that speech a New Deal for the American people, so Eleanor demonstrated her enthusiasm for aviation by taking her social life aloft. In December 1932, as her large transport plane circled over New York City, she and three friends played a rubber of bridge while half a dozen members of the press sat and observed, generating some clever publicity, for the Roosevelts, of course, but also for aviation.[12]

Among the other day-to-day routines that enthusiasts made into flights of the mundane was, of course, travel. Commuting by air fascinated Americans, as we've noted, one of them being Senator Hiram Bingham of Connecticut. Bingham had learned to fly during the World War and put behind him his former career as a scholar-explorer during which he had taught Latin American history at Harvard, Yale, and other universities, and had discovered in Peru the ruins of the ancient Inca civilization at Machu Picchu. In the 1920s Bingham became an ardent disciple of the gospel, accepting the presidency of the National Aeronautic Association and, in

1928, being elected senator from Connecticut. One summer day in 1929, Bingham startled his fellow legislators by arriving at the Capitol by Army blimp, alighting on the steps to attend a meeting of the Senate Banking Committee, to which an urgent telegram had summoned him. Two years later he previewed another gambit in tomorrow's aerial lifestyle when he arrived for work in an auto-giro (a precussor of the helicopter), carrying his golf clubs, after an early morning game at a nearby country club. In these actions, Bingham was not merely displaying the politician's endemic fond-ness for publicity, although surely he was not averse to press cov-erage. Rather, he fervently believed in the vision of personal flight and sought to back belief by action. In 1931 Bingham told a re-porter that the autogiro was "the solution to the air-commuter needs for the future" and that it offered almost "the safety of a church pew."[13]

Another believer in the vision of mass personal flying, Harry H. Culver, made a flight in 1929 that possessed characteristics of both the flight of the ideal and the flight of the mundane. In the sense that he simply used a personal plane to travel to speaking engage-ments, Culver's flying hardly evidenced any special idealism. But when one considers that his "flight" was some 100,000 miles long, that he gave talks at his own expense in some 650 cities, and that he did not expect personally to benefit from the trip, it takes on atributes of a personal crusade. Indeed, Culver made the tour on behalf of his vision of tomorrow's air age. He believed rural land in America was on the verge of "the most drastic changes that have ever occurred to this class of property in the history of the world." A mass exodus was about to occur as Americans aban-doned their cities to take up residence in semi-rural settings—while still staying in close touch with the metropolis through airplanes. Culver himself had become rich through real estate development, most notably through the building of Culver City, a new commu-nity outside of Los Angeles, and in that work he had hopped around the greater Los Angeles area by personal plane. His own experience, then, lent credibility to his message.[14]

Culver's self-chosen ministry on behalf of the gospel relied heavily on the power of words to supplement the fact of flight, but a few individuals conceived of flights that they hoped would change the world directly. These were the purest flights of the ideal. An example that did not even get off the ground was Clif-ford Harmon's effort to use airplanes to end war. Many prophets had claimed the air age would be an era of peace, but Harmon, a wealthy aeronautics enthusiast and early pilot, actually tried to form an organization pursuant to that belief. In 1929 he proposed to the League of Nations what he called the "Silver Wings of Peace." The organization would enlist the leading male and female pilots of the world to create a kind of flying counterpart to the League. In the event of an international crisis, the pilots of the Silver Wings would fly over the quarreling nations and drop peace leaflets. This, Harmon thought, would cause most disputants immediately to cease any bellicose behavior. The mere demonstration of aerial brotherhood, it seemed, would end the crisis and restore peace. Sentiment for international action, as opposed to discussion, on behalf of peace was then missing in the League, a problem compounded by the United States not being a member. Thus, Harmon's effort came to naught. It testified, however, to his faith in the gospel. This was hardly diminished by the fact that, as if sensing the utopian quality of his Silver Wings, Harmon posited a second international group to go with the first, this one comprised of pilots and planes representing 10 percent of each nation's air force. In the event the Silver Wings did not keep the peace, this armed international air force would prove, he believed, the ultimate deterrent.[15]

Another flight of ideals was the Inter-American "Good Will Flight" made by Dr. Albert Forsyth and C. Alfred Anderson in 1934. The fliers, both blacks, conceived of the effort as an antidote for racial prejudice and as an explicit instrument of bettering race relations. Forsyth and Anderson, respectively an Atlantic City physician and a former mechanic and chauffeur for a well-to-do Philadelphia area family, projected a 12,000-mile flight around the Caribbean. Forsyth believed Caribbean blacks held an even more negative opinion of American Negroes than did whites in the United States, thinking them all either "slaves or servants," unable to vote, and incorrigibly "shiftless and lazy." The Good Will Flight, he believed, would once and for all disabuse prejudiced observers of the idea that American blacks had "never done anything worthwhile." By generating "favorable publicity" for the race, the flight would bring about a new era in inter-racial harmony.[16] Aided by a committee of "Good Will Flight Boosters," the two aviators purchased a new plane which they christened the *Booker T. Washington* in ceremonies at Tuskegee Institute in Alabama. They prepared carefully, making a number of long-distance practice flights and consulting with Charles Lindbergh about safety equipment. Despite their preparations, they had to abandon their flight after visiting four of the twelve countries on their planned itinerary. Bad luck plagued them and a series of mechanical failures, coupled with a minor landing mishap on the island of Santo Domingo, ended the Good Will effort.[17] Even had they completed their flight, it is unlikely that Forsyth and Anderson would have measurably diminished racial prejudice. Yet if their attempt was peripheral to the history of improving race relations, it fit strongly into the tradition of believing in the airplane as an instrument of social reform. Forsyth and Anderson, along with Harmon, Bingham, and many others, considered aviation a secular religion which promised tremendous benefits. In witness to their faith, they laid their various sacrifices on the "altar" of the winged gospel.

Celebrants of the gospel of wings had no church that brought them together, of course, yet one observance united virtually every airminded man, woman, and child in a kind of spiritual communion. This was the celebration of the airplane's birthday. On every December 17th, just as Christians honored the birth of Christ, believers in the winged gospel solemnly paid homage to the original "miracle" that took place at Kitty Hawk in 1903. This tradition seems to have begun in 1909, the year after the Wright brothers made their public debut at Ft. Myer and demonstrated their flying machine. In December of 1909 the Smithsonian Institution hosted a dinner in honor of the Wrights, who were presented with the first Samuel P. Langley medal, named for the recently decreased head of the Institution who had also been an enthusiastic aeronautical experimenter.[18] There were not as yet any public events held to mark the passing of another year of the airplane age, although in 1909 the press widely reported the anniversary, applauded the progress made in the air since Kitty Hawk, and speculated about aviation's future prospects.[19]

As airplanes came into wider use and more people became airminded, commemoration of the airplane's birthday changed from an occasion celebrated in private by a few aeronautical insiders to a popular and public event. Particularly after Lindbergh, December 17th became a day of public remembrance, made official when in 1934 President Franklin D. Roosevelt designated it as National Aviation Day. Airminded men and women kept December 17th as a veritable holy day, an occasion that demanded "feasting and rejoicing," according to Senator Hiram Bingham.[20] As will be evident, no aviation activity borrowed more heavily upon Christian terminology. Furthermore, the rituals directed at commemorating the airplane's birthday possessed striking parallels to those performed by Christians in celebrating the birthday of Christ.

First there was the ritualistic retelling of the original miracle. Just as the clergy would repeat the story of Christ's birth every December 25th, aviation enthusiasts would each December 17th recite the events that had taken place at Kitty Hawk. Providing new information was not the point: the audience invariably knew the salient facts anyway. Rather, the telling itself was important, for it affirmed one's faith in the winged gospel and gave believers a sense of collective purpose in their support of aviation. For Christians, of course, the cornerstone of their faith was the belief in personal salvation; for believers in the winged gospel, it was the belief in some kind of social salvation through flight. A second point of congruence between the two birthday celebrations, then, involved a reiteration of those promises, a reciting of the respective creed of each faith. Finally, the celebrants, whether on December 17th or on December 25th, demonstrated their faith not only through words but also by deed. They laid some kind of symbolic sacrifice on their respective altars, some small offering to their respective gods.

These points of similarity to Christian ritual, along with the extravagant and public celebrations of the airplane's birthday, may be illustrated by considering the ceremonies held in 1928, the twenty-fifth year of flight. Although festivities occurred in many places around the country, the most important one was at Kitty Hawk. A governmentally sponsored "pilgrimage," led by Secretary of War Dwight F. Davis and including congressmen from Ohio and North Carolina; a contingent of officials and citizens from the Wrights' birthplace in Dayton, Ohio; numerous aviation celebrities, including Senator Hiram Bingham, Amelia Earhart, and Orville Wright; and representatives of many foreign countries—all these people traveled to the remote site on the North Carolina coast. In the morning on December 17th the group laid a cornerstone for a large monument that would soon be erected atop Kill Devil Hill, from which site the Wright brothers, beginning in 1901, had made their first glider flights. In the afternoon, the pilgrimage retired to the flatter ground beneath the hill, where they dedicated a tablet marking the precise spot where, at 10:35 a.m. twenty-five years earlier, the world's first airplane had left the ground.[21]

In the two ceremonies speakers characterized Kitty Hawk as "already sacred" ground and predicted it would soon become a "national shrine." Many would journey "to this spot in centuries to come" and "pay reverent tribute" to the airplane. "Today the homage of the world is given here. Tomorrow it will become the pilgrimage and the Mecca of those whose happiness [will] have been enhanced." Besides worshiping the airplane by deeming its birthplace holy, the speakers reiterated their belief that the airplane was wondrously transforming the world. As Secretary Davis laid the cornerstone for the hilltop monument, placing within it a sealed metal box containing the original manuscript of the first news dispatch reporting the Wrights' first flight along with other aviation relics, he emphasized this fundamental tenet of the winged gospel. "Even as we today lay the corner stone of this memorial," he said, "so aviation of today is building the foundation for a great structure—the aviation of tomorrow.[22]

In the major address of the day, accompanying the dedication of the first-flight marker, Senator Bingham emphasized another tenet of the gospel: the airplane was a dove of peace. Acknowledging the presence of the guests "who have come to this sacred spot from many lands," Bingham claimed that airminded people everywhere were "guided by one principle. That principle is profound faith in the art of flying." Bingham then told the familiar story of what happened at the very spot on which they were standing, some twenty-five years earlier. He described the cold weather and the biting wind against which Wilbur and Orville had to contend and their primitive "device that looked like a cross between a box kite and the skeleton of a bird." Then, after lovingly recounting the events leading up to the first miraculous moment, Bingham measured aviation's progress since Kitty Hawk by comparing those first flights with present world records. From a flight lasting under a minute and covering less than a quarter-mile, aviation had developed to the point where men had stayed aloft without refueling for 65 hours and flown 4,466 miles. Yet even those wonderful achievements, Bingham predicted, were but a prelude: "What we have today is but an indication of what we shall have in the future."[23]

This same three-part ritual, featuring the retelling of the original Kitty Hawk miracle, prophecies of aviation's dazzling future, and deeds evidencing people's commitment to the aviation cause, continued to characterize public commemoration of the Kitty Hawk anniversary through the 1930s and into the Second World War. Within this common format, however, believers in the winged gospel developed variations on their December 17th celebrations. They consecrated other sites as sacred ground for the aviation religion, such as Dayton, Ohio, the home of the Wright brothers. Wilbur Wright had died in 1912 and was buried in Dayton, but by the late twenties his grave had become a spot where aviation enthusiasts gathered every December 17th to deliver appropriate speeches and decorate his grave with a wreath. Believers in the gospel also elevated the Wright brothers' bicycle shop to hallowed ground. There the brothers had conducted their early flight researches and constructed their first flying machines. Henry Ford had bought the building in the twenties and moved it to Greenfield Village, his museum of Americana and technology which was opened to the public in Dearborn, Michigan, in 1927. Like Kitty Hawk and Wilbur's grave, the bicycle shop became a place where the airminded gathered on December 17th to retell the story of the airplane's birth, rejoice in subsequent aeronautical progress, and to voice their faith in a wondrous aerial tomorrow; the place was, as Dayton publicists liked to call it, "the shop that became a shrine."[24]

Enthusiasts could celebrate the birth of flight virtually anywhere, it seemed, as long as they incorporated an airplane into their ritualistic observances. In 1933, for instance, on the thirtieth anniversary of the air age, Philadelphia's Franklin Institute honored the airplane's birth by dedicating an aviation exhibit featuring the Lockheed aircraft that Amelia Earhart the previous year had flown alone across the Atlantic. At the ceremony were Earhart, Orville Wright, and other aviation dignitaries. Because Wright invariably declined to make speeches, Frank H. Russell, president of the Manufacturer's Aircraft Association, retold the obligatory Kitty Hawk story. He read, however, from an account published decades earlier by Orville Wright, a kind of sacred text as it were of the 1903 miracle. Amelia Earhart then delivered the major address of the day, running over aviation's tremendous progress since then, developments that she believed portended further progress in the future. She also extolled the beauty of flight and its influence on the imagination, "one of the most important things the Wright brothers gave to humanity."[25]

At the very same time Earhart, Wright, and others were commemorating the airplane's birthday in Philadelphia, another group stood around a glass exhibit case at the Smithsonian Institution in Washington, D.C. They too were honoring the airplane's birthday, focusing their attention on a small model of the original Kitty Hawk Flyer. After the traditional speech making, members of the local unit of the Women's National Aeronautic Association reverently placed a wreath against the exhibition case containing the miniature plane. In the absence of the real Kitty Hawk Flyer, the model airplane served as an object of worship. It became a kind of icon, a symbol of the winged gospel and its promise.[26]

Whenever possible, enthusiasts included aerial observances as part of their celebration of the birth of flight. The most dramatic and flamboyant aerial ritual was held on December 17, 1934. Eugene Vidal, President Roosevelt's Director of Air Commerce who was charged with regulating and promoting civil aviation, had written an open letter to all pilots and aircraft owners requesting that on December 17th all licensed airplanes in the country make a "flight of remembrance." He wanted as many planes as possible to take off at 10:30 in the morning and to stay in the air for half an hour. They would thus be aloft at the precise time at which, thirty-one years earlier, Orville Wright had also been airborne. The response to Vidal's call was impressive. According to the New York *Times*, all available planes in the New York metropolitan area took to the sky "in honor of the first flight," while nationally an estimated 8,000 aircraft participated in the ritual. So aerial was the celebration, in fact, that the *Times* subheadline noted, almost as an afterthought, that "aviation officials also mark the anniversary on the ground."[27]

More typical than Washington-directed mass maneuvers were individually initiated flights of remembrance. On the thirty-third anniversary of Kitty Hawk in 1936, for instance, a National Park Service pilot dropped a wreath over the newly completed Wright Memorial at Kitty Hawk, and an airline pilot circled above Wilbur Wright's grave in Dayton while Orville, on the ground below, placed a wreath. Another pilot flew from North Carolina to Dayton carrying two bags of sand from the Kitty Hawk dunes. The sand was to be spread on the runway so that the first scheduled transcontinental transport plane, shortly to arrive there, would land on the very same sand from which the world's first airplane had risen, years earlier.[28]

The spreading of sacred sand from Kitty Hawk on the runway in Dayton reflected for aviation enthusiasts their faith in the airplane as an instrument of social reform and messianic transformation. The action, like the dedication in 1928 of a marker at the sites of the first flight at Kitty Hawk, the laying in 1933 of a wreath on the model airplane at the Smithsonian Institution, or the carrying out in 1934 of "flights of remembrance," symbolized the tremendous optimism and hope which Americans invested in flight. Throughout the 1920s and 1930s such rituals expressed enthusiasts' belief in the promise of the winged gospel. Yet by the 1940s, many Americans were becoming estranged from the "holy cause" of flight. For the Second World War produced a change in the way Americans thought of aircraft. People began to view the airplane not as a messiah but rather as an ambivalent agent in human affairs, even as a menace. Greater realism entered into public discussion of aviation and popular perceptions of its future. These new sentiments invariably showed up on December 17th, in the rhetoric and behavior surrounding the commemoration of the airplane's birthday.

The outbreak of war seemed at first merely to interrupt the aerial part of the Kitty Hawk rituals. On December 17, 1939, just months after the Nazis stormed into Poland, the Army and Navy refused to allow any of their planes or pilots to participate in the thirty-sixth anniversary observances, because of the urgency of war preparations. In 1940, military aircraft helped commemorate the day, but the next year the Japanese attack on Pearl Harbor prompted the immediate cancellation of all flights of remembrance planned for the thirty-eighth birthday. For the duration, all non-essential flying remained prohibited, although in speeches and writings many Americans continued to treat December 17th as a day of reverence and thanksgiving.[29]

But new tones of ambivalence, anxiety, and above all realism obtruded into these ceremonies. Assimilating the news from Pearl Harbor, Midway, London, Dresden, Okinawa, and eventually Hiroshima and Nagasaki, Americans inevitably came to think of the airplane first and foremost as a weapon, as an instrument capable of unprecedented destruction and horror. As a result it became harder to believe unequivocally in the flying machine as a messiah, as an unalloyed blessing and panacea. One symptom of this new perspective, unthinkable earlier, was that people raised, on the airplane's birthday, the question whether it was an evil or salutary influence in human affairs. In 1943, for example, Senator Bennett C. Clark of Missouri called the airplane's invention the "greatest disaster that has ever happened to mankind." Few were willing to go that far, but Americans commonly in the early 1940s aired ambivalent sentiments about the airplane on the Kitty Hawk anniversary. "Aviation," said John K. Northrup, a prominent aircraft manufacturer, on the airplane's fortieth anniversary, "is perhaps the strongest force that man has created and let loose upon the earth—be it for death and destruction, as it is at present, or for the glorious future of understanding and brotherhood that we hope awaits it."[30]

Immediately after Pearl Harbor, Orville Wright had registered a similar lament, claiming that the airplane was presently "in the hands of barbarous men" and wreaking terrible damage. He nevertheless predicted that it would "be instrumental in establishing for the entire world a guarantee of human liberty and lasting peace." After two more years of aerial horror, Wright still had no regrets for having invented the airplane. There was no need to feel guilty on that score, agreed Alexander Seversky, aircraft designer, builder, manufacturer, and vocal advocate for air power, who told Americans that they were entitled "to an easy conscience in relation to the airplane." Other countries bore the entire blame for the carnage being wrought from the sky. Seversky argued, and confidently predicted that the airplane would be "the greatest instrumentality of world peace despite its baptism in blood."[31]

In this wartime rhetoric, hymns to nationalism are superimposed on the once purer paeans to the airplane and the winged gospel. Clearly enthusiasts were now perceiving the airplane as a political tool, as an instrument of Allied strategy rather than a self-acting agent of beneficial change. It was only friendly planes, after all, that Seversky, Wright, and others saw as promising a future that was anything but terrifying. Only by assuming Allied victory could they consider the airplane an "instrumentality of world peace." But the cause of Allied air power gave the winged gospel a new and less utopian interpretation that would weaken it considerably.

A full-page advertisement placed by the Curtiss-Wright Aeronautical Corporation in major newspapers on the airplane's fortieth birthday typified the new emphasis. The advertisement depicted a family, consisting of husband, wife, and child, standing together in a field looking skywards. Behind them was a giant monument to the Wright brothers. The family gazed toward the skies as three heavy bombers, B-17 Flying Fortresses flew overhead. The text of the advertisement read as follows: "At 11:00 a.m. today, the people of 33 nations are watching the sky, united in a common hope of victory, for liberation, and for a better world to come. Look to the sky, America!" In its reference to a "better world to come" and the image of the family gazing toward the heavens, the advertisement was pure winged gospel. Yet by limiting the worship of the airplane only to the people of the Allied nations, it reflected the narrower, more political, and secularized gospel that emerged during the war. Americans would continue to pay homage to the airplane, particularly on its birthday, but the rise to prominence of military aviation and the ascendancy of air power as an arbiter of international affairs lent a new thrust to such rituals.[32]

The new strategic and military tone of the airplane's birthday celebrations continued after VJ Day. Gone forever was the purer and more idealistic spirit of earlier anniversaries. December 17th was now a time to parade airforce equipment and demonstrate American air power. The ceremonies at Kitty Hawk in 1949 illustrate the changed spirit. Hundreds of airplanes participated in the rituals that day, but every one of them belonged to the military. In fact, the U.S. Air Force Association handled the planning for the event. Although some of the civilians made remarks that echoed the purer gospel of old, it was strategic and military air power that dominated the proceedings not only at the podium but also in the sky.

To begin, Congressman Herbert C. Bonner of North Carolina read to the assembled audience a letter from President Harry S. Truman. The letter itself had already traveled by plane around the world to symbolize the fact that, thanks to aircraft, "most of the world is now linked together." Yet the circumstances behind the letter's 25,000-mile trip to Kitty Hawk had little to do with visions of a world united by flight into one harmonious brotherhood such as earlier aviation prophets predicted. Rather, the intent of the flight was to demonstrate that one could fly around the world exclusively on U.S. flag carriers, a goal of American diplomatic negotiations and corporate lobbying ever since the early 1930s. The Air Force veteran who carried the letter on its globe-girdling flight rode entirely on scheduled U.S. airlines. The letter, then, testified much more to American faith in free competition and to the political policy of "open skies" than to the winged gospel.[33]

In the letter itself, President Truman similarly preached the more political and military message of air power and anticommunism. "The task which faces us today," he wrote, "is no less challenging than the task which faced the Wright brothers on that historical December day:

> It is for us to use the instrument they gave us as a force for peace; to make the peoples of the world spiritual neighbors as well as physical neighbors.
> This is a responsibility which free men the world over owe each other. We Americans and many of our neighbors across the seas stand ready to do our part—to make the world's airways paths of peace—to use our planes for travel, for pleasure, for commerce and for all the peaceful pursuits that make up our daily lives.[34]

This was rhetoric for a world ideologically divided between communist and free, a world threatened by the possibility of nuclear annihilation. It still carried the message of the gospel, but now the airplane was the key to peace only through its force as a weapon.

If Truman's words left any doubts on this score, they were removed by the Air Force with thunderous emphasis. Immediately after Congressman Bonner finished reading the President's letter, planes of the 156th and 157th Fighter Squadrons of the Air National Guard swept overhead in a "V" Memorial formation, that is, a chevron with two places in the "V" empty. This was a military tradition signifying that two fliers were missing. In this case, the two pilots were civilians: Orville and Wilbur Wright, symbolically inducted into the Air Force in the spirit of the day. Wilbur, it will be recalled, had been dead since 1912, but Orville had died in January of 1948. As the planes passed, two wreaths were placed to commemorate the brothers on the Memorial atop Kill Devil Hill. Next came what the Air Force Association called an "Air Progress Formation," consisting of a flyover by bombers, fighter

planes, and patrol craft. After it passed, the F-86 jets in the formation peeled off and doubled back over the Memorial. As they came
in low over the crowd, the announcer started to count the seconds,
ticking off the twelve seconds that Wilbur Wright had remained
in the air forty-six years earlier. The jets drowned out his voice as
they leaped toward the horizon with a deafening roar, covering
nearly two miles in the time the first Flyer stayed aloft.[35]

Compared with Hiram Bingham's verbal description of post-
Kitty Hawk progress in 1928, this demonstration of aviation's
advance must have been impressive indeed. But it also was somewhat terrifying. In fact, terror was an emotion that since the war
could not be disassociated from airplanes. It lay just beneath the
surface at Kitty Hawk on December 17, 1949. This was not simply because the aircraft overhead were such powerful and destructive weapons. It owed much to the act that the Soviet Union had
recently exploded its first nuclear bomb, raising the specter of
atomic war. In a nuclear age, the relationship of flying machines
to the future no longer could be wholly sanguine. Nobody could
easily believe the older, more buoyant hopes regarding the air age.
When speakers from the podium that December morning predicted great improvements in future aircraft, their words simply
could not dissipate the fear of possible nuclear war and even human extinction. Unlike earlier aviation prophets, in 1949 they
could not even promise survival, not to mention perpetual peace
or transcendent social reforms. The rhetoric and behavior at Kitty
Hawk made it abundantly clear that by mid-twentieth century
aviation's position as a holy cause was considerably weakened.

Yet for almost half a century, large numbers of Americans had
worshipped the airplane as if a god. They had read in "the new
sign in the heavens" a wondrous promise, and much of their behavior was devoted to praising flight and spreading the message of
the winged gospel. Their faith in the gospel influenced not only
their expectations for and their use of the airplane. It also affected
the way they promoted aeronautics and even the kind of aircraft
they developed. In the next three chapters we shall consider three
such instances of promotion and development. Each represents a
case study of a group of aviation enthusiasts and their beliefs and
activities. A chapter on women pilots considers how the gospel
combined with traditional stereotypes of women to permit female
fliers to play an important role in fostering popular acceptance of

flying. A second chapter focuses on the efforts of individuals who believed in the possibility of an airplane in every garage. Their effort to devise machines appropriate for a truly democratic air age reveals how the gospel affected even the planning and design of aircraft and airports. A third chapter looks at the attempts by parents, educators, and other adults to make their children air-minded and thereby assure, at least in the next generation, the coming of the long-promised air age.

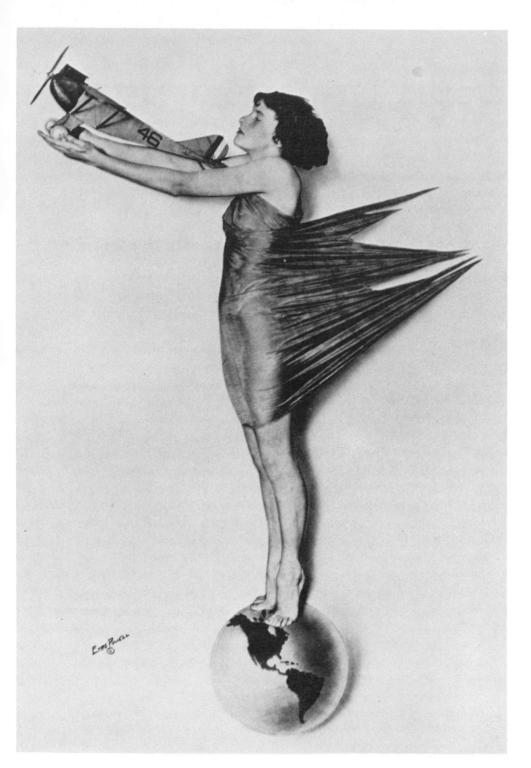

Looking back to classical precedents in sculpture, photographer Eyre
Powell created this *Goddess of Flight* in 1922. He posed his model on a
miniature globe, had her hold a model airplane, and simulated the effect of
wind and speed on her costume. (Library of Congress)

Many songwriters celebrated the airplane in music, just as they had earlier written songs about the bicycle and automobile. One of these was Alma Ives, whose 1919 tune, *Wed in an Aeroplane*, reflected the growing number of aerial nuptials. (Author's Collection)

On November 22, 1935, Pan American Airways inaugurated Clipper service between California and the Orient. Here an officer receives a mailbag delivered by a Wells Fargo stage coach, an action symbolizing the passing of mail transport from land to air. To symbolize flight's ultimate destiny, another mailbag was dropped into the hold of the flying boat electrically, triggered by a signal from a distant star, sent to the Alameda dock from a nearby astronomical observatory. (Pan American Airways)

In 1922 opera singer Miss Jeannette Vreeland posed with her pilot Bert Acosta just before taking off to give an aerial concert. (Author's Collection)

A most spirited aviation evangelist, Senator Hiram Bingham of Connecticut stood on the wing of an autogiro on his return from a round of golf during the summer of 1931. Bingham later told the press that the autogiro was almost as safe as "a church pew." (Library of Congress)

Lindbergh's flight prompted the creation of all kinds of aviation ephemera, some of which simulated the appearance of his plane, the *Spirit of St. Louis.* Here a Los Angeles girl holds "The Spirit of Savings," an airplane-shaped aluminum savings bank designed by a local inventor. (Author's Collection)

As Americans became more airminded in the late 1920s and 1930s, the Patent Office received many ideas for objects designed to look like airplanes. For the aviation conscious lady, this 1930 patent showed the perfect handbag.

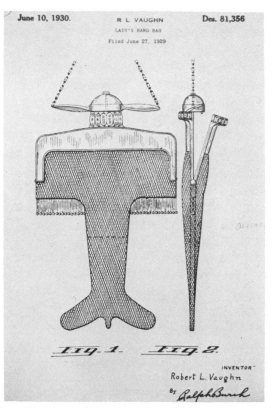

June 10, 1930.   R L VAUGHN   Des. 81,356

LADY'S HAND BAG

Filed June 27, 1929

Fig. 1.   *Fig. 2.*

INVENTOR
Robert L. Vaughn
By *Ralph Bunch*

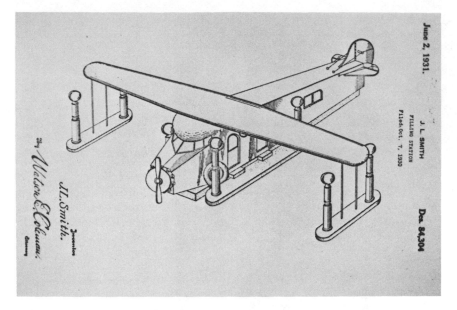

Patents for various airplane-shaped buildings were common in the period.
Here is one for a filling station, issued in 1931.

An electric motor turns the propeller of this "Airplane Fan" of about 1930.
It is typical of various airplane-simulative appliances and household objects,
such as clocks and lamps, that were produced for an airminded market.
(Private Collection)

Artists also became airminded, creating works that dealt with flight or aviation themes. When Aline Rhonie received a commission for a mural to decorate a hangar at Roosevelt Field, Long Island, she painted the history of early flight. Miss Rhonie was not only an artist but also a pilot. (National Air and Space Museum, Smithsonian Institution)

One of the rooms filled with aviation relics in the home (called the "hangar") of "Mother" Tusch of Berkeley, California, seen in a late 1940s' photograph. (National Air and Space Museum, Smithsonian Institution)

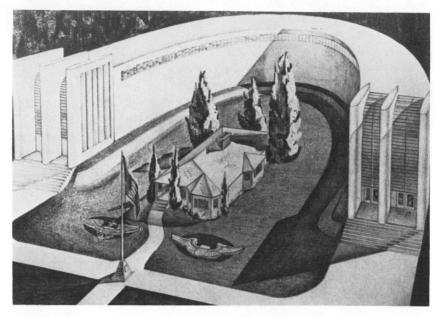

When "Mother" Tusch's hangar was threatened with demolition in 1947, some enthusiasts proposed transporting it by ship from California to Washington, D.C., and making it the centerpiece of a large aviation museum and shrine. This contemporary sketch illustrates the proposal which never materialized. (National Air and Space Museum, Smithsonian Institution)

As this pre-World War I broadside makes clear, some of the "World's Greatest Birdmen" were women. One was Blanche Scott, who with her male colleagues of the period performed daring aerial feats at flying exhibitions and air shows. (National Air and Space Museum, Smithsonian Institution)

Some of the post-Lindbergh generation of women aviators were employed by the U.S. Bureau of Air Commerce as Air Marking Pilots. Their job was to persuade communities and businesses to paint identifying signs on rooftops, roadways, and airfields to aid pilots in navigation. From left to right, Louise Thaden, Blanche Noyes, Helen MacClosky, and Helen Richey. (Elizabeth Hiatt Gregory Collection, Special Collections Library, University of California, Los Angeles)

The most famous woman pilot, the "Lady Lindbergh" of the day, was Amelia Earhart, shown here with pilot Wiley Post in 1935. Later that year Post lost his life in a crash which also killed Will Rogers, the beloved humorist and aviation enthusiast. In 1937, on the final leg of an around the world flight, Earhart disappeared over the Pacific. (Elizabeth Hiatt Gregory Collection, Special Collections Library, University of California, Los Angeles)

In 1929 women pilots established an all woman pilots organization, the Ninety Nines, and organized the First National Women's Air Derby. Dubbed by Will Rogers the "Powderpuff Derby," the race went from Santa Monica to Cleveland and generated great publicity, helping women pilots find a place in aviation. (Author's Collection)

In the 1930s Americans looked to Washington for all kinds of assistance to weather the hard times. For airminded individuals, Eugene Vidal, Roosevelt's Director of the Bureau of Air Commerce, personified the hopes for a new deal in the sky. Vidal stands here next to Waldo Waterman's "Arrowplane," one of the so-called "safety planes" subsidized by his agency and touted as forerunners of the machine for the masses. (National Air and Space Museum, Smithsonian Institution)

The most publicized of the Bureau of Air Commerce subsidized aircraft was the Roadable Autogiro, capable of being flown in the air and driven on the highway. Here the machine has been photographed after delivery to the Commerce Department in 1936. (National Air and Space Museum, Smithsonian Institution)

Vidal's Roadable Autogiro on the Highway. (National Air and Space Museum, Smithsonian Institution)

Waldo Waterman, builder of one of Vidal's safety planes, receives a "ticket" in a later, roadable version with removable wing, his so-called "Arrowbile." (National Air and Space Museum, Smithsonian Institution)

A 1938 promotional brochure for Waldo Waterman's roadable "Arrowbile." (Author's Collection)

While aircraft builders designed machines to put the masses in the cockpit, a number of architects struggled with the problem of where to store the family flying machine. Architect George Keck showed this "Home of Tomorrow," complete with planeport, at the Chicago World's Fair of 1933-34. (Ken Hedrich, Hedrich-Blessing)

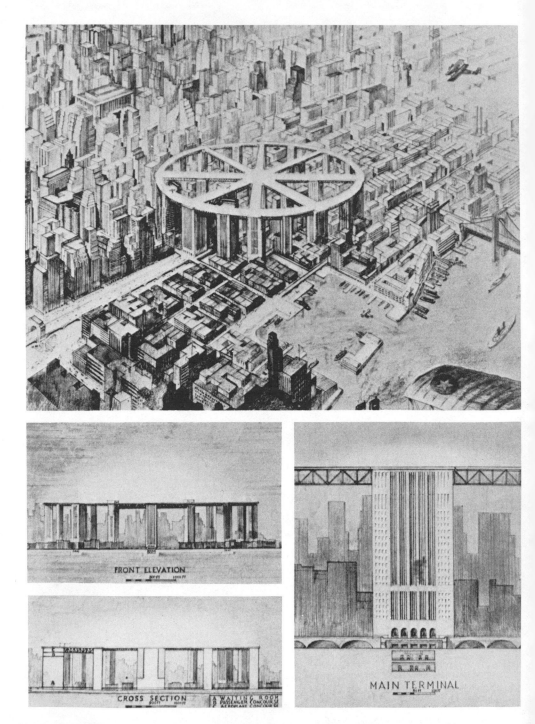

Early aviation enthusiasts proposed various solutions to the problem of how to bring airplanes into the city. This design, an entry in an airport competition conducted by the Lehigh Cement Company in 1928, envisioned a giant, spoked-wheel-shaped landing platform supported by a ring of skyscrapers.

This "Airport of the Future" was designed by E. P. Goodrich, city planner, and Francis Keally, architect, both of whom were advisers to the Lehigh Airports Competition in the late 1920s. It was exhibited at the Grand Central Palace Air Show in New York. (Author's Collection)

Frustrated by the inability of passenger planes to cross the ocean, inventors in the twenties and early thirties proposed building airports in the ocean so that planes could refuel and thereby extent their range. Here Edward R. Armstrong stands in the lobby of the Hotel Roosevelt in New York with a model of his "Seadrome" or "Ocean Utopia," intended for a location 250 miles east of New York in the Atlantic Ocean. (Author's Collection)

Chief Engineer O. R. Angelillo of Los Angeles is shown with a model of a "skyscraper air terminal." Twelve stories high and 980 feet by 152 feet at the base, the combined office building and airfield was expected to cost ten million dollars. (Author's Collection)

When the U.S. Government imposed sixteen years as the minimum age for pilots in 1927, Jack Chapman had just become the country's youngest aviator at age eleven. Here he stands by his plane just after soloing—and on the eve of his youthful retirement. (Author's Collection)

Boys and girls showed their airmindedness by building model airplanes. In February 1930 some of them posed with their model planes and zeppelins on exhibition at the Grand Central Palace Air Show in New York City. (Elizabeth Hiatt Gregory Collection, Special Collections Library, University of California, Los Angeles)

By organizing flying competitions and model clubs, adults encouraged youngsters to make model airplanes. One of these clubs, the Junior Birdmen of America, was the creation of publishing magnate William Randolph Hearst. Junior Birdmen flew their planes at a meet in Central Park, New York, in the mid-1930s. The circle in the sky identifies a high-flying model. (Author's Collection)

Nurses at the University of Pennsylvania learned about model airplanes from Victor R. Fritz, field director of the Philadelphia Model Aeroplane Association. The nurses planned to instruct their boy and girl patients in model airplane construction. (Author's Collection)

These boys posed for the press with their models at the dedication of the first "Junior Airport" in the United States. Under the supervision of the Los Angeles playground commission, in the 1930s the facility was exclusively devoted to model airplane activities. (Author's Collection)

In the 1930s radio spread the winged gospel to the young. One radio adventure was the "Jimmie Allen" show, sponsored by the Richfield Oil Company of California and starring a company pilot, Dudley Steel. Through the free *Jimmie Allen Club News*, available at local Richfield gas stations, youngsters learned about model airplane building contests and how to get this autographed photograph of "Jimmie Allen." (Elizabeth Hiatt Gregory Collection, Special Collections Library, University of California, Los Angeles)

Jimmie Allen Club members at the Burbank, California, airport greet their hero, "Jimmie Allen," alias Dudley Steel. (Elizabeth Hiatt Gregory Collection, Special Collections Library, University of California, Los Angeles)

Susie and Johnnie

"Who's a Sissy?"

Proponents of the winged gospel preached egalitarianism in the skies, as this cartoon strip from the *Jimmie Allen Club News* shows. (Elizabeth Hiatt Gregory Collection, Special Collections Library, University of California, Los Angeles)

Because girl model airplane builders competed at a disadvantage, Amelia Earhart put up trophies for girls whose models stayed aloft the longest. Here, one of the first winners of the Earhart trophy, thirteen-year-old Betty Hind of San Francisco stands with her successful airplane model. (Author's Collection)

The late 1930s brought a new form of power to flying models, gasoline engines, and a new link between junior aeronautics and patriotism and preparedness. This news photograph of two contestants, posed in front of their flag, typifies the spirit of model aviation as the world entered the Second World War. (Author's Collection)

THROUGH the ages man has carried the dream of a magic carpet—a wonderful conveyance capable of whisking him about with the ease of a wish. Of all his endeavors to attain this happy dream, the Airphibian comes perhaps the closest.

It carries him as the eagle flies, over mountain, river and desert. Nor does it fail him when he again touches ground. There it still provides continuous private transportation capable of running him to and fro at any time of the year, the day and the night.

Engineering achievement of the Airphibian, with all its successful research and government testing, marks an important milestone in man's endeavor to travel with more ease, pleasure and mutual profit among his fellow men.

As the war came to an end in 1945, the longstanding dream of wings for everyone seemed close to attainment. Returning GIs wanted to buy planes, as apparently did millions of other Americans. New firms appeared, offering enticing new flying machines, such as the Fulton Airphibian, pictured on this 1946 promotional brochure. (Author's Collection)

THE FULTON AIRPHIBIAN

"The airphibious age is upon us," announced the Fulton Airphibian brochure in 1946, "the beginning of a new era in transportation." (Author's Collection)

Changing from driving to flying would be simple, according to the designer of the Fulton Airphibian, who promised "5-Minute, 1-Woman Conversion Time." The model's white dress emphasized that conversion, "a strictly light-handed job," was also a clean one. (Author's Collection)

Moulton Taylor's "Aerocar" was another of the air-road hybrids to appear after the Second World War. In designing his Aerocar to pull its wings and stabilizer along with it when on the highway, Taylor avoided the difficulty owners of Fulton Airphibians would face if caught somewhere without their wings. (National Air and Space Museum, Smithsonian Institution)

Just before the outbreak of war in 1939, Fred Weick introduced the Ercoupe, a two-seat, all-metal plane that featured a simplified control system and tricycle landing gear, both innovations designed to make flying safer and easier. When production resumed after the war, Ercoupes sold well. In 1946 Santa Claus arrived in Chicago in an Ercoupe, riding in the fourth plane of the jeep-drawn parade. (National Air and Space Museum, Smithsonian Institution)

FEBRUARY 1951   35 CENTS

POPULAR
MECHANICS
MAGAZINE
WRITTEN SO YOU CAN UNDERSTAND IT

See page 118

If an airplane-in-every-garage was impossible, how about a helicopter? By 1950 this was the vision of many Americans who still looked to the sky for mass personal transportation. The cover of *Popular Mechanics* for February 1951 illustrated a jet-powered job and enticed readers with the story, "Here Comes Your Helicopter Coupe."

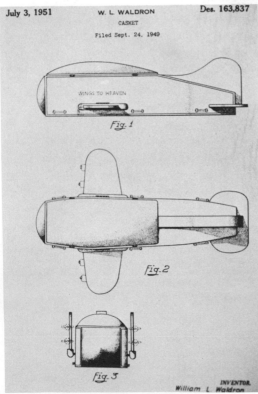

July 3, 1951   W. L. WALDRON   Des. 163,837

CASKET

Filed Sept. 24, 1949

WINGS TO HEAVEN

Fig. 1

Fig. 2

Fig. 3

INVENTOR.
William L. Waldron

Perhaps the ultimate expression of the winged gospel is this airplane-shaped casket, emblazoned with the words "wings to heaven," which a Texas enthusiast patented in 1950.

IV

Making Flying "Thinkable": Women Pilots and the Selling of Aviation

As they turned to their newspapers on the morning of September 5, 1936, many Americans looked for the results of the previous day's Bendix Trophy air race. In an airminded era, such racing resonated with romance, excitement, and import for the future. And the Bendix, a transcontinental speed dash, in 1936 from Floyd Bennett Field on Long Island to Mines Field in Los Angeles, was always front-page news—the "most important" of all air races, according to the New York *Times*. For days Americans had been following preparations for the race. They had read how a crash had forced both Col. Roscoe Turner and Bennie Howard, the winner of the previous year's race, to withdraw; they knew that the Bendix, with $15,000 in prize money, would have top competition. But now the headlines told them who won: Louise Thaden and Blanche Noyes, "two veteran women pilots."[1] They covered the coast-to-coast distance in their sleek cabin Beechcraft in 14 hours, 54 minutes, and 59 seconds, besting the seven-plane field. Bendix entrants did not have to start together as in a foot race, but rather they had to make the flight within a stipulated time period. The plane of Henry L. Doherty, the first to arrive in Los Angeles, finished fourth on the basis of flying time. When all the planes arrived and the results were computed, they were dramatic: behind Thaden and Noyes, in second place, was Laura Engalls, flying solo. In third and fourth place came planes flown by men, but then in fifth, still in the money, landed Amelia Earhart and Helen Richey, in Earhart's Flying Laboratory plane, given her by Purdue University.[2]

Women won three places out of five. Outstanding, yes, but not unusual. Throughout the late 1920s and 1930s, numbering at most about 500 and constituting less than one-thirtieth of all aviators, women pilots were highly visible in aeronautics and played an important role in spreading the winged gospel. Not only did they race against men and often beat them, but they also held positions in commercial aviation. In one sample of women pilots, fully one out of five flew professionally. Women sat in the cockpits as test pilots, flight instructors, aerial photographers, and flying chauffeurs. Some ran one-woman aviation enterprises, such as the Florence H. Boswell Flying Service of Cleveland, Ohio. The 1936 Bendix winners themselves had worked in a variety of flying jobs: Louise Thaden had been an airplane salesperson, while Blanche Noyes flew as a company pilot for Standard Oil of Ohio before accepting a piloting position with the U.S. Department of Commerce. Helen Richey was an aerial colleague of Noyes with the government. She had previously served as a regular pilot with one of the scheduled airlines. And Amelia Earhart had played many parts in the drama of aviation development. Before her untimely disappearance in 1937, she had sold airplanes, piloted aircraft on publicity tours for manufacturers, done promotion for airlines, and spoken and written widely on behalf of flying. She also had flown both the Atlantic and Pacific Oceans alone and was the best known of the aviatrixes, the "Lady Lindbergh" of her time.[3]

Earhart's generation of women pilots was not the first. No sooner had the airplane been invented and publicly demonstrated than women joined men in the air. One of the first American women to fly was Bessica Raiche, who, with her French aviator husband, built a Wright-type plane in their Mineola, Long Island, living room. In this machine, without any previous flying instruction, she took off on her first flight in September 1910 and shortly afterwards, received a gold medal inscribed, "First Woman Aviator of America, Bessica Raiche," from the New York Aeronautical Society in honor of her effort. Another pioneering aviatrix was Harriet Quimby, a Californian and former actress who came to New York, turned to writing as a drama critic, and became airminded through exposure to the very active Long Island aviation scene. In 1911 Quimby learned to fly and acquired the first international license issued to an American woman. The next year she accomplished another first, becoming the first woman to fly across the English Channel. In 1912 she also became a martyr to the aviation cause when her plane went out of control and crashed during an air meet in Boston. By the time war broke out in Europe in 1914, other women had joined Raiche and Quimby in the air. There was Ruth Law, an aerial daredevil and holder for a while of the American long-distance flying record. And there were Katherine and Margaret Stinson, who with their younger brother Eddie became known as the "Flying Stinsons" and were long active, running flying schools, performing in air meets, and contributing to other aviation activities.[4]

The attraction of women to aviation was a strong one, for no activity better symbolized the freedom and power which was lacking in their daily lives. As pilots women experienced feelings of strength, mastery, and confidence which, particularly at a time when Victorian norms still rendered all strenuous effort and most public activity by women suspect, seemed delicious indeed. It was this giddy sense of liberation they found in the sky which prompted so many women to predict that the new field of aviation promised great opportunities to their sex in the future. Yet for that first generation of female aviators, the place for women in the sky was narrow, a fact symbolized by the experience of Ruth Law and Katherine Stinson in 1917. In that year the United States entered the European war and pilots were in very short supply, both because of poor preparedness by the military and because of the nascent state of American aeronautics. Law and Stinson volunteered to become military pilots, but despite their considerable experience the Army responded predictably and turned them down. The "fruitful opportunity" that Quimby had once predicted for women, thanks to the coming of airplanes, still remained in the future.[5]

It arrived in the late 1920s and 1930s, and Amelia Earhart's generation of women pilots found considerably broader opportunities in the air. In this period, flying possessed the same romantic excitement and symbolized the same prophetic promise as it had in earlier years, even more so. But the "rush to the cockpits" by women also reflected new opportunities, which stemmed mainly from the peculiar needs of the aeronautical industry at a time of transition. By the latter half of the twenties, the airplane had emerged as a practical and reliable means of transporting people and goods over great distances. No longer was it merely an exciting but somewhat useless toy, as it had remained for so long after the Wright brothers invented it in 1903. The most obvious sign of the airplane's coming of age was Lindbergh's dramatic solo flight from New

York to Paris in 1927. His flight was but one testament to the fact that engineers were designing safer and more reliable aircraft. Further evidence of the airplane's coming of age technically lay in the many new airlines founded in the period, not to mention the beginnings of widespread recreational flying. Yet another indicator of the airplane's new-found utility could be found in the hundreds of airports under construction in the towns and cities of the nation.[6]

Although poised on the brink of maturity and promising great profits, the aviation industry faced a paradox. The public was enthusiastic about airplanes and about flying in the abstract, yet in great numbers they refused to fly. People would go up in an airplane, ran a popular joke, only as long as they could keep one foot firmly on the ground. "Fear not fare," airline executives maintained, kept potential passengers out of the air. Similar anxieties were said to be retarding sales of planes to private users. In part a fear of heights and of falling, also of the unknown, underlay such anxieties. But more important, Americans had an image of the pilot and of flying that greatly retarded aviation growth.

The public still thought of fliers as "intrepid birdmen," a phrase common in the 1900s. The birdman, a popular magazine had explained in 1908, required "an extraordinary combination of active energy, courage, decision of purpose, a quick eye, clearness of judgment, the utmost presence of mind, and great physical dexterity." Other characterizations of the pilot from those years—an athlete of "the lithest sort," "a breed apart," the "modern superman"—still gripped the popular mind in the 1920s and 1930s. They added up to what may be termed the intrepid birdman stereotype, a sense that flying was not for ordinary mortals. Why even science had been cited in support of the proposition, for a medical doctor had invoked Darwin's theory of evolution in claiming that pilots were descended from birds whereas the vast majority of humankind descended from fish and therefore would never be able to pilot a plane.[7] The view that flying was only for birdmen possessed greater credibility during the infancy of aeronautical technology, when planes were fragile creations of wood, wire, and cloth which, even with the most circumspect piloting, often killed their occupants. In the later 1920s, however, when planes had become much safer and reliable, as well as easier to fly, the public's continued acceptance of the intrepid birdman stereotype seriously retarded aviation development. Of little help was the more recent gloss on that stereotype, the pilot as "Ace," as a fatalistic and chivalric aerial warrior, an image popularized by the First World War. In the twenties the "Ace" dazzled and terrified millions of Americans, flickering across the screen in the many war films that Hollywood, recently become airminded, was cranking out. The aerial dogfights, crashes, and perilous escapes that one saw in the movies kept alive the reluctance to fly and the belief that only supermen might become pilots. Even the barnstormers may have contributed to these perceptions. Although they introduced many Americans to the airplane and fostered great enthusiasm for aviation, they also perpetuated, through their daring stunts and participation in flying circuses, the same intimidating birdman stereotype.[8]

Only in the latter twenties did the aviation industry recognize the harm being done by this attitude and try to do something about it. By this time the economic consequences of such perceptions were undeniable, and the industry launched a major campaign to change the public's image both of piloting and of flying. It tried hard to convince the public that a new era had arrived, that modern aircraft were safe and easy to operate, and that virtually anybody could fly. The remarks of an editor of an aviation periodical in 1928, complaining of the excessive lauding of Lindbergh's piloting abilities, typified the industry's new tack. "No special 'air sense' or divine gift is required," he wrote. "Nor may a person suppose that because he has not been a star football player" he must stay grounded. The ordinary automobile driver, in fact, could pilot his or her own airplane, claimed Eugene Vidal, the head in 1933 of the Air Commerce Bureau and a proponent of producing a "poor man's" airplane. A contemporary of Vidal's, writing in *Collier's* went even further and assured his readers that "you and I and cousin Libby can all be Lindberghs."[9]

Exhortations and rhetoric may have disabused some people of their fear of flying, but something more was needed. The industry found its answer in women. The female pilot became the antidote for the intrepid birdman stereotype. As 1936 Bendix winner, Louise Thaden, once put it, "Nothing impresses the safety of aviation on the public quite so much as to see a woman flying an airplane." If a woman can handle it, she said, "the public thinks it must be duck soup for men." Another woman, Manila Davis, observed that "if I can fly and land a plane successfully, weighing as I do but 105 pounds, almost anyone ought to be able to." Aviatrix

Ruth Nichols agreed. People will believe "it must be easy" to fly a plane, she believed, if they see the "fragile sex" setting aerial records just like men. These comments assumed, explicitly or otherwise, that women were frail, timid, unathletic, and unmechanical, the very antithesis of the stereotypical birdman. The women were voicing another stereotype, what might be called the lady-flier stereotype. It was of course men who phrased it most absurdly and cruelly. One male pilot, purporting to speak for his fellow aviators in the *North American Review* in 1929, characterized the woman pilot as "impulsive and scatterbrained," incapable of monitoring her plane's instruments or even of remembering to put gas in her ship, and a menace to society because she might fall out of the sky and injure innocent persons. In addition, a woman pilot lacked "air sense," that indefinable something allegedly needed for successful piloting. Quoting a contemporary witticism, he concluded that "women as pilots made good passengers."[10]

Paradoxically, prejudice begat opportunity. The stereotypical image of the lady pilot formed the cornerstone of the opportunities women pilots found in the air in the late twenties and thirties. Because they appeared to the public as less capable than they really were, women fliers became marvelous advertisements for the ease of piloting and the safety of flying. But if the lady flier stereotype helped women find a place in the sky, it simultaneously circumscribed that place. And this created problems and tensions. Because the women pilots of Earhart's generation believed in expanded occupational and public roles for women, they often chafed at restrictions on what they might do as pilots. But complaint or protest was difficult, for they also considered themselves evangelists of aviation and sought to do nothing that would in any way damage the cause. To the extent that their feminism conflicted with their airmindedness, the women fliers invariably subordinated the cause of equality for women to the cause of aviation.

Of all the jobs women pilots found in the period, demonstrating and selling planes for the private market was the most common. Airplane sales, in fact, was really woman's work in the sense that female sales personnel were common at airfields around the country. At some point in their careers, almost all of the better-known female aviators worked in sales, including Amelia Earhart, Louise Thaden, Blanche Noyes, and Ruth Nichols. Of fifteen professional women pilot listed in a 1932 aviation directory, five sold airplanes. By comparison, among 143 male professionals (excluding military fliers) whose biographies appeared in the same directory, only twenty-four had anything to do with selling planes. Twenty-one of these, moreover, owned or managed aircraft distributorships and were thus entrepreneurs or executives, not simply salespersons as were the women pilots.[11] The disproportionate number of women selling planes had much to do with the popular belief that aircraft would soon supplant automobiles, a story taken up in the next chapter. But before Americans flew with anywhere near the frequency that they drove cars, their fear of flying and their belief that piloting was difficult would have to be allayed. Thanks to the lady flier steretoype, the pilot saleswoman was uniquely equipped to accomplish this task. As a 1930 aviation writer put it, she represented "the greatest sales argument that can be presented" to the potential buyer of a family plane.[12]

Women pilots may well have presented a powerful sales argument, but their sales did not always come easily. Bendix winner Louise Thaden's experience working for the Travel Air Corporation, a manufacturer of small planes, was probably shared by many women. From 1929 to 1931 she sold twenty-five aircraft, an enviable number considering the depressed economy and the fact that planes were not yet widely sold on credit. But Thaden's male customers often made her a target for their hostility toward women. She would take men up in her demonstrator plane, hand over the controls, and suddenly some of them would become demons, throwing the ship into violent, airframe-bending maneuvers. A few times she had to seize the controls to prevent disaster. "Some psychological reaction," she tersely concluded, compelled men to display their "prowess" in her presence.[13]

Women secured other opportunities from aircraft manufacturers besides the chance to sell planes to obstreperous men. Their services were in demand for all kinds of flying. They raced, set records, made long-distance tours, and flew on promotional flights, all at corporate expense. In the 1936 Bendix race, Thaden flew to first place in a plane lent to her by the Beech Aircraft Corporation. Once when Earhart wanted to challenge the women's speed record (separate categories for each sex having been set up on the initiative of women pilots), she simply turned to the Lockheed Aircraft Company, which provided her with a new streamlined monoplane. On another occasion she made a four-week promotional tour in a Monocoupe made available free of charge by the Mono Aircraft Company. Wherever she stopped, Earhart addressed civic and women's groups about flying while the factory representative accompanying her took orders for Monocoupes. In the early 1930s Mono Aircraft also hired women pilots for its racing team, and Phoebe Omlie and Florence Klingensmith logged many hours in the air flying the fast aircraft.[14]

That the Monocoupe sold so well and earned a high reputation among business and private fliers owed much to Omlie, Klingensmith, and Earhart's public appearances with the machine. For women pilots, all else being equal, "received far more attention" and generated greater publicity for an airplane manufacturer than did a male pilot, thanks to the lady flier stereotype. This could be, of course, a two-way street. While the prejudicial view of women as simply lady fliers guaranteed them a role in the selling of aviation, the same stereotype could also be invoked to deny them any opportunity. Clearly, some men in the industry were leery of putting a woman in the cockpit. Amelia Earhart reported being refused the loan of an aircraft by a manufacturer who worried that, were she to have an accident, the resulting publicity would be lethal to the business.[15] Because the media did in fact pay more attention to women fliers, his concern was not without validity.

Inevitably women encountered other instances of discrimination, starting with the day they first decided to fly and continuing even after their death. In taking up flying, men might defray the cost of lessons by working at the airfield, but women seldom had the mechanical background to get such jobs and often were not welcome around the hangars. As a result they generally had to pay cash for their lessons. Once a woman accumulated the required hours in the air for her license, she faced the hurdle of the exam. Just to pass she often had to meet a higher standard than would a man, a phenomenon familiar then and now to women in male-dominated fields. This was especially true of the more advanced licenses. "That wife of your had better be good," a federal examiner told Blanche Noyes's husband prior to her examination for a transport rating, the government's highest category of license, "or I'm going to flunk her on general principles, because she's a woman."[16] Noyes passed with flying colors, as did many other women. As professional pilots, however, women encountered almost daily instances of male prejudice.

Blanche Noyes's experience while working for the aviation department of Standard Oil of Ohio was hardly unique. From the outset of her employ, the male employees resented her "wandering around the hanger," she later recalled, wearing the same flight suit and goggles as the men pilots. They ridiculed the notion of a female flier and joked about her supposed mechanical incompetence. She rebutted these prejudices slowly, but on one occasion gained quick respect among her Neanderthal colleagues. She was to fly the company's autogiro to southern Ohio and had completed preparations for take-off when all of a sudden the sky turned ominous and she cancelled her trip. The vice president in charge of sales argued with her and said that "if you're going to be afraid, maybe we'd better get a man pilot." She stood her ground and taxied the aircraft back into the hangar. Moments later a tornado hit, destroying the airplanes on the field and blowing off a piece of the hangar roof.[17]

For some women pilots, even death did not free them from the barbs of prejudice. The lady flier stereotype often surfaced in discussions of fatal accidents, such as the one that killed Muriel Crosson in 1929. Crosson was competing in the First National Women's Air Derby, from Santa Monica, California, to Cleveland, Ohio, when her plane crashed in the mountains near San Bernardino, California, the first control point in the event. A male reporter explained her death as due to the fact that she "neglected" to open her parachute after bailing out when her airplane's engine failed. A government official investigating the crash rejected out of hand the possibility of engine failure and speculated that Crosson simply became faint or ill from intense heat and thereby lost control of her plane. Although it is impossible to know for sure what caused the accident, such conclusions appear to have reflected male prejudice as much as any objective assessment of the evidence. For one thing, Crosson's body was found draped in her partially opened parachute, close to the wreckage of the plane, totally rebutting the charge that she neglected or forgot to open her chute. That she managed to get out of the cockpit and jump at all casts doubt on the assumption that she fainted or became ill from heat. Furthermore, the temperature in the cockpit of an open airplane, flying over mountains at over a hundred miles an hour, was unlikely to have been high enough to cause heat exhaustion. The most probable cause of the accident was engine failure at low altitude, a danger that could kill a man as easily as a woman. Before the start of the competition, Crosson had mentioned to a number of people how poorly her engine was performing, but she took off anyway. As a six-year veteran of flying with her brother in the Alaskan bush, she might be faulted for poor judgment. Had she not taken off, however, she would have opened herself to the criticism of being timid and overly cautious, thereby encouraging yet another invocation of the lady flier stereotype.[18]

The lady flier stereotype was freely available in the culture to those who wished to discriminate against women. It operated most rigidly in the field of air transport. For a woman to parlay a transport license into a job flying with the airlines proved almost impossible. In no other branch of aviation, save of course for the military, did discrimination and the limits of woman's place in the air show so clearly. "The public simply doesn't have confidence in women fliers," noted Louise Thaden, not without bitterness. "That is, not enough confidence to ride with them to any great extent." Until the 1970s, only one woman found a place flying with a scheduled airline, and even then, discrimination cut short her tenure. In 1934 Helen Richey beat out seven male candidates for a position as co-pilot on Central Airlines' Washington, D.C. to Pittsburgh route. The company's male pilots, however, resented her appointment and claimed she was too weak to fly the airliner safely in the bad weather frequently encountered over the Alleghenies. Central's management turned a deaf ear to these complaints, but the men then complained to their pilots' association, an exclusively male body, and to the male officials in the Air Commerce Department, the agency then charged with regulating the airlines. The Department earlier had considered grounding all women for nine days each month, during each woman's menstrual period, and was therefore receptive to the weakness argument. It backed the pilots' association and issued a regulation limiting women pilots on scheduled air carrier routes to fair weather operations, thereby gutting Richey's job. She resigned in protest in November 1935.[19]

It was not simply male prejudice that made Richey the only regular female airline pilot. Many women believed their sex *should* not pilot airliners. Ruth Nichols, for instance, claimed women had no more place in an airliner cockpit than they did "as sea captains or truck drivers." The issue was not so much competency or even strength—Nichols herself had ably flown large multi-engined transport aircraft, both with and without passengers aboard, and never doubted her ability to fly anything a man could. Rather there were "other spheres" in aviation, she believed, to which women were "better suited." Primarily they should be exemplars of "safe and sane" flying, helping to "steer men away from the spectacular." Pilot Barbara Southgate held "woman's place" in the air to lay in guiding "the footsteps of the younger generation in aviation." After all, claimed another aviatrix, women were flying "for their children and their children's children," not primarily for themselves. Just to raise kids for the dawning air age every mother had the responsibility of acquiring "first-hand flying experience," Amelia Earhart believed. Teaching young people to fly, along with tasks such as leading safety crusades at the local landing field—these constituted what another woman termed aviation's "housekeeping functions" and the proper field of endeavor for female pilots.[20]

Women pilots themselves, then, posited a kind of aerial domesticity seemingly at odds with their daring work. As they talked about the new technology and their role in the dawning air age, their language looked back to older and more traditional womanly roles. The emphasis on making safe and sane flights and on rearing aerially adept offspring reiterated in a surprising modern context the nineteenth-century paradigm of the female as exemplar and nurturer. Dorothy Lynn, national commander in 1933 of the Betsy Ross Corps, a voluntary organization of women pilots, struck precisely this older chord. "We are not trying to bring forth a freakish lot of women," Lynn assured those who might frown upon any change in customary sex roles.

> Nor are we contemplating any theatrical, hysterical or sensational activities. Our work is the same humanitarian relief work which has always been done by women, only we are using the latest most modern medium for our service. Most of our members are married and many of these have children. The requirements of the corps will never interfere with a member's first duty—her children and her home.[21]

As Lynn's statement suggests, women aviators did not merely speak the rhetoric of aerial domesticity. They also comported themselves in accordance with traditional notions of the feminine. This behavior enhanced their effectiveness as evangelists for the aviation cause and helped them dislodge the prevailing image of pilots as birdmen and in general domesticate the image of flying in the popular mind.

Being married was definitely an asset in this work. Not all women pilots flew with wedding bands on their fingers, to be sure,

but most of the better-known aviatrixes were married, including
Earhart, Cochran, Thaden, Omlie, and Noyes. The fact that they
could say that their husbands did not worry about them, coupled
with the fact of their own flying, made these pilot-wives doubly
effective in allaying people's fears of flying. When the woman
pilot was herself married to a pilot, her visibility and impact on
popular acceptance of flying grew. In 1932 about 100 women
fliers, or one out of five, had an aviator spouse. Typical flying
couples were Gladys and James O'Donnell of Long Beach, California, and the "Flying Omlies," Phoebe and Vernon, of Memphis, Tennessee. Both couples operated flight-related businesses
together and both wives raced professionally. In 1930 Gladys
O'Donnell won $8,000 racing, more than any other woman that
year; in her moments on the ground she still found time to mother
two small children, as did Louise Thaden, herself the better half
of a flying couple. Blending family, marriage, work, and adventure, "Mr. and Mrs. Pilot" provided an appealing role model to
Americans who, from the twenties forward, were increasingly
embracing a shared, cooperative ideal of marriage.[22]

The most famous flying wife and mother was Anne Morrow
Lindbergh. The daughter of a banker and diplomat, Dwight W.
Morrow, Anne met Charles Lindbergh in December 1927, in
Mexico City, where her father was U.S. Ambassador. Lindbergh
had flown there from Washington, another of his good-will efforts
on behalf of the aviation cause. Anne and Charles fell in love and
in 1929 were married. Quickly Anne learned to fly from her pilot
husband. Charles gave tremendous impetus to aviation development, but Anne also furthered the cause of flight. Her contribution was partly literary. A gifted writer, she evoked in prose the
sensations and magic of flying with a passion and force that rivaled
the French airman-writer Antoine de Saint Exupéry. Anne Morrow Lindbergh's two books about aviation, both best sellers, were
North to the Orient (1935) and *Listen, the Wind!* (1938). They
emerged from two distance flights she made with her husband to
demonstrate the feasibilty of intercontinental air transport. In
1931 the Lindberghs had flown to China via the Arctic Circle.
Two years later, skirting the coasts of Europe, Africa, and South
America, they circumnavigated the Atlantic Ocean.[23] In her accounts of the two flights, Anne depicted flying as sensual, joyous,
and inspirational, not at all a terrifying proposition.

Had Charles made such flights alone, no doubt the media would have shown great interest. Yet the impact would have been different. Reading about two more aerial odysseys by men would do little to smooth the goose bumps that many people still developed contemplating the prospect of air travel. To people who read about "Lindy and Anne, First Flyers of America," however, or who watched the couple in the newsreels, flight took on a cozier, less intimidating cast. There was diminutive Anne, relieving her husband at the controls or operating the plane's shortwave radio. She did not look afraid. On the ground, acting the cultured and well-bred lady she was, Anne further exorcised the intrepid birdman image. In interviews she always deferred to her husband's aviation expertise and, playing the mechanically inept female, falsely denied any knowledge of what she called flight's "clean-cut and steely technicalities." Although she privately resented questions about where she kept the "lunchboxes" on the plane, in a sense she asked for them by rhapsodizing over maternity and housekeeping.[24]

If the woman pilot's marital status, domestic bent, and demure manner all helped purge flight of manly terror and thus further the aviation cause, so too did her choice of clothing. A few women wore the regular male pilot's attire, which tended toward one-piece flight suits or pants and bulky leather jackets, topped off with helmet and goggles. Sometimes such garb could not be avoided, as when flying in open cockpit planes in cold weather. But many women, including Louise Thaden, Amelia Earhart, and Ruth Nichols, dressed differently whenever possible. They believed figure-veiling, unfashionable flight suits repelled many non-flying women, while helmets and goggles, with their obvious protective qualities, suggested discomfort if not danger. Whenever she could, Earhart avoided public appearances with helmet and goggles and flew in simple blouses and tailored slacks. For personal use as well as the market, she and other of her sister pilots also designed female sports and flying clothes, costumes which blurred the distinction between ground and sky and rendered the latter more accessible emotionally and psychologically.[25]

In other ways women pilots conformed, sometimes against their wishes, to feminine stereotypes because they felt it would help the cause of aviation. During the first running of the Women's Air Derby in 1929, the race in which Muriel Crosson was killed, the competitors reluctantly accepted the role of social butterflies. The race organizers and promoters at the various cities visited by the

Derby fliers had scheduled nightly banquets and receptions, not thinking that the women would prefer to spend their evenings tinkering with their aircraft or preparing navigation charts for the next day's leg of the race. Amelia Earhart, one of the competitors, explained that she and her sister pilots endured the weary socializing because to have refused the invitations would have seemed ungrateful, perhaps alienating people from flying. A sympathetic female journalist covering the Derby said that the women wished simply to be treated as fliers, but everywhere "they had to be 'sweethearts of the air,' 'flying flappers,' 'angels,' " and the like. By acquiescing in the social whirl, however, no matter how well-intentioned, the Derby pilots inevitably gave support to those who would claim women fliers were frivolous and unprofessional.[26]

Jacqueline Cochran's habit of putting on make-up after landing in a race, before she got out of her plane, was another instance of feminine behavior that both worked for the cause of aviation and against the reputation of women pilots. Cochran headed a cosmetics firm but had more than merely business or vanity reasons to wear lipstick. She well understood the impression her appearance in an air-race, not just her performance, would make on spectators and the press. If she *looked* fresh and glamorous after a flight, it would show flying as being smooth and restful. In the 1938 Bendix, in fact, Cochran emerged from her cockpit with such an out-of-the-boudoir freshness that somebody started a rumor that she really had not flown all the way from Burbank, California to Cleveland, Ohio. According to the rumor, Cochran had landed to pick up a male pilot shortly after take-off and, while he raced across the country, she slept! Somewhere near the finish, she supposedly dropped off her chauffeur and flew in to victory. The story was preposterous; she did not take first place in the race, "beating nine men," by making two extra stops. Furthermore, she won the Bendix in a prototype fighter plane, a single-seat pursuit ship lent to her by the Seversky Aircraft Company. But the rumor testified both to the strength of male prejudice and, presumably, to the success of her cosmetic strategy in convincing people of the ease and restfulness of flying.[27]

What red lips and rouge did to sell flight on one occasion, a little white lie accomplished on another. In the 1935 Bendix, Cochran withdrew shortly after take-off because mechanical failures, beginning with a faulty engine and culminating with gasoline flooding her cockpit as she fought her way through a night thunderstorm, made continuing impossible. When asked what had happened, rather than "give an alibi which put the blame on the plane or engine," Cochran told reporters she "just got tired and quit." By shifting the blame from the machine to herself, Cochran saved the public from further anxiety about flying. But her airminded sacrifice at the same time compounded the indictment of women pilots as frail and timid.[28]

Ruth Nichols once said that pilots "made every sacrifice" to ensure that people thought of flying "in the best light." She might more accurately have said that *women* pilots made every sacrifice. Cochran dissembling over fatigue, the Derby racers subordinating piloting to politeness, and women accepting a sex-limited place in aviation generally—all sacrificed personal reward or reputation for the cause of aviation. But their sacrifice, while of a sort unfashionable today, must be kept in historical perspective. Women pilots exploited the feminine to their own advantage and did not simply act out scripts implanted by their socialization as little girls. They stood in the tradition of figures such as Jane Addams, Florence Kelley, and Eleanor Roosevelt, all of whom manipulated the symbols of femininity and domesticity to expand woman's role in the world. As Addams legitimated her sex's entrance into municipal and public life under the rubric of "housekeepers" to the nation, so women pilots staked out an important place in aviation under their own banner of aerial housekeeping.[29]

Still, at some level, no doubt every woman pilot resented the subservience imposed upon her by the idea of womanly spheres and feminine norms. The experience of flying, after all, opened to her a world of seeming power and freedom which belied the rhetoric of domesticity, the sacrifices on behalf of others, or the suffering of discrimination. The fact that women aviators, more than the men, wrote about the sensations of flight supports this view. Cochran reported feeling "equal with all things" when alone in her plane and "exalted" in self-importance. Louise Thaden wrote that "flying is the only real freedom we are privileged to possess," a telling slash at prevailing sexual discrimination. Celebrating the power of her "own hands managing this fierce and wonderful machine," Ruth Nichols alluded to the physical exaltation women pilots found at the controls of their planes. The airplane, after all, did equalize the condition of the sexes by rendering muscle power unimportant. Not equipped by biology to fly, human beings flew only as high, as fast, or as far as his or her mechanical wings allowed.[30]

Frustrated by earthly prejudice yet intoxicated by the liberation they felt in the sky, women pilots commonly thought about the connections of flying and equality. Some prophesied that aviation would bring about a fundamental change in male-female relations, while others envisioned alternatives to their sex-typed aerial spheres. Anne Morrow Lindbergh covertly wished for some of the technical knowledge of her husband, for emancipation from responsibility for the lunchboxes. Ruth Nichols mused about starting an airline that would be wholly owned and operated by women, even while she rejected a place for her sex in transport aviation as outside woman's proper sphere. But Louise Thaden voiced the most poignant discontent with existing sex roles in aviation in her short story, "Noble Experiment," tucked into an otherwise factual autobiography published in 1938. There Thaden invented heroines who, while serving as non-combat auxiliary pilots in some unspecified future war, got the chance to fly bombers against the enemy after casualties decimated the regular male crews. Thaden's fictional pilots and crewwomen exceeded the expectations of their male commanders. They fought well, bore death and suffering stoically, and dispelled all vestiges of male doubts concerning their abilities. As a result the women won promotions, assignments to the most hazardous missions, and commissions as regular officers in the air corps.[31]

Frustrated flights of fancy were not women's only response to their limited aerial sphere. They organized. On Long Island in 1929 Earhart, Nichols, and a number of women attached to the airplane sales staff of the Curtiss-Wright Company took steps to found an all-women pilot's group. The group sought through organization both to further women's aerial opportunities and to foster traditional womanly activities among female pilots. They also aimed to promote aviation. These goals inevitably conflicted and produced an organization that was partly a women's rights organization, partly a sorority, and partly a kind of female aviation chamber of commerce. From the outset, these aims were in tension. At the organizational meeting held on Long Island in 1929, the founders fought over what to call their group. Some of the women suggested names such as "Breezy Girls," "Gad Flies," and "Queens High," reflecting the social motives behind their organizing. Amelia Earhart, a member of the National Woman's Party and a strong believer in total equality for women, viewed the new organization more seriously and urged something less frivolous by way of a name. She suggested that the name be a number, the number being that of the charter members, who enrolled and paid dues by a certain date. Earhart's suggestion was accepted, and soon the "Ninety-Nines" came into existence.[32]

In the spirit of Earhart's no-nonsense name, the Ninety-Nines protested various forms of sex discrimination in aviation. When the government contemplated banning women from flying during menstruation, the organization pressured the officials into changing course and in the process brought about the appointment of the first woman medical examiner in the Air Commerce Department. The Ninety-Nines also complained vigorously against the discriminatory rules which the Department promulgated to force Helen Richey out of her co-pilot job with Central Airlines in 1934. In that instance, however, the women pilots had no impact. In the same year, when male racing pilots decided to bar women from participating in the national air races, the Ninety-Nines co-sponsored an all-women meet. And the *99'er*, the monthly magazine of the women pilots' organization, regularly reported news regarding women's aerial status such as new licenses granted, records established, occupational firsts for women in aviation, aeronautical activities in women's colleges, and sex discrimination in fields such as aeronautical engineering.[33]

Along with these feminist concerns, however, the Ninety-Nines also supported its members' more traditionally feminine interests. This is readily apparent by looking through the pages of the *99'er*. In the January 2, 1934 number, for instance, the "Planely Personal" column gossiped about pilot Clara Gilbert, "the one with the beautiful blond hair and those green eyes." Readers learned that Gilbert was "23 years old, weighs 100 pounds, is five feet two inches tall, wears a size four shoe, has exceedingly long and brilliantly red fingernails." Another column called "Pots and Pan Mechanics," on cooking, and "Fashions in Flight," with advice on clothing, also appeared in the magazine regularly. In 1935 the *99'er* started its "Betsy Barton" column, directed at girls eight to eighteen who were invited to become members of a Betsy Barton Cloud Club. While the Cloud Club inculcated an awareness of the "importance and fascination of aviation," at the same time it prepared young girls to be perfect little hostesses. One column suggested Cloud Clubbers hold aviation luncheons and serve "flight-y" food such as little sandwiches shaped like airplanes.[34]

Plane-shaped canapés, protest, and piloting—the mixture today might not qualify as feminist, but the Ninety-Nines stood squarely in the muddy mainstream of the interwar woman's movement. Few American women then called themselves feminists, thinking like Amelia Earhart that the word connoted an undesirable mannishness and pushiness. Yet Earhart and her sister fliers, by combining flying and adventure with marriage and nurture, personified the ideal of so many women of the era, the liberated yet feminine woman. More significantly, the fact that they were at home both with canapés and cockpits made it possible for them to be extremely effective advertisements for flying. Indeed, they were arguably the most effective evangelists of aviation in the period, for they "made flying thinkable to so many people." The words were written in 1939, in memory of Amelia Earhart, two years after she disappeared while on one of the last legs of an attempted around the world flight. But they sum up succinctly the achievement of all the woman pilots of her generation. Those women made flying "thinkable" by making it seem safe as well as easy, and they accomplished that by comporting themselves like traditional ladies, thereby turning the existence of the lady flier stereotype to advantage. By eschewing behavior that would have been perceived as aggressively feminist or as unfeminine, they played a pivotal role in selling flying to the American public. More than the men who barnstormed around the country or crossed the oceans by plane, women pilots domesticated the sky, purging it of associations with death and terror.[35]

Once flying became thinkable, once Americans not only were excited about airplanes and their promise but felt comfortable using them, what then of women's opportunities in aviation? The answer was obvious. Because women pilots carved out professional opportunities in the sky by functioning as nurturers of public confidence in flying, they were no longer in demand, once that confidence had been acquired. When Americans no longer had reservations about being a passenger in an airplane—when aviation had arrived, so to speak—the women who helped bring about that arrival in effect had worked themselves out of a job. This had happened by the time the United States went to war in 1941. By then private flying no longer seemed exotic, even if it was not yet as universal as the prophets of an airplane in every garage were predicting. As a result, the rationale for hiring women as sales and demonstrator pilots disappeared. Airline travel also had become common by Pearl Harbor, and the war gave further thousands of Americans a chance to fly as passengers. Even though the real explosion of air travel lay in the postwar period, it was already clear that the public's fear of flying was no longer economically significant. By the 1940s the males who built the planes and ran the industry had no further business need to recruit women pilots as part of a strategy to sell flying to an airminded but timid public.

Women pilots never totally disappeared from the aviation scene, of course, During the Second World War, in fact, hundreds flew as Women Air Service Pilots, or WASPS. They taught basic flying, flight-tested and delivered military aircraft, towed aerial targets for gunnery practice, and performed other aerial tasks so as to free male pilots for service in combat zones. Their work was understood to be temporary, however—for the duration only. Even before the war was officially over, their organization was eliminated. More typical of female presence in aviation from the 1940s on was the stewardess, who of course was not a pilot. Yet her role in the selling of flying in the mature air age possessed ironic similarities to the work performed earlier by Amelia Earhart, Louise Thaden, Blanche Noyes, Helen Richey, and the other female evangelists of the winged gospel.

United Airlines hired the first stewardesses in 1930, recruiting attractive, personable women who had completed nursing training but who were not pilots. By the latter part of the decade, other companies were imitating United's practice. More than saving weight, the usual reason advanced for hiring stewardesses rather than stewards, the companies wanted females because they would better allay passengers' anxieties and domesticate the flight experience. The airlines wanted, as a journalist in the 1930s explained, "professional women" who were "skilled in the domestic services." In nurses, he explained, companies gained women who had learned how to groom themselves and how to meet strangers with charm and politeness. The choice partly backfired, however, for some people concluded that the presence of nurses on airliners proved how likely it was that one would be hurt riding in one. The airlines viewed their stewardess-nurses, however, not as medics but as professional nurturers.[36]

The strategy of United and the other early airlines was really quite the same as that which had led to the hiring of many women pilots. In both cases men hired women because they would make air travel seem safe and comfortable. Just as the woman pilot demonstrated the safety of flying and the ease of piloting in an earlier period, the stewardess salved anxieties regarding air travel in a later era. Both held jobs premised on the female's supposed superiority as a nurturer, and both succeeded to the extent they appeared feminine and ladylike. The stewardess put passengers at ease by making conversation, by serving refreshments, and by exemplifying calm whatever the situation. For her part the pilot defused anxiety over flight simply by operating a plane and by behaving as unlike the intrepid birdman as possible. That the skies today seem "friendly," as an airline advertising slogan puts it, results less from the fact that flight attendants do their jobs with a smile but rather from the fact that an earlier generation of women, all pilots, embraced the winged gospel and sacrificed so much to the aviation cause.

V

"An Airplane in Every Garage?" The Gospel's Most Pervasive Promise

In February 1951 the cover of *Popular Mechanics* ventured a glimpse of the aerial future. It showed a man in hat and overcoat pushing a sleek little yellow helicopter into the garage of his suburban home. Over his neighbor's house hovered a similar machine, bright red in color. The cover story, "Here Comes Your Helicopter Coupe," claimed that in only two hours virtually anybody could learn to fly the two-seat, jet-powered machines. According to its inventor, Stanley Hiller, the helicopter was virtually foolproof; unless one "deliberately" flew into a building or a power line, it would be hard to hurt oneself. In an emergency the pilot could always "slow down to a halt in the air and think things over." But the best news was that the little copters were already "in production." Because of the war in Korea, Hiller's entire output was going to the military, but there would be civilian deliveries "just as soon as circumstances permit."[1]

Our helicopter coupes never arrived, of course, and the idea of mass ownership of family flying machines today seems fanciful and utopian, not to mention hazardous. Belief in such a possibility, however, was a key tenet of the winged gospel. For nearly half a century preceding the *Popular Mechanics* article, millions of Americans expected to own a flying machine in the near future. Prophets considered the airplane, and later the helicopter, to be the "horseless carriage of the next generation" and wrote enthusiastically about the prospect of an "airplane in every garage" or of a coming "helicopter land boom." Like most Americans who gazed into their crystal balls to glimpse the future air age, these prophets were not excited just because people would fly tomorrow. It was rather the way of life that flying would make possible which sent them into rapture. Instead of "rushing like moles" into dark subways and breathing "foul subterranean air," wrote a 1922 enthusiast, tomorrow's sky commuter would escape the "push and struggle" with the urban "masses" and whisk swiftly and pleasurably through the clean, clear air alone or with a few friends. Inevitably, prophets envisioned the coming aerial lifestyle as a rural one. The airplane "would create the countryside," just as the automobile had created the suburb. As the comparison to suburb suggested, air-car prophets envisioned the further spread of commuting. The future would see thousands of city workers at day's end "rising like homing birds" and flying off "to cool mountain retreats." Aircraft would become the means not only of linking rural residence and urban workplace but also of shopping, making social calls, and taking vacations. Rather than once-a-year outings to a favorite lakeside or mountain retreat, hymned an advertisement during the Second World War, the "family car of the air" would facilitate "vacations every week end" and "magic trips to everywhere."[2]

So ran the gospel's promise, but the vision of wings for all was much more than rhetoric. Numerous Americans worked devotedly to fulfill the dream. Airminded architects designed houses with planeports in lieu of garages; towns constructed airparks or small airports and offered high school flight instruction in anticipation of the day when everyone would fly; the federal government planned a "poor man's airplane"; and inventors designed aircraft that were easier, safer, or more practicable to fly.[3] These and other concrete accomplishments made prophecy credible and nourished the dream. One such accomplishment was the use of airplanes to travel to and from work. In 1913 Alfred W. Lawson and Harold F. McCormick became the country's first aerial commuters, generating a great deal of publicity and optimistic prophecy. Lawson is the same man who authored "Natural Prophecies," looking forward to the year 10,000 A.D. to glimpse the ultimate implications of flight. It was by flying to work, however, that he first became publicly known. In a seaplane or what was then called a flying boat, Lawson commuted between his home at Seidler's Beach, New Jersey, on Raritan Bay, and his office near the New York City waterfront. A thousand miles to the west, in Chicago, Harold F. McCormick purchased not one but two flying boats and erected substantial hangars for them on the shore by his Evanston, Illinois, residence. He also engaged a professional pilot as his flying instructor and aerial chauffeur. First as a passenger and then, as he gained in experience, as pilot, McCormick commuted the twenty-eight miles from home to office in minutes. He berthed his "air yacht," as sea-going aircraft like his and Lawson's sometimes were called, at the nearby Chicago Yacht Club.[4]

"Yacht" aptly described a vehicle that had a mahogany-panelled cockpit and cost $7,000. As an heir to the International Harvester fortune, McCormick could well afford it. But at a time when an automobile cost $500—more than the average laborer brought home in a year—most Americans could not buy a car, let alone an airplane. If the dream of wings for all was to be realized, the cost of aircraft would have to be drastically lowered. Yet cost was only the first problem retarding the popular adoption of aircraft, then or later. Another was their inability to offer door-to-door convenience. McCormick and Lawson solved the convenience problem by using a seaplane, but not everyone lived on a lake or wanted to fly to a destination on another body of water. Conventional landplanes demanded relatively large, flat areas without trees or other obstacles to take off and land, and such places seldom existed in residential districts or next to one's place of employment. A third impediment to the widespread adoption of personal planes lay in the difficulty of piloting them. Flying, in part because it demanded sensitivity to three dimensions rather than two, required special training and experience. And of course the risk of mistakes in the air was far greater than with other modes of travel. Safety, then, was the final obstacle in the way of mass personal flight. Somehow popular fears would have to be allayed and the real dangers of airplanes minimized. Early aircraft, it has been noted, not only looked frail and dangerous but often were. With disheartening regularity their wooden frameworks collapsed, their controls jammed, and their engines failed. And even when engineers began to understand better the forces involved in flight and build stronger and safer aircraft, the popular perception of flying as dangerous, of pilots as intrepid birdmen, would have to change before people would regularly fly.

Although aeronautical technology improved rapidly in the decade after Lawson and McCormick made their debut as aerial commuters, it was in the latter twenties and thirties—again, the post-Lindbergh years—during which various developments, technical as well as social, converged to make the dream of an airplane in every garage seem just about to materialize. Relative to the cost of living, airplanes became much less expensive. Inventors also devised machines that promised greater convenience and simpler operation. Moreover, flying ceased to appear so daring and dangerous in the period. Another major impetus to the dream was the automobile revolution, which seemed to provide a model for the future direction of aircraft development. In less than a generation, the automobile had gone from being a plaything of the rich to a fixture in the lives of the millions. In 1906 Princeton University president, Woodrow Wilson, had charged the horseless carriage with fostering class antagonism and raising the specter of socialist revolution. so unattainable were cars by ordinary working Americans. A quarter of a century later, even the destitute refugees from the dust bowls drove automobiles as they migrated west in search of opportunity. To adults who had witnessed the rapidity by which a nation got wheels, it seemed only logical to think the airplane's development would be similar. Soon "everybody would fly, everybody would have a plane, and aerial traffic cops would soon be busy handing out tickets," predicted the Assistant Secretary of War for Aeronautics in 1930.[5]

No man contributed more to putting Americans in the driver's seat than Henry Ford, the lean mechanical genius from Dearborn, Michigan. In 1908 Ford first introduced his famous Model T, and, through quantity production of that single model on a novel moving assembly line, reduced its price so that by the early twenties virtually anyone could afford one. Over the next eighteen years Ford sold more than fifteen million of the stark, solid, and sure-footed flivvers or tin lizzies, as the Model Ts were affectionately called. In the early 1920s, in fact, over half of all the cars sold in the country were Fords. In the latter part of the decade, however, Ford also seemed to be giving Americans wings. Encouraged by his airminded son Edsel, Ford had started the manufacture of airplanes in 1925, building first an eight-passenger all-metal aircraft for airline operation and introducing the next year the Ford trimotor, which carried twelve passengers and offered a new standard of performance for commercial operators.[6] Although Ford shrewdly perceived that it was the commercial market which was significant, the public inevitably expected the flivver king, now that he was airminded, to build some kind of aerial equivalent of the Model T. Even before Ford's name was associated with aviation, people were awaiting "some Henry Ford of the aeronautical world" who would bring the price of airplanes down "where al-

most anybody will be able to have his private air car." Now that
Ford was actually building airplanes, talk of "air lizzies" and aerial
"flivvers" multiplied.[7]

When in the summer of 1926 Ford announced a prototype "Ford
flying flivver," it was a big day for the air-car dream. To those
expecting an aerial version of the family-toting, cargo-hauling
Model T, however, the flying flivver proved disappointing, for it
was a diminutive single-seat machine. Yet it prompted incredible
enthusiasm. On an airplane reliability tour similar to the ones held
for automobiles in the early years of the century, the little Ford
was flown to a number of cities, where airport crowds excitedly
flocked to the machine, at times threatening to crush it. The press,
too, treated Ford's flying flivver exuberantly.[8] A New York *Evening Sun* columnist, imagining himself already aloft in the little
machine, penned what he termed the "hallucination" of a new
flivver owner:

> I dreamed I was an angel
> And with the angels soared
> But I was simply touring
> The heavens in a Ford.[9]

Outside the big city, on the farms and in the workshops where
Ford, himself a country boy, had his most devoted following,
many took Ford's effort as prophetic. One country journalist, for-
getting how skittishly farm animals had reacted to the automobile,
claimed that "when Mr. Farmer lands in the farm yard" in his family plane, his chickens "will be there to welcome him." Another
grass roots flivver enthusiast wrote to Ford, poetically expressing
her faith in mass flying:

> Now Henry is in Clover
> For he had some tin left over
> He will use for making Air Plains big and small
> All the world is in a hurry
> But the people does not worry
> For they know he will make an
> Air Plain for them all.[10]

But the little Ford failed its maker, as well as the prophets. In 1928,
while flying the flivver over the beach in Miami, Harry Brooks, a
pilot and friend of Ford's, crashed and was killed. Grieved over
the loss, Ford temporarily suspended aircraft production. Five

years later he withdrew from airplane manufacture altogether.[11] If Americans were to tour the heavens, it would not be in Fords.

With the onset of the depression in the 1930s, one might have expected interest in an "Air Plain for them all" to ebb. But hard times retarded neither experimentation nor optimism. Indeed, the thirties saw many developments that seemed to point toward rapid fulfillment of the dream. Some members of the aeronautical community, for example, devoted themselves to building what was commonly termed a "foolproof" airplane, a machine that could be safely flown by people with no more skill than was required to drive an automobile. It was not the larger airplane manufacturers, firms such as Beechcraft or Mono Aircraft, that pursued this vision. They built more traditional small aircraft for family and business use. Instead the quest in the thirties for a foolproof or safety plane was led by small-shop owners, backyard experimenters, and a few government engineers.[12]

One of these engineers was Fred Weick, employed at the government's aeronautical laboratories at Langley Field, Virginia. Working off-hours with some of his colleagues, Weick in 1931 began to evolve a plane that would not stall and spin (tailspins killed many pilots at the time); that could be landed safely on rough fields or in cross-winds; and that had a simplified system of controls. On the eve of World War II, after years of development and the testing of prototypes, Weick and his partners introduced the "Ercoupe," a two-seat, all-metal aircraft that satisfied his criteria for "foolproof" flight. The plane would sell well in the postwar market, and its spin-proof design and tricycle landing gear were lasting contributions to flying safety that have become almost universal. Its simplified control system, however, proved a passing fad, an innovation that unwisely traded off mastery of the airplane in flight for easier operation by neophytes.[13]

To understand the two-control innovation and the motives of its developers, and to explain why it failed to catch on, let us take a brief flying lesson. Climbing into a conventionally controlled plane, we notice a control stick (or a steering wheel) and a pair of foot pedals. The stick or wheel, along with the pedals, really comprise three separate controls which can be used to independently govern the plane's movement in the air (the throttle is also used in these maneuvers, but we shall omit it in the interest of simplicity). Push the stick (or steering wheel) forward and the plane descends; pull it back and the plane climbs. Move it (or turn the wheel) to one side and the plane banks or rolls to that side. Finally, depress one of the foot pedals connected to the rudder and the plane's nose moves left or right, turning the ship. This three-control system, standard since aviation's earliest days, provides maximum control on three separate axes—what pilots term pitch, roll, and yaw. Yet the three-control system inevitably frustrated beginners when they tried to make smooth banked turns in the air. To turn to the right, for instance, one has to move the stick or turn the wheel to that side, taking care not to pull or push the controls, for the plane would then gain or lose altitude. Simultaneously one has to apply right rudder with the foot pedal. Too much bank and the plane sideslips downwards in its turn, while too much rudder causes it to skid rather than turn. Getting just the right positions, and coordinating one's hands and feet, required considerable practice and a soft touch.

In Weick's simplified control system, however, there were only two controls, not three. The rudder was linked to the ailerons, with the stick or wheel activating both. Thus the rudder pedals were gone. To turn an Ercoupe or other two-control plane, the pilot simply turned his steering wheel as in a car. The plane automatically banked the proper amount as it turned, thereby preventing any skidding. Neophytes loved it, but experienced pilots were often less than enthusiastic. If a gust of wind raised one wingtip while landing, for instance, the pilot could not level his plane—achieved with aileron control—without simultaneously turning it. Near the ground, in the presence of trees or obstacles, that could be fatal. And there were other things a pilot could not do with two controls: he could not sideslip, a means of losing altitude quickly without increasing forward speed; nor could he fly acrobatically. To be sure, not everyone would want to do acrobatics, but few pilots of any kind wanted to trade off the versatility represented by three controls for the simplified system. They knew that in flying such a plane, even with prudence, one might get into a dangerous situation avoidable with a conventional aircraft. The two-control system simply was not foolproof, as its developer Fred Weick was the first to admit. It therefore never caught on and became an interesting technical monument to the gospel promise of everyone a Lindbergh.[14]

The period witnessed numerous other efforts to improve the safety of aircraft or to make their operation simpler. In 1927 the Daniel Guggenheim Fund for the Promotion of Aeronautics, a philanthropy interested in fostering scientific, educational, and promotional activities connected with aviation, launched its safe aircraft competition. It led to some important technical innovations which enabled aircraft to land and take off at slower speeds and in shorter distances. The most publicized efforts having to do with safer aircraft, however, were those of the federal government in the early 1930s. Orchestrating these activities was Eugene L. Vidal, Director of the Bureau of Air Commerce in the Commerce Department during Franklin D. Roosevelt's first administration.[15]

Vidal had been a West Point football and track star, an Olympian, a military pilot during the World War, and then an airline executive. He also believed fervently in the winged gospel and particularly the dream of wings for all. As head of the agency then empowered to regulate and promote civilian aeronautics, the Bureau of Air Commerce, Vidal in November 1933 announced that the government would soon spend half a million dollars to produce a "poor man's airplane." The machine would sell for $700, Vidal said, about the cost of a medium-priced automobile. It would be a two- or three-seat plane, built of metal so as to "look right" to a public that admired the new all-metal silver airliners and had grown accustomed to metal automobiles. The plane would be cheap because it would be mass-produced by "conveyor belt." It would also be rugged and easy to repair, with the cost of owning and maintaining the machine "less than that of an average-priced automobile." Vidal imagined that one might fly the plane "for the full span of its life without major overhauls" or, alternatively, find it more economical to replace the engine or even the entire plane rather than repair it. A market definitely existed for such a craft, Vidal believed, not only among car drivers but also among more experienced fliers. He had queried some 34,000 licensed pilots, student fliers, and mechanics as to their interest in a $700 plane, and three-quarters of the 18,000 returning the survey responded affirmatively.[16] This was hardly surprising, given the fact that the plane's $700 projected price tag was about $300 to $500 lower than anything else on the market. Furthermore, what one could buy for $1,000 was a fabric-covered, one- or two-seat, low-performance aircraft, suitable for training or recreational hops around the countryside in daylight but hardly the miniature airliner of Vidal's vision. Of the 25 percent who responded negatively, a disproportionate share were licensed pilots, men and women who knew from experience that low price meant low performance and often a lack of safety.[17]

Vidal did not let such criticisms worry him as he moved ahead with plans for the poor man's airplane. He planned to launch the project with a grant from Harold Ickes's Public Works Administration (PWA), one of the numerous government agencies established in the depression to battle unemployment. Federal funds, channeled, he thought, perhaps through a consortium of existing airplane builders, would be used to hire unemployed engineers, draftsmen, and craftsmen who would design and manufacture the federal flivvers. Before a man was hired or a blueprint drawn, however, politics grounded the scheme. PWA lawyers insisted money could only go to public works, and that there was nothing at all "public" about private planes for the masses. Some members of the administration objected to rewarding the aircraft industry at a time when some manufacturers were under suspicion of antitrust violations.[18] Firms already building planes for the private market vehemently attacked the plan, charging that the publicity already was causing potential buyers to wait for some chimerical government plane rather than buying existing aircraft. Manufacturers also knew that building simpler, one- or two-seat, light planes for much under $1,000 was difficult enough, so they thought Vidal's proposed $700 price tag for an all-metal plane absurd. The metal alloy alone would cost $360, claimed a critic. Most experts considered an all-metal machine such as Vidal described an impossibility and derided it as the "all-mental" airplane.[19]

Not to be thwarted by less airminded administrators, Vidal devised an alternative approach. Liberally interpreting the legislation which had created the Bureau of Air Commerce and given it the power to promote civilian flying, Vidal formed a Development Section in his agency to foster "the design, construction, and development of safer, easier operated, more comfortable and lower priced airplanes for private owners." The Bureau had no budget for development, but it did have monies for purchasing aircraft to be flown by its inspectors as they traveled around the country pursuant to the agency's work of examining pilots and licensing aircraft. Using these funds, his newly created Development Section now turned to the task of setting up design criteria for what Vidal called a "safety plane." Once the specifications were drawn, he solicited bids from the aircraft industry. He planned to purchase twenty-five safety planes from the firm submitting the best design. Cost was not to be the determining factor in the competition, and Vidal was no longer talking about the "poor man's" airplane or planes at the price of a car. He envisioned the safety plane, however, as a "proving ground" for the mass-produced, inexpensive aircraft of tomorrow, expecting that the Bureau's adoption would generate a growing demand that would eventually lower the plane's price and put it in reach of the masses.[20]

Vidal opened the final bids in the safety plane competition at a small Washington ceremony on August 27, 1934. If he had not been such a believer, he might then have had some second thoughts about the project. Only one bid came from an aircraft manufacturer of any size and reputation; another was crudely penned on a hotel letterhead and came from a complete crank. All the others had been submitted by small firms or backyard inventors of limited experience. Because the designs were all so untried, or possessed significant faults, Vidal decided against ordering twenty-five from any one bidder. He momentarily considered reopening bidding for a dozen each of the two most promising designs but rejected the idea because, as his superior, Secretary of Commerce Daniel Roper, privately explained, the public would think "we had not succeeded in getting the safe airplane they were expecting and that we had to modify our requirements." In the end, modifying once again his strategy for promoting mass, personal flight, Vidal awarded contracts to five different builders, each for a single prototype which the government then would test and evaluate.[21]

As these government subsidized prototypes rolled out of the workshops in 1935 and 1936, they attracted considerable publicity, both in the popular as well as the aeronautical press. Each aircraft was an effort to address one or more of the four obstacles that had been retarding the acceptance of personal flying since Harold McCormick's air-yachting days: high cost, lack of safety, difficulty of operation, and inconvenience for door-to-door travel. One possible answer to the high cost of flying was represented by Vidal's "Plymacoupe," a plane having the engine of a Plymouth automobile. Because an airplane engine cost three times as much as an automobile engine, and because it comprised approximately half of the plane's total cost, this approach seemed to promise great savings. Unfortunately, pound for pound, auto engines were less powerful, so the savings in dollars came at the expense of performance.

Putting automobile engines in aircraft, therefore, was hardly a breakthrough in the effort to put an airplane in every garage.[22]

Two of Vidal's prototypes, the Waterman "Arrowplane" and the Hammond Y-1, embodied design features to make them safer and easier to fly. Both had the same tricycle landing gear introduced by Fred Weick, and both were resistant to tailspins. In August 1935, Fred Geisse, Vidal's Chief of Development and an amateur pilot, successfully flew the Waterman from its factory in San Diego to Washington, D.C. Impressed by his flight, Geisse told reporters that the Waterman was "very close" to being foolproof. Some journalists who came out to Bolling Field just outside the capital to observe or fly the plane went much further. The Waterman gave "soul-satisfying evidence" that the sky would soon be "a general traffic highway for private and family airplanes," reported the New York *World Telegram*, which concluded that "the idea of a cheap, safe automobile of the air seems at last out of the dream stage." Other writers heralded the plane as ideal for the "average working man" or for the "layman pilot." If its engine quit on take-off, the Associated Press pointed out, instead of falling into a spin and crashing, it would "land itself safely . . . no matter how rattled the pilot may become." Dropping down onto Bolling Field from a flight one day, Amelia Earhart took a short hop in the Waterman and proclaimed that it handled "nicely." Similar responses greeted the Hammond. One journalist, airminded but with no experience as a pilot, took off in the ship, flew several times around the field, and even made a number of perfect landings. The Hammond, he concluded, was "far easier to take off, fly and land, than an automobile was to drive."[23]

Despite these encomiums, both the Hammond and the Waterman had limitations. They may have been easy to fly, but they were slow and unresponsive to their controls. This was largely because the planes were pushers—that is, they had rear engines and their propellers pushed them through the air rather than pulled them as with conventional aircraft. All else being equal, the pusher configuration is less efficient than the so-called tractor design because the pusher propeller operates in air already disturbed by the passing of the plane's fuselage. The Hammond and Waterman were pushers, however, because the configuration seemed to better match the vision of making automobile drivers into pilots.

Indeed, both planes strongly reflected the influence of the auto-

mobile on the thinking of the airminded. Vidal's safety-plane specifications had required that the successful designs provide visibility
equivalent to that of a car for both pilot and passenger, and there
was virtually no way to obtain the stipulated area of windshield in
a design without going to the unconventional, rear-mounted pusher
engine. So the Hammond and the Waterman achieved the visibility
of a car but at the cost of their performance as aircraft. Both, in
fact, looked a bit like cars, with their short, stubby, teardrop-
shaped fuselages, reminiscent of the streamlined, automobiles being proposed by inventors and industrial designers in the 1930s.
Had the Hammond or Waterman ever gone into production, the
visual similarity of their fuselages to automobiles might have helped
sales, but, instead, the designs remained one more instance where
pursuit of the vision of wings for all shaped technology in ways
that failed.[24]

The Waterman plane reflected yet another automobile-inspired
compromise in pursuit of the dream: it was designed from the outset to be "roadable," that is, to be capable of being driven like a
car on the highway, in which mode the pusher configuration would
make sense, both to protect the propeller and to increase visibility
for the driver. A few years after delivering the original Arrowplane to the government, Waterman built a roadable version, which
he called the "Arrowbile." Its single high-mounted wing (it had
no tail) was removable, and the plane had a clutch and transmis-
sion that permitted the driver-pilot to transfer power to the wheels.
For road use, the machine had headlights, diminutive fenders, and
license plates. By the time Waldo Waterman was flying and driving around in his Arrowbile, Vidal had already had some experience with another air-road hybrid, one of his safety-plane prototypes.[25] In August 1936, in a small park near the Bureau's downtown
Washington offices, a large lunch-hour crowd had assembled to
watch test pilot John Ray land a weird-looking aircraft. The spectators saw a wingless, lozenge-shaped machine with a gigantic
overhead rotor like a helicopter but with a propeller on its nose
like an airplane. It was an autogiro, a precursor of the helicopter.
It could not rise straight up and down or hover motionless like a
helicopter, but it required a fraction of a conventional airplane's
take-off and landing space. What lifted the machine onto the front
pages of newspapers, however, was that it was half automobile. It
could be driven on the road as well as flown through the air. Its

pilot-driver could transfer power from his propeller and rotor to his single rear-drive wheel just by throwing a clutch.

On the ground, pilot Ray demonstrated the features of the road-able machine. Climbing out of the aircraft's diminutive cabin, he folded the overhead rotor blades back along the craft's black and orange fuselage and returned to his cockpit. He then drove the autogiro, looking now like a giant grasshopper, around to the front of the Commerce Department building on Pennsylvania Avenue. There in a brief ceremony Vidal accepted the machine on behalf of the government. Ray then motored off through the mid-day traffic to the nearby Mall, got out, unfolded the overhead rotor, shifted the machine into flying mode, and took off for nearby Bolling Field. A little later he provided an unplanned encore to an already impressive performance. Cruising over the capital area, the autogiro's engine oil pressure suddenly fell. Worried, Ray scanned the ground for a lightly traveled road; spotting one he rotored down, landed, and drove off to find a gas station. There he diagnosed his problem as simply a lack of oil. He topped off his supply, and once again took to the air, this time completing his trip without further incident.[26]

Surely the hybrid, air-road vehicle represented the answer to the dream of wings for everyman. With such machines, it seemed, not just the rich, with their waterfront homes, downtown yacht clubs, and air yachts, but virtually everyone might have the door-to-door convenience of the automobile plus the speed and freedom offered by the flying machine. But this route to the fulfillment of prophecy proved equally illusory. Neither the roadable autogiro nor any other air-road vehicle, including Waldo Waterman's Arrowbile, ever entered production, let alone triggered a travel revolution.[27] The reason was simple. In solving the convenience problem, designers of air-road hybrids made too many compromises. Their machines were analogous to frogs and other amphibians which, although they manage adequately on land as well as in water, are easily outperformed by mammals and fish which are specialized for life in a single environment. So it was with roadable aircraft. In the air, the weight of their clutches, transmissions, brakes, lights, and other necessary highway equipment made them poor fliers compared with pure airplanes. On the ground the light construction of these hybrid vehicles rendered them vulnerable while parking or moving in traffic; their wheels, small to minimize weight and air resistance aloft, limited driving speeds. A Ford sedan might, conditions permitting, idle along at fifty miles per hour, but Vidal's autogiro cruised at only twenty-five. And the Ford's interior was a virtual living room compared with the tiny, cramped, two-person cabin of the autogiro.

While Vidal and inventors like Waldo Waterman focused on aircraft in their effort to make flying as convenient as driving, others sought the same result by rethinking the metropolitan landing field. During the late 1920s and early 1930s, a number of engineers, architects, and city planners, devised ways to permit conventional aircraft to fly directly into the modern city. Instead of adapting the flying machine to the urban or suburban environment, as Waterman did, these enthusiasts imagined downtown airfields, landing facilities erected in the heart of the metropolis. They proposed schemes for airfields on stilts, atop skyscrapers, or floating on man-made islands. For various reasons, no such structure was ever built, yet even at the level of concept, drawing, or model the idea of the urban landing facility brightly symbolized the promise of future air travel. For a brief moment in history, they appeared to be the public works of tomorrow.

As early as 1920, the manager of San Francisco's Fairmont Hotel approved preliminary plans for building an "airdome" on the roof of the building and announced that inter-city airplane service would be inaugurated following trials. The announcement was premature, of course, but San Francisco's extremely hilly terrain, difficult for ordinary aircraft operations, seemed to encourage such schemes. In 1927 a number of San Francisco business organizations were proposing to erect an elevated landing platform above the Embarcadero for the use of passenger and mail planes, and similar structures were suggested for other cities. In Los Angeles the city engineer developed a plan for a landing deck atop an industrial warehouse and even had a model of the building constructed. In the late 1920s, the Babson Statistical Organization, an early business advisory service, urged investors to buy up roof rights in towns and cities in anticipation of a boom in downtown landing field construction.[28]

Much grander conceptions for the urban landing field of the future emerged from the drafting boards of those engineers and architects who projected solutions to New York City's airport problem. By the late 1920s, the city desperately needed a metropolitan airport, yet the most central location, Manhattan, was already too built up to permit construction of a conventional air-field. Airminded New Yorkers, like their brethren elsewhere, were not yet reconciled to the idea of placing a city airport out in the country, half an hour or more away by old-fashioned ground transport. Sites in Queens or New Jersey, therefore, chosen even-tually out of necessity, seemed to countermand the very speed and efficiency that caused one to embrace flight in the first place. It was such thinking that underlay, for example, the giant, wheel-shaped landing field resting atop a ring of skyscrapers, proposed by a contestant in an airport design competition conducted in 1928 by the Lehigh Portland Cement Company, or the "rotary airport" that floated in New York Harbor right off the tip of Manhattan, anchored permanently to the harbor bottom but capable of turn-ing so that aircraft could take off and land into prevailing winds, suggested in 1930 by industrial designer Norman Bel Geddes.

An architectural competition conducted in 1925 by the New York Beaux Arts Institute of Design generated even more dra-matic proposals. Dedicated to promulgating the Beaux Arts aes-thetic and ideal in architecture, the Institute offered a $100 prize for the best design for "an aeroplane landing in a metropolis." The design put forward by first-prize winner Martin Beck was a gigan-tic skyscraper-airport that filled an entire city block. The building was to have an interior court created by four 950-foot-high tow-ers, taller than any edifice in the world at the time, one in the mid-dle of each side of the block. The towers in turn would support "a superstructure 300 feet more in height, comprising the landing proper with a level 30 feet beneath for repair shops, waiting-rooms, and other accommodations for passenger and mail service." Compared with this towering structure, the third-prize design, by Raymond P. Hughes, was almost puny: just a flight deck erected atop the piers of one of Manhattan's existing bridges. Hughes's design envisioned easy interchange between air transport and land and water transport, for it included ramps that ran from the bridge up to the landing area as well as access to the river below.[29]

For a number of reasons, even the least ambitious of these struc-tural and architectural proposals to meet the airport needs of the metropolis was never realized. Too many obstacles stood between vision and reality. For one thing, even in 1930 urban dwellers were sensitive to the noise of aircraft and would have protested mightily were such landing facilities ever built in their vicinity. That they were not, also reflected economics, a second problem. In the mid-twenties, when the Beaux Arts Institute competition was conducted, aviation simply lacked the prosperity to warrant constructing anything like Beck's skyscraper airport or even a deck atop a large bridge; by the early 1930s, when Bel Geddes proposed his rotary, island airport, aviation had demonstrated the potential to generate revenue, but economic conditions made the launching of such projects unfeasible. But the primary obstacle to their realization was technical. It was virtually impossible to meet the take-off and landing requirements of conventional aircraft, save on terra firma. In 1925, for example, experts stipulated that runways should be 2,700 feet in length. The skyscraper-airport design that won a prize that year, however, was only 1,400 feet square, gigantic for a building but far too small to be practicable as an airport. No building ever constructed, in fact, could hold on its roof a runway long enough for the largest planes of the mid-twenties. And that was before a cluster of interrelated technical changes—streamlining, all metal construction, cowled engines, retractable landing gear, and wingflaps—combined to increase significantly the runway requirements of commercial passenger planes. By the early 1930s, then, if not much earlier, all talk of "an aeroplane landing in a metropolis" was purely utopian, save possible with reference to autogiros or small personal planes. Yet it was precisely that sort of aircraft, the machines which Eugene Vidal's favored automobile driver might have flown which, ironically, were the least suited to operating in the city. Much more than larger planes, small aircraft would have been treacherous to fly in the unpredictable and often strong air currents that swirl around city buildings and other urban structures. If urban Americans were ever to enjoy easy access to flight, it was clear by the 1930s that conventional planes, operating from man-made landing structures erected in the heart of the metropolis were not the solution.

Yet the dream still burned brightly. Indeed, the 1930s offered much to buoy the hopes of those who subscribed to that tenet of the winged gospel. Eugene Vidal's safety plane program, although it ended in 1936 with the delivery of the roadable autogiro, had developed some interesting prototypes and broadly publicized the idea of planes for all, even though none of his machines ever made it to production, let alone sold at the cost of medium-priced automobiles as originally promised. Despite talk about planes for the poor man, owning an airplane remained something most Americans could only dream about—the average fly-away cost of a new two-seat, light plane in 1937, the year Vidal left government, was $1,935, about three times the price of a new Ford sedan. On the more sanguine side, however, the number of small planes flying had increased fourfold during his four years in office, notwithstanding the depressed state of the economy. Moreover, in the same years the number of licensed pilots increased by 25 percent. When Vidal resigned in 1937, such statistics could be taken as supporting the air car dream. Vidal himself still believed in the feasibility of mass-produced personal planes, and in private life began experiments with molded plywood, a material he thought appropriate for the purpose.

Believers in the vision might, however, have taken pause from one other statistic: in 1937 the *total* number of private planes licensed in the United States was fewer than 3,000, compared with 25 million registered automobiles, a figure also up 25 percent during Vidal's tenure in Commerce.[30] The numbers revealed the trivial place of personal planes in the transportation picture, but few Americans in the late 1930s seemed to sense the futility of expecting aircraft to rival, let alone to supplant, automobiles.

Indeed, with the coming of the Second World War, air car enthusiasm rose to an unprecedented level. In newspapers, popular magazines, and aeronautical publications; in corporate board rooms as well as government offices; and in schools, architectural firms, and even museums—in a wide variety of contexts during the years from 1941 through 1945 Americans debated the question, as one enthusiast phrased it: "What and when will Mr. and Mrs. John Q. Public be flying after the war?" Most people answered the "what" question as they always had, pointing to the airplane. A growing number of enthusiasts, however, considered the recently perfected helicopter a much better answer. At the immensely popular exhibition called "Airways for Peace," held at the Museum of Modern Art in New York in 1943, a film produced by the Sikorsky Helicopter Company was one of the most popular features of the exhibit, transfixing thousands by its image of tomorrow. Viewers saw a man take off in a helicopter from the roof of a New York apartment building, presumably heading for the office. Moments later he returned to hover motionless a few feet above the roof while he reached through the cockpit window to get from his wife the lunch he had forgotten! The Sikorsky film, along with other promotional materials from helicopter manufacturers, implanted the idea that soon everyone would be hopping off from city roofs in what *Cue* magazine called the "Poor Man's Pegasus."[31]

The question as to *when* Mr. and Mrs. John Q. Public would be flying, and the implied question of how many new aircraft would be in the air once peace returned, generated the most extensive discussions, particularly during the last years of the war. Not only simple predictions but also market research and public-opinion polls addressed the question. Businessmen trying to forecast postwar buying trends, aircraft manufacturers planning peacetime production, and government planners thinking about future airfield requirements and the reconversion of the economy, were just some of the groups wanting information regarding the public's aerial expectations and intentions. All the surveys and studies pointed toward a crowded peacetime sky. One poll suggested that as many as 85 percent of Air Force pilots, once they returned to civilian life, planned to own planes. A study of the largely female readership of *Woman's Home Companion* showed that 39 percent planned to take flying lessons, indicating that the postwar sky would be an egalitarian one. According to yet another study, 43.5 percent of all professional and business people expected to own a plane after the war.[32]

Of all the wartime surveys, the one conducted by the *Saturday Evening Post* in 1945 employed the largest and most careful sampling. It showed that 32 percent of the adult American population wanted to own a plane after the war and that 7 percent definitely planned to buy one. These percentages, if projected onto the population at large, represented 3 million definite airplane purchases and a potential of 15 million. Government crystal-ball gazers, only slightly less sanguine, reinforced such predictions. A Civil Aeronautics Administration report published the same year as the *Post* study made the familiar assumption that personal plane development would duplicate automobile history. "Under proper conditions," the report claimed, the rate of increase in the number of new planes during first postwar decade would match that of automobiles during the period from 1902 to 1912, a period chosen apparently because it straddled the introduction of various mass-produced, moderately priced automobiles, including Ford's Model T. This worked out to 2 million planes, the report's "most optimistic" estimate, which was offered along with an "ultraconservative" estimate of merely 400,000 planes in the air ten years after the war.[33] Accepting any of these predictions, and recalling that as late as 1937 there were fewer than 3,000 planes licensed to private pilots, it becomes clear why one out of every three new car dealers was said to be planning to sell airplanes after the war![34]

The air-car fervor of the war years grew from a number of causes. Probably all wars encourage speculation about the future, either because of the impulse to define collective goals or only as a kind of wishful escape, a respite from the horrors of battle. During the Second World War, however, Americans commonly spoke of the future—and justified the struggle against the Axis—under a rubric centered on the "American way of life." This formulation called attention to elements of American culture beloved and missed by servicemen overseas, such as girlfriends, movies, ice cream parlors, and baseball games, but it also encompassed the consumer goods which citizens everywhere viewed as distinctly American, as a prize for victory in the war: new cars, houses, refrigerators, televisions—and family planes.[35] This tendency to conceive of the future in material terms was strengthened by the fact that the war came on top of a decade of depression and severe shortages. Furthermore, the family disruption and suffering wrought by war and depression gave family-related consumer goods, including the family plane, great appeal. Finally, the extravagant wartime expectations regarding postwar purchases of personal aircraft also reflected the aerial nature of the conflict. Just reading the newspapers or watching the newsreels, it was hard not to become airminded. Millions of Americans came to know aviation first hand, flying for the armed services, working in aircraft factories, and serving as civil defense aircraft spotters in their communities. Many of these people saw personal wings in their immediate future. And, as we shall see in greater detail in the next chapter, the younger generation eagerly studied aviation-influenced curricula in the public schools, readying themselves for the day when "millions of inexpensive planes" would be available, as U.S. Commissioner of Education, Dr. John Studebaker put it.[36]

The war ended in 1945 with the dream of an airplane in every garage stronger than ever, and within a year of VJ Day numerous signs indicated that it might, at last, be coming true. In 1946 alone Americans purchased 33,254 personal planes, five times more than in any previous year. Backlogged orders for personal aircraft ran into the millions of dollars, a situation that attracted numerous new companies into the market. Among the prototypes demonstrated to postwar consumers were the "Skycar," "Airphibian," "ConvAircar," and "Aerocar," air-road hybrids of the sort Eugene Vidal had encouraged fifteen years earlier. (None of these machines ever made it into production). Wheaties, "the breakfast of champions," gave away a new airplane in a contest advertised on the back of a cereal box. The winner, a ten-year-old girl, was too young to fly but her father took lessons and became a pilot. Thousands of veterans, flush from newly legislated G.I. benefits, were also learning to fly, another hopeful augury of the arriving air age. Many of these new pilots flew out of newly constructed "airparks," small grass-covered flying fields being built by airminded communities to anticipate the expected burgeoning aerial population. If few of these fliers bought new planes from local automobile dealers, as had been predicted just a few years earlier, there were signs that obtaining aircraft would be much easier. In 1945 Macy's Department Store in New York added the all-metal, two-seat Ercoupe to its inventory. Quite matter of factly Macy's elevator operators, as they stopped on the fifth floor, chimed out, "ladies' girdles, gentlemen's socks, airplanes, and household appliances."[37]

Airplanes, of course, never became personal necessities like socks, underwear, and appliances. The symptoms of an impending buying spree and mass adoption of personal planes proved illusory. By 1950, in fact, the postwar flying boom had already faded. Airfields closed, pilots allowed their licenses to lapse, and many investors lost money, including the builders of the various roadable aircraft that briefly flitted across the postwar sky. And while helicopter coupes appeared on the cover of *Popular Mechanics*, they never showed up in people's garages. The most graphic index of collapse, however, was the precipitous decline in airplane sales: from a high of over 30,000 units in 1946, sales fell off by half in 1947 and by half again in 1948.[38] The downturn was not a recession. Other consumer goods—the girdles, gentlemen's socks, and household appliances at Macy's, not to mention homes and automobiles—all sold exuberantly. Postwar consumers were making up for their lack of money during the depression and for the lack of things to buy during the war. But they were not purchasing the hundreds of thousands—let alone millions—of family planes which prophets, just a few years before, so sanguinely had predicted.

By mid century the dream of personal wings ceased to resonate in popular culture. Never again would serious discussions of aerial flivvers or poor man's airplanes compel the attention of a major automobile manufacturer, the federal government, or private business. Never again would women's or family magazines cover developments in small aircraft as they had in the years from Lindbergh through the Second World War. The public, encouraged for decades to think that personal planes were just around the corner, had been disappointed once too often and now viewed the prospect of owning a plane or helicopter as improbable, if not utopian. Increasingly Americans realized that flying, at least for those who lived in and around the great metropolitan centers, was and would likely remain a costly, inconvenient, and dangerous way to travel compared to driving.

With the ebbing of faith in the dream of mass personal flight, the winged gospel itself lost much of its appeal. As it became clear that the sky was not to be a democratic arena filled with individuals in their own machines, that flying was to be dominated by giant corporations just like in the heyday of railroads, aviation became much less interesting.

VI

Adults and the
"Winged Superchildren of Tomorrow"

A 1929 advertisement in the *Saturday Evening Post* showed a young boy seated at his workbench building a model airplane. The boy had paused in his labors and gazed dreamily upwards, as if to the heavens. He looked beyond the tattered pictures of George Washington and Abraham Lincoln pinned to the wall and dreamed of more modern heroes, perhaps Lindbergh, or maybe of his own future as a mail pilot or war ace. The text of the advertisement, extolling the ability of Monarch Foods to give youngsters strength for careers in the air age, was typical commercial hyperbole, but the image captured a fundamental truth. For airminded adults believed that the boys and girls who were building and flying model airplanes were irrefutable proof that the prophesied air age would, in time, be realized. No matter if consumers failed to buy personal planes, if the present generation dragged its feet in taking to the air, or if adults persisted in their wars and squabbles—the next generation would surely deliver on the gospel's grander promises. Youngsters, after all, appeared far more airminded than their elders. As educators formulated the popular expectation, adults constituted the "last earthbound generation," while youth would grow up to become the "winged superchildren of tomorrow."[1]

For this reason the image of youth and model plane was extremely popular. It appeared not only in advertisements like that of Monarch Foods but also, for example, on the cover of a 1936 U.S. government pamphlet on aviation in the public schools, where a boy stood in front of his school holding his miniature airliner while, in a small inset, the full-scale transport is illustrated; in a giant mural painted in the 1930s for the San Francisco stock exchange by the famous Mexican artist, Diego Rivera; and on the cover of the *Saturday Evening Post* for April 1940, where a boy, dwarfed by the large flying model he is holding, stands gazing up at a giant seaplane flying low overhead. In these and the other representations of youth and model plane which were common during the years from Lindbergh through the Second World War, we have a most powerful symbol of the public's faith in aviation as a transforming force in human affairs. The Wrights themselves had become interested in flight as children when their father gave them a small flying toy, so it seemed that the model-making propensity of today's young would lead to even greater things in the future. The image of youngster and model airplane, therefore, served the believers in the winged gospel as a kind of icon.[2]

Almost from the beginning of the airplane age, members of the older generation sought to encourage aeronautical interest among the young. In 1912 a spokesman for the Aero Club of America called upon its members to help prepare youth "to take up our work intelligently and create, ten years from now, a race of Americans to whom flying is as familiar as automobiling has been to us." At first such calls generated relatively little response. In the 1910s and early 1920s, a few industrial arts teachers introduced model building into their classes; a handful of model airplane clubs appeared; and some airminded faculty organized informal aero clubs on college and university campuses.[3] With the explosion of airmindedness in the late 1920s, however, a more systematic and energetic effort to nourish—and to implant—youthful aeronautical interest emerged. Parents, teachers, recreation leaders, municipal officials, pilots, and various others involved with airplanes now actively promoted the building of model planes and learning about aviation. Amelia Earhart, Jacqueline Cochran, and Charles Lindbergh were just three of the famous aviators who devoted time to the clubs, organizations, and contests which proliferated around the model airplane hobby in the period. Even nurses were learning to build models for use in therapy with young patients. During the late 1920s and the 1930s the national press covered miniature aeronautics with almost the same intensity as the real thing, and model airplanes became big business for retailers and manufacturers. Building model planes became much more common in the schools, too, where teachers were now frequently introducing aeronautical subject matter into their classes. Educators from the primary level through college developed syllabuses and course materials around flight related topics and, by the time of the Second World War, were touting "Air-Age Education" as a revolutionary new pedagogy.[4]

As adults pursued the gospel through their children, they imposed organization and structure upon the hobby of model making. This happened most pervasively in urban areas. In Los Angeles, Kansas City, Wichita, and Detroit, then emerging as centers of the burgeoning aircraft industry, municipal recreation leaders led this organizational movement, establishing model clubs for children, conducting classes on model building, publishing instruction manuals for young practioners, and holding flying meets. Los Angeles opened the first "Junior Airport," a specialized playground dedicated exclusively to flying model airplanes. Representatives from companies that manufactured model airplane engines would come out to the model airport on weekends and give advice or help youngsters with problems. In Detroit, where Henry Ford started building aircraft in 1925, an airminded population supported one of the biggest municipal youth programs. In 1928, the first summer of the city's model-making program, 600 children built models under the supervision of municipal staff. By the summer of 1936, some 45,000 youngsters were receiving instruction in the craft and, two years later, 120,144 boys and girls attended neighborhood model clinics. By then Detroit had ten full-time model-building instructors on its payroll. Periodically the city sponsored flying meets, and as many as 25,000 spectators would turn out to watch the young people fly their models.[5]

A number of large city department stores also began to sponsor clubs and to run competitions for young model builders. Jordan Marsh in Boston: Bamburger and Kresge in Newark; Stix, Baer and Fuller of St. Louis; and Gimbel's and Stern Brothers in New York City all offered model workshops or clubs. Stern's provided its "Sky Cadets" with a special workshop in which to build their models and employed an expert model-maker to supervise the youngsters.[6] Profit could not have played much of a part in the stores' efforts, as the volume of nickel and dime purchases at their hobby counters would hardly have justified the even modest costs of the programs. Rather, Stern's and other department stores sponsored model programs for good will, itself a profit maker, of course, and because store executives themselves often sincerely believed in the gospel of aviation and wanted to do their part in ushering in the air age. The depression provided another reason.

Widespread unemployment made it all the harder for adolescents to find remunerative work, and building models was thought to help keep teenagers off the streets. Some observers claimed these programs helped control juvenile delinquency, and the rate of juvenile delinquency in Wichita, Kansas, was said to have dropped 55 percent in two years following the inauguration of a model-building program. Miniature planes, enthusiasts seemed to think, just like their larger counterparts, would prove a social panacea.[7]

The fact that model building became a preoccupation for many American youngsters in the late twenties and thirties owed much to its promotion by the media. Both newspapers and radio stations started model-building clubs. By far the largest of these was the "Junior Birdmen of America," launched in 1934 by publishing magnate William Randolph Hearst and conducted in 17 "Junior Birdmen Wing City Newspapers," all part of the Hearst empire. Sundays brought youngsters the "Junior Birdmen Feature Page" containing information about aeronautics and model-building techniques as well as how kids might obtain official membership cards and identifying wing-pins and how they could organize their own flight squadrons. In the various Junior Birdmen Wing Cities, Hearst newspapers sponsored model contests in which boys and girls flew their planes for prizes. Hearst denied that the organization was another "newspaper stunt" to boost circulation and characterized it rather as a "permanent youth movement devoted to the boys and girls of the United States who are interested in aviation." In reality, Hearst's Junior Birdmen was like many other air-minded efforts, simultaneously an expression of the winged gospel as well as good business, a social "movement" as well as a promotional ploy.[8]

In the 1930s broadcasters also beamed the gospel of model building to youth by radio. NBC's Model Airplane Club of the Air, for example, reached boys and girls who lacked access to big city model clubs or even Junior Birdmen columns in the newspaper, giving them expert advice on model building and flying along with a feeling of camaraderie. One of the aviation radio programs of the period, the "Jimmie Allen Club," was not itself about models although model making was a key part of the sponsor's, Richfield Oil Company, strategy of promoting youthful aeronautics—and the sales of its automobile and aviation gasolines. "Jimmie Allen" was the radio name of Dudley Steel, a pilot and the head of aviation petroleum sales for the California-based petroleum company.

Every weekday evening, over half a million Jimmie Allen Club members tuned their radios to the Richfield-sponsored adventure serial and vicariously flew with their hero through various aerial episodes. Interest in the Jimmie Allen show prompted a movie, *Sky Parade,* the first of a projected series starring Dudley Steel, but the film failed at the box office, despite Steel's strenuous promotion of it over the air and in the Club's *Jimmie Allen Club News.* He also used the radio show to direct club members to their nearest Richfield filling station, where they could pick up free membership cards and copies of the *News,* while their parents might buy some gas. The *News,* a four-page tabloid-size monthly, included aviation fiction, model-building tips, and reports on the activities of members and of the local Jimmy Allen Clubs, organized by youngsters in their communities.[9]

The Hollywood branch of the Jimmie Allen Club in the mid-1930s included both Mickey Rooney and Shirley Temple, thereby reflecting the faith of many airminded Americans that tomorrow's sky would have an equal place for boys and girls. In the period, model making was not at all the male preserve it became later. The names of girls appeared often in the Club's newsletter, and one of the adult advisers to the Jimmie Allen Club was Gladys O'Donnell, a leading racing pilot of the period. The comic strip that appeared regularly in the *Jimmie Allen Club News,* "Johnny and Susie," also drove home to young readers the idea that the air age would be egalitarian. In one of these comics, Johnny cries. "Let's play Jimmie Allen," as he prepared to parachute off a roof with his mother's umbrella. "No, I'll be Jimmie Allen—I want to jump too," countered Susie. Johnny believed his sister was a sissy and told her she had to be "ground crew." But Susie was not so easily grounded. She grabbed the umbrella, climbed onto the roof, and successfully parachuted to the ground. When Johnny tried the stunt, however, the "parachute" failed, and he crash-landed, a clear warning to boys who denied their sisters a place in the air.[10]

The evidence for girls' involvement in the building and flying of model planes is overwhelming. During the thirties 25 percent of all the youngsters in Cleveland's municipal model-building clubs were girls, and five of Detroit's neighborhood clubs were all female in membership.[11] Girls also competed in local and even national contests. But just as there were handicaps to being a woman pilot, there were problems encountered by girl modelers. Model aeronautics in the period, reflecting the larger world of full-scale airplanes, did not offer true equality. A contest conducted by the Jimmie Allen Club highlighted one of the problems facing girls. Entrants had the choice of building a non-flying, scale model of one of four planes. These ranged in complexity from a small private aircraft, the Curtiss-Wright "Baby Bunting," to a large twin-engined commercial transport. If any girl built the transport, her model must have been judged unworthy of any prize, for every one of the five contestants with obviously female names among the winners listed in the *Jimmie Allen Club News* built the simplest model, the "Baby Bunting." No mystery underlay this result. Although girls felt the lure of flight just as strongly as boys, they did not bring the same knowledge of tools and shop kinks or the same experience to model making, and surely did not receive the same encouragement in tackling complex, time-consuming model projects. As a response to this situation, Amelia Earhart, who knew well the difficulty of acquiring mechanical know-how as a female, created in 1929 a special trophy to be awarded the girl who entered the best model in the annual National Playground Miniature Aircraft Tournament. This competition, started in 1927, was the first truly national model airplane contest and through the 1930s attracted a small number of expert female model-builders.[12]

Another problem for girls was the bias of schools and curriculum. Ironically, corporate sponsored organizations such as the Jimmie Allen Club or the municipal model-airplane groups offered airminded girls more opportunity than the public schools. Some of the civic or commercially sponsored clubs and groups started informally as all-boy organizations, like Kresge's Junior Aviation League in Newark, New Jersey, but most of these organizations welcomed girls if they wanted to join, which they did in significant numbers. All of these extracurricular institutions escaped the more fixed, sex-role expectations of the schools, where model building had been introduced early but usually in the context of manual arts or shop classes that were generally confined to boys. As early as 1929 almost every junior and senior high as well as some elementary schools in airminded Detroit offered some instruction and supervision in plane building, and by the 1930s it was a rare high school that did not have some boys building planes in shop. But girls could not participate in this airminded learning.[13]

Whether pursued by boys or by girls, whether carried on in basements or bedrooms, schoolhouses or department stores, the model-building boom of the late twenties and the thirties owed a great deal to business and technical changes having to do with miniature aircraft. It was only in the late 1920s, for example, that hobby shops first appeared in the large cities. One of the first in the country was the Albatross Model Aero Supply Shop, opened in Newark, New Jersey, in 1929. It and other stores like it provided young enthusiasts with a convenient source for buying model airplane supplies and construction kits. These shops became meeting places where boys, and probably less often girls, could talk shop to more experienced modelers and get advice, encouragement, and inspiration. The hobby shop had become commercially feasible, not only because of the vastly increased interest in the building of model aircraft but also because of the proliferation of kits for building model planes.[14]

The planes that youngsters built from these kits were themselves innovative. In design, construction materials, and even its source of power, the flying model of, say, 1935, was a significant departure from its equivalent of twenty or even ten years earlier. The most popular and best flying model of the 1910s had been the so-called A-frame pusher. Built with a hardwood frame of spruce, cedar, or bamboo, and powered by rubber-band motors, this type of model had twin fuselages which were connected in the front of the plane and which diverged toward the rear at an acute angle. At the rear of each fuselage boom was a propeller. Crossing the two fuselages was a wing and stabilizer, which made the model look like the letter "A," hence it's name. The long twin fuselages permitted more powerful rubber motors, which meant longer and higher flights. But the A-frame models resembled no real airplane. It was their performance in the air, not their realism, which made them appealing.[15]

Soon after Lindbergh's flight, the A-frame pusher became obsolete, the victim of a technological revolution no less dramatic than that which was affecting full-sized aircraft. Balsa wood, first imported from South America in the twenties, had all but supplanted the heavier and harder-to-work hardwoods for flying model construction. With the newly available material, the delicate stick and tissue-paper models still familiar today came into existence. Because of the ease with which manufacturers could cut and mill balsa, the price of model airplanes fell dramatically. Whereas earlier kits with hardwood parts seldom cost less than a few dollars, now children might purchase a model for as little as a dime. The parts were printed on thin sheets of balsa, and youngsters could easily cut them out with a knife or razor blade. They would glue the pieces together to make wings, tail sections, and fuselages, and then cover the delicate structures with doped tissue. The result was an extremely light yet strong model which could be powered by rubber motors or tiny engines running on compressed air or gasoline. As fliers the models were to their predecessors as Lindbergh's *Spirit of St. Louis* was to the Wrights' Kitty Hawk machine. They flew higher, longer, and more realistically. It took great skill to build a kit so as to get the best performance out of a model, but with the new technology even a beginner could build a plane that flew well.

But perhaps the greatest consequence of the balsa wood revolution was the impetus it gave to realism. In the pre-balsa period, if a model were realistic—that is, a scale miniature of a real plane— almost by definition it was a poor performer. Hence the popularity of the A-frame pusher. With balsa wood, however, the boy or girl who built a flying model of, say, Amelia Earhart's ocean- crossing Lockheed or of Eddie Rickenbacker's World War I Spad could now expect their miniature planes really to fly. Here the impact on experience, although subjective, was immense. As boys and girls watched the machines which they built with their own hands climb skywards, perhaps after rising off the ground on their own wheels, they could imagine themselves at the controls in a way not possible earlier. The new flying models blurred the line between model aeronautics and the real thing, especially so with superdetailed craft, like the one entered in a 1931 model contest that had working lights, a completely furnished cockpit, and auto- matic devices that dropped bombs and laid down a smoke screen in the air. For the builder and operator of such a model, the motto of the Junior Birdmen—"Today pilots of models, Tomorrow model pilots"—hardly seemed prophetic; he or she was, in a more than trivial sense, also its pilot.[16]

Although nobody denied the benefits of youth's involvement with model airplanes, by the late 1920s an increasing number of teachers and educators believed that a more systematic approach to aviation learning was needed. Lindbergh's flight had awakened them to the fact that aviation—as Stanford University aeronautics professor William F. Durand told a meeting of school superin- tendents in 1928—was one of the great "movements" of their time, one that all citizens must be prepared to participate in and direct.

The influence of progressive education reformer John Dewey was high among educators at the time, and his idea of education as a preparation for life led logically to introducing aviation into the school curriculum. A survey of almost 3,000 school systems conducted by the Guggenheim Fund for the Promotion of Aeronautics in 1928 revealed that most airminded educators were trying to "infiltrate" aviation material into existing courses rather than introduce new ones because the present school curriculum was already "overcrowded."[17]

The forms that infiltration took were many. Some junior high teachers added a ten-lesson unit on aeronautics to their general science course, leading students to examine the history and principles of aviation, to survey existing aeronautical occupations, and to speculate about the future implications of flight. Some mathematics teachers brought airline flight schedules into class and gave their students problems involving airline flight schedules that required the manipulation of speed, time and distance formulas, while English teachers incorporated the myths and legends of flight into their syllabuses or drilled students on vocabulary taken from aeronautics. Physics instructors added topics on meteorology or aerodynamics. Even airminded health and art instructors pursued the gospel through pedagogy, setting up the pilot as a goal for physical conditioning in the one instance and having their students sketch airports, airplanes, and imaginary aerial landscapes in the other. Although the breadth of these curricular changes in American education cannot easily be gauged, the teachers involved expected this infiltrating strategy to produce greater motivation in the classroom as well as to ground students in the aerial "movement." Outside of class, such teachers often became involved with aeronautically oriented extracurricular activities. The Air Cadets group that was organized in 1929 at Lafayette Junior High School in Elizabeth, New Jersey, and which provided social opportunities, model-building activities, and a general spur to boys' and girls' airmindedness typified the kind of group that was becoming part of school culture throughout the country.[18]

The ultimate airminded pedagogy would be to teach the young to fly. "Flying should be learned by every young man," argued the editor of *Western Flying*, in 1927, simply as an adjunct to living in the air age. While some educators and teachers shared the sentiment, little was done to implement it until the Second World War. Yet in the 1920s and 1930s some beginnings were made. Extracurricular flying clubs emerged at a number of colleges and universities, including Harvard, Stanford, William and Mary, and Purdue University, which had its own airport where students could take lessons at reduced rates. Purdue even had an aviatrix in residence during the 1935-36 academic year, the inspiration of its airminded president, Dr. Edward C. Elliott, who brought Amelia Earhart to the Indiana campus that year to live in one of the women's dormitories and meet informally with female students. At the high school level, at least one institution offered flight instruction, beginning apparently as early as 1925. This was Galt High School, located in the central valley of California, near the state capital and the U.S. Army's Mather Field. In the late 1920s Galt's 300 students attended classes in buildings that adjoined it's 75-acre flying field, with repair shops, hangar facilities, and three school-owned airplanes. Although Galt's program seems to have had no imitators, not a few people praised its "farsightedness" and saw the school's curriculum as truly prophetic.[19]

It was the appearance of military dictatorships and the rise of armed conflict in the 1930s that prompted many Americans to rethink the need for flight training in the schools and to reassess the overall relationship between youth and aviation. As Hitler and the Nazis rebuilt German military might, the fact that fourteen-year-olds were building real gliders and learning to fly them under the supervision of the German government led some Americans to conclude that the United States was not doing enough to prepare its own youth aeronautically. A growing number of people began to view the connection between the young and aviation through the lens of national and military necessity. Even the promotion of model airplane activities took on military coloration: the Junior Birdmen formed "flight squadrons," while the Jimmie Allen Club "cadets" took orders from their "Chief of Staff," who was Dudley Steel of Richfield Oil, alias Jimmy Allen, and the various "major generals" who were the adult sponsors of the organization. The use of military ranks and terminology familiarized youthful enthusiasts with hierarchy, discipline, and obedience in a way that could in the future make them better real cadets. This gentle militarization of the young had older roots, going back at least to the early years of the century, as in the case of the scouting movement, yet to some airminded Americans in the 1930s it seemed totally inadequate. These individuals wanted to form explicitly military organizations for the young—immediately. A bill to create aerial reserves for boys and young men was introduced into Congress, but with the isolationist sentiment of the time it had no chance of passage.[20] So various individuals and private groups set up their own quasi-military organizations, such as the Air Cadets of America, founded by the American Legion in 1933. Air Cadets, chosen from boys fifteen to twenty years of age, were to receive pre-flight or ground school instruction so that they could more readily be processed into pilots in the event of a war. Another outfit, the Falcon's Civilian Air Corps, was established at about the same time. It was intended to be "slightly military in procedure" but also, somewhat contradictorily, a "uniformed, disciplined organization." Its recruits, young men from eighteen to twenty-five, would become pilots and then be stationed around the country in eighteen-man squadrons, a kind of private air force ready for a national emergency.[21]

Although none of these schemes for enlisting youth on behalf of aerial preparedness went very far in the mid-thirties, they are an indication of the direction adults were moving in their thinking about youth's place in the air. With Germany's attack on Poland on September 1, 1939, the most strident demands for escalated air training and aeronautical education suddenly appeared quite reasonable. Concerned individuals launched a number of new programs and organizations aimed at strengthening the country's readiness to fight a war in the air. One of these was the Civilian Pilot Training Program (CPTP) set up under the auspices of the Civilian Aeronautics Administration. It established ground schools on many college and university campuses and subsidized flight instruction, for male and female students, at local airports. CPTP flight training was not expressly pre-military, yet it expanded greatly the pool of beginning pilots that would be available in a national emergency, and in fact many CPTP graduates did eventually become military aviators. Another important effort was Air Youth of America, founded in 1940 by Laurence S. and Winthrop Rockefeller out of their realization that European countries were far ahead of the United States in developing their youthful aerial reserves. Air Youth of America had offices at Rockefeller Plaza in New York, a national council of prominent educators and aviation leaders, and ample financial resources to pursue its stated goal of providing "the youth of the country with wider opportunities for recreation and self-development in aviation, and to teach a citizen's understanding of our national aviation program." The organiza-

tion quickly emerged as an important force in the lives of youngsters as well as adults. It published a monthly magazine, *Air Youth
Horizons*, and handbooks on different aspects of model building
and conducting model contests; designed and put into production a
series of model airplanes, carefully graded as to difficulty; and
offered scholarships for the young and ran symposia for their
elders, like the four-day conference on "Youth and Aviation,"
which met at the Museum of Modern Art in New York in August
1940.[22]

The conference, held against a backdrop of the Battle of Britain,
as England's beleaguered RAF valiantly staved off the superior
numbers of the German *Luftwaffe*, catalyzed new levels of commitment to aviation education. One after another, educators went
to the podium and called for more aviation subject-matter throughout the curriculum, more pre-flight aeronautics, more pilot training. Dr. Robert W. Hambrook of the U.S. Office of Education
told the high school teachers in the audience that nationwide only
12,000 students were enrolled in aeronautical vocational programs,
while a million workers were desperately needed in the various
aviation fields. That need became acute with the Japanese attack
on Pearl Harbor, a matter of national survival. Educators now
rushed to recast education to meet the needs of aerial war. No
longer was it enough for youngsters to be simply airminded; youth
now had to be "air-conditioned," in the popular phrase coined by
Assistant Secretary of Commerce for Air, Robert H. Hinckley.
"Something deeper is needed than a mere consciousness of the
airplane. There must be a universal familiarity with it, and basic
understanding of why and how it operates," Hinckley said.[23]

As members of the educational establishment turned their attention to air-conditioning the young, they jettisoned their earlier
tactic of infiltration and in many ways turned schools into vocational adjuncts of the military.[24] For the purpose of victory, anything could be justified. Inevitably this new vocational and military emphasis eroded the idealism and prophetic optimism that
once characterized the adult view of the youth-aviation connection. By turning their young charges into airminded warriors,
educators would lose forever the promise symbolized by the child
with a model plane. For educators, as for so many other Americans, the war disillusioned them with the winged gospel and
changed their emotional relationship with the airplane.

From 1942 through 1945, however, teachers embraced aviation

education with enthusiasm. They welcomed what would have been anathema in peacetime, direction and support from the federal government. Through two agencies, the Office of Education (OE) and the Civil Aeronautics Administration (CAA), teachers proceeded with their air-conditioning of American youth. The agencies oversaw the development of texts and class materials, organized in-service training for teachers, and helped professionals establish networks to plan "air-age education," now the preferred phrase, for the postwar era. One of the major government projects was the textbook project of the OE and the CAA. This proceeded under the aegis of an Aviation Education Research Group, composed of academics based at the schools of education at Columbia University and the University of Nebraska. These experts facilitated the preparation of an "Air-Age Education" series of textbooks. During 1942 and 1943 some twenty titles appeared under Macmillan's imprint and sold well. *Human Geography for the Air Age* exemplified educators' faith in the airplane as an instrument of world peace and simultaneously reflected their preparedness work during the war. It treated geography from a global perspective, telling young readers that isolation was no longer possible, and that the policy evidenced "rowboat geography rather than airplane geography." But the text also oriented young Americans to where they might soon be fighting—places like Micronesia, North Africa, or Southeast Asia. Some titles in the series, such as *Flying High*, an anthology of fictional and non-fictional writing about aviation for English classes, showed how even the humanities could be air-conditioned, while others, such as *Physical Science in the Air Age*, simply added some aeronautical topics to a fairly conventional syllabus.[25]

The most widely adopted text in the Air-Age Education series was *Science of Pre-Flight Aeronautics for High Schools*. The book covered, in considerable detail, the reasons why an airplane flew and how it was controlled in the air. By the end of 1943 this book, or one of its competitors, was being used in over half of the nation's high schools to teach the one- or two-semester-long, pre-flight aeronautics courses which had joined biology, chemistry, and physics in the American high school science curriculum. These courses, taken almost exclusively by male students, wearing uniforms in many schools, symbolized more than anything else the military thrust of aviation education in secondary teaching.[26]

In the grammar schols no such military presence existed. But during the war teachers further enriched their traditional classes with material on airplanes, airports, and pilots. Yet they sanctioned their young students' participation in the war through a model-building program. Some junior high students constructed non-flying, constant-scale models for use as aids in aircraft identification training, both by the military and by local Civilian Defense volunteers. The Navy chose the aircraft to be modeled, selecting from among American, Allied, and enemy types, and the Office of Education developed plans and instructions for the models and handled relations with the high schools and junior highs involved in the program. The models, carved of solid wood, had to meet exact specifications as to size and be finished in a standardized, flat-black color. Although the work was quite regimented and lacking in the creative challenge of other kinds of model making, children loved it. By the end of 1942, when the Navy in the interest of greater uniformity turned to molded plastic for the construction of identification models, youngsters had produced hundreds of thousands of the little wooden planes.[27]

Compared with their students, who were actively building model planes, wartime school teachers often knew much less about aviation. Many youngsters could tell at a glance the difference between a P-51, a Spitfire, and a Zero, and use aviation terminology easily; they festooned the margins of their notebooks with sketches of planes, a favorite being the P-40 fighter, with its shark-tooth nose decorations. The disparity of knowledge between young and old concerned educators, one of which complained that "you can't develop an airminded child with an earthbound teacher." One effort to solve the problem came from the federal government, which started to sponsor day-long "Operations Institutes" for schoolteachers. These were held during the war at airports, where teachers viewed airfield procedures, traffic control, and communications and airline operations. During summers, the OE and CAA also organized in-service aviation courses for the teachers, holding classes on dozens of college and university campuses throughout the country. The in-service training upgraded teachers' information about aviation and often included visits to airports or other facilities. Had resources been available, educators would have liked these courses all to be like the one held at the University of Illinois during the summer of 1944. There the participating teachers received eight hours of dual flight instruction along with their earthbound work. Most were leaving the ground for the first time and were reported to have been very enthusiastic about their experience.[28]

The feelings of teachers about aeronautics in the school curriculum, however, were varied and complex. Some were uneasy about the pre-flight aeronautics courses on the grounds of their military discipline and uniforms, yet most teachers seem to have accepted the regimentation that inevitably went along with these classes. The issue of whether aviation was an effective motivating force in the curriculum also divided pedagogues. Some attributed to aviation education virtual miracles, like the case where a "very poor student" with an I.Q. of 90 and "no interest in anything" became, thanks to airplanes, a purposeful and exemplary student and eventually an Army Air Cadet. No doubt such stories exaggerated matters, for patriotism as well as the lure of military service and adventure also operated in wartime high schools. Some teachers' comments make it clear that an air-conditioned curriculum was no panacea for student indifference. Just by putting some material on aeronautics into a history course, reported a teacher from experience, one did not cure boredom. Although students were fascinated with present-day aviation, they had little interest in the Wright brothers or even in Lindbergh. Those names resonated with past miracles for the older generation, but to youngsters they could be Roman emperors, for all some knew about the past. Students' preoccupation with the present went so far that some laughed at the illustrations of airplanes in their textbooks, just because the machines were a year or two out of date.[29]

Whatever reservations they held about recent airminded curricular reforms, by 1944 and 1945, as the war ground on toward a conclusion and victory began to seem certain, educators gave increasing thought to the future, to what was now being universally called "air age education." Part of the impulse here was professional. The war had greatly boosted high school attendance levels, particularly among boys, and strengthened science and technical education. Teachers acquired a new sense of importance which they did not wish to relinquish. By promoting air-age education they in effect sought to preserve and enhance this rising professional status. Their embrace of it also reflected the aviation consciousness the war had given all Americans. Like so many others, for example, teachers assumed that the return of peacetime routines and prosperity would usher in an age of family airplanes. Schools, they felt, should be ready for this new air age. To some educators this meant pre-flight instruction and even pilot training. But at least, according to one expert, a high school curriculum worthy of the air age should prepare young men and women to be good citizens, to be able to decide issues such as the size of aerial police forces or the location of school landing fields.[30]

Far more important than local issues, however, were the international ones. "Waging peace" on a global scale might be far more difficult than waging war, according to a 1944 report by that title, produced by a committee of the influential American Association of School Administrators. "Somehow," the report advised school people, "boys and girls, pilots, mechanics and factory workers—all persons—need to develop a vivid and thorough understanding of the principles of the Air Age and the importance of wings to mankind." The report noted that postwar Americans would live in a world "shrunken" by aircraft, a world in which no individual on the planet lived more than fifty hours by air from anyone else. Under the conditions generated by modern aviation, continued the authors, "the yellow, red, black, brown and white people of the earth" now lived together, "in the great common ocean of the air."[31] Given the awesome destructive powers of modern weaponry, and given mounting talk of World War III, they had *better* live peacefully, educators believed. It was truly "one world," to use the phrase popularized by Wendell Willkie in a book he wrote with that title. In 1943 the onetime Republican Presidential candidate had flown around the world as a special envoy of President Roosevelt. Willkie's flight was one more demonstration of the necessity of developing "global minds" for living in the new "global world." With the dropping of an atomic bomb on Hiroshima in August 1945 this necessity grew instantly larger—and with it the challenges of air-age education. Educators knew they were engaged, as one of them put it, in a "race between education and catastrophe," but with customary optimism and faith in the gospel they moved confidently into the postwar era.[32]

In some respects air-age education in the latter half of the 1940s differed little from what went on during the war. Teachers continued to attend institutes, conferences, workshops, and symposia devoted to air-age education. Indeed, the federal government's sponsorship of these activities increased in the latter half of the decade, reflecting the growing power of the teachers' lobby in Washington and the intense airmindedness that suffused the country immediately following the war. Pedagogues also continued to write articles about air-age education, publishing more during the three years from 1944 through 1947 than they had during any three-year period before or since. Special numbers of professional journals devoted to the subject also appeared in the immediate postwar period.[33] And in the classroom, teachers continued to infuse aeronautics into their courses, adding some new wrinkles, such as air-age home economics, with units on the interior decorating of airplanes and airline meal preparation, a course introduced in Los Angeles. One innovation, much discussed but tried it seems only briefly, was "flight experience." The concept called for students to be taken up in small planes for a kind of aerial laboratory session. They did not receive pilot training but rather observed the pilot operate the plane, studied the effects of wind on its performance, and noted the geographical features of their community from above.[34]

What really distinguished postwar air-age education from earlier efforts was its global emphasis. In the heady years of establishing the United Nations and relishing the return of peace, the internationalist climate nurtured some dramatic, although short-lived, curriculum innovations. One was the use of "Air Globes." These were entirely white and showed no continents, no nations, and no oceans, rivers, or any other physical or political features of the planet. Only cities were indicated on the globe, by black dots. The globes symbolized in tangible form the new world which Americans believed the airplane was about to create, a world of peace where national boundaries and topographical features were no longer pertinent. Another novelty of the period was the "general language" course. The need for language instruction in American schools had been driven home by the war and took on added importance for preserving peace in the atomic age. Yet students in general language courses bypassed the multifold and frustrating complexities of a foreign language and instead sampled perhaps half a dozen tongues, smorgasbord style. They learned to say "hello" to many of their new neighbors in the world, but in effect they were also learning, however inadvertently, to be the ugly Americans of the 1950s and 1960s, smugly confident in the phrases of marketplace and restaurant but wholly unable to speak enough of a language to find out what foreigners really thought or felt.[35]

Another innovation in aviation education in the later 1940s was the entry into the field of a number of airlines, including American, Transworld, and Pan American. TWA and American each set up separate educational departments, staffed by professional educators. TWA hired Dr. John H. Furbay, a Yale graduate and former college president, to be the first head of its Air World Education Program, while American placed Dr. Nickolaus Engelhardt, Jr., a graduate of Columbia University Teachers' College, at the head of its non-profit affiliate, Air-Age Education Research, Inc. Started in 1945, Air-Age Education Research was the biggest and most active of the airline ventures into education. Engelhardt's organization developed a wide variety of innovative teaching aids, most of which were distributed to schools free of charge. These included wall charts, maps and pictures, film strips, movies, reading matter, and the popular "Air Globe."[36] In 1946 the American Airlines affiliate made a dramatic gesture toward global thinking when it sponsored in New York City the first World Congress on Air Age Education. For eight days, some 350 delegates from 22 countries, all of whom had traveled on American's budget to New York, talked about curricular reforms required by the air age and listened to speeches affirming the airplane's role in world peace.[37]

The airlines did not, of course, embrace the winged gospel with total altruism. They saw, as a Pan American executive candidly explained, a "vast travel market" in the eleven million American administrators, teachers, professors, and students who it was thought would be traveling widely by air in the coming future.[38] And as the publisher of *Time* put it, the war had ushered in the "American Century," which meant markets on a global scale, ones that American airlines wanted for their own. Air-age education corporate style aimed at developing this market, both by getting potential customers to think of a particular carrier for their foreign travel and, even more importantly, by convincing the American public of the merits of the airlines' political vision of how postwar international aviation should be organized and conducted.

In the service of these goals, as well as more idealistic ones, Pan American and American Airlines both published weekly school newspapers, *Classroom Clipper* and *Air-Age Education News* respectively. Neither airline directly advertised itself in the papers, although the message came through indirectly in photographs, which always depicted the company's own aircraft. Readers would see American Airlines DC-3s flying over Egyptian pyramids or

Pan American Stratocruisers landing on tropical atolls in the South Seas. Much less elliptical was the publications' prosyletizing on behalf of free enterprise in the air and an "open skies" policy, that is, free air access for the planes of all nations to all parts of the globe. This policy, promoted by both the Roosevelt and Truman administrations, opposed the creation of any government air transport monopoly that might enjoy privileged landing rights in a country. Because such practices would threaten the potential markets of U.S. flag carriers, the airlines strenuously fought them and let pass no opportunity to inculcate teachers and students in the wisdom of their position. The Pan American and American magazines told readers that United States firms were efficient because they engaged in free and open competition, while foreign flag airlines gave poor service because they were state monopolies. To balance their shriller political sermons, the *News* and *Clipper* also preached the gospel of one-world through flight in articles such as "An Air View of Brazil Today," or "Your Neighbors, India and Pakistan."[39]

The vision of global neighborliness animated many educators after the war, including Engelhardt of American Airlines. They developed noble plans for waging peace. "Let our children travel around the earth," Engelhardt urged, "experiencing the physical unity of the air world." Another educator suggested a "post graduate year of world understanding" or a year spent in "world wide explorations by air" in which every youth would have "an opportunity to meet with youths from other regions of the world." To carry the young on these odysseys, Chancellor Ben Cherrington of the University of Denver called for fleets of "educational airplanes."[40]

International youth exchanges did develop after the war, although nothing on the scale envisioned by Cherrington, Engelhardt, and other airminded educators. Even with the tremendous cheapening of air travel in the jet era of the 1960s and 1970s, the economics of aviation never permitted anything approaching the universal flying they projected. In any event, no amount of air travel could alone have produced the result they hoped for: perpetual peace. By placing their faith in "fleets of eudcational airplanes," educators continued to invest the flying machine with messianic promise. Instead of seeing the airplane as a transportation tool, they saw an instrument of world peace, a substitute for politics—in short, a messiah. Like other Americans who emerged from the war with grand dreams for the wondrous air age, the educator's version of the winged gospel would also be disappointed. Their euphoric hopes of 1944, 1945, and 1946, as with the vision of personal family planes, turned to frustrations and then collapsed altogether. There was simply no way that their idealistic faith in the power of winged youth could have survived the events of the late 1940s. The 1947 Soviet blockade of Berlin, the 1948 India-Pakistan war, the 1949 Communist takeover of China and the Soviet Union's detonation of an atomic weapon, and the outbreak of war in Korea in 1950—these and many lesser international alarms jolted them, along with Americans generally, out of any illusion that the air age would be one of peace and harmony.

In the cold-war climate of 1950, as strategic bombers droned overhead on permanent aerial alert, nuclear weapons at the ready, air-age education seemed frivolous, quaint, or even dangerous. Although a global approach to geography survived, along with bits and pieces of aeronautics in the physics and general science curricula, the type of thinking symbolized by the "air globe" was obsolete. Teachers now used maps, usually delineated graphically into areas of freedom and communism. Many other of the more visionary and exciting vestiges of the air-age education movement— aviation English, air art, and flight experience—followed the air globes into obscurity. Other features of the air-age education movement also faded in the late 1940s. In-service training courses for teachers fell off by the end of the decade to a trickle. The whole subject of air age education no longer interested educators as it had just a few years earlier. In the three years after 1947 they published half as many articles on the subject as they had during the three years from 1944 to 1947; in the three years after 1950, they wrote a third fewer still.[41] In 1947 Dr. Nickolaus Engelhardt, director of American Airlines' Air-Age Education Research, Inc., resigned to take up a career more appropriate for the times, the planning and designing of suburban schools. The next year American Airlines closed its non-profit affiliate and stopped publication of its classroom newspaper. Pan American continued publishing its *Clipper*, but by the early 1950s it had lost much of its idealistic content and had become essentially a travel primer for teachers.[42]

Many youngsters, of course, still found aviation fascinating, and some of their elders encouraged them in their interest. Yet the magic and sense of promise linking airplanes and the young had largely faded. In 1950, when adults looked at a boy with a model airplane—the girl model makers had also faded away—they no longer thought automatically of a better tomorrow. All they saw was a kid with a toy.

VII

Epilogue

Between 1910 and 1950 two generations of Americans kept faith with the winged gospel, raising aviation to the status of a technological religion. They worshiped the airplane as a mechanical god and expected it to usher in a dazzling future, a virtual millennium.

In the dawning air age, prophets predicted, society would transcend the problems and inequities which for centuries had plagued it. The airplane would at once banish the struggles and conflicts stemming from industrial capitalism, put an end to urban congestion, and even eliminate the inequalities between men and women and different races. The world would become more beautiful, too, once the heavens became a common thoroughfare, and architects, designers, and planners took inspiration from the new aerial vantage point to produce works of aesthetic superiority. According to some prophets, airplane flight would even alter human nature, eventually producing a new breed of human being, far superior to earth-bound types. The rapid development of aeronautics gave support to these convictions and made it seem that the airplane was indeed producing social and moral benefits beyond calculation.

In one respect the creed of the winged gospel simply restated, in twentieth-century terms, the idea of progress. Since the eighteenth century Americans had believed that, were reason consistently applied to the direction of human affairs, a steady and inexorable advance in the levels of culture, justice, prosperity, and happiness would be the inevitable result. This concept of progress, beholden to intellectual currents generated by the Enlightenment, took a new direction in the nineteenth century as Americans experienced the coming of industrialization. Noting the dramatic improvements wrought in manufacturing, transportation, and agriculture, it was hard not to conclude that mechanical innovation, not simply rationalism, was the primary catalyst of social and moral improvement. Machines produced not only other machines, it seemed, but also progress itself. More than that, nineteenth-century commentators also viewed machines as moving society toward the millennium. Technology and the Saviour, they thought, both were working toward the same purpose. This perspective reflected the pervasive Protestantism of nineteenth-century American culture and suffused the winged gospel in the twentieth century.

The winged gospel, however, was always more than simply a belief in the airplane as the source of progress. Aviation was a religion. Like traditional faiths, its belief system gave meaning to existence and provided a grand design for future life. This faith not only could give aviators courage but they also could motivate airminded men and women to great efforts on behalf of the cause. The evangelical, crusading quality to the selling of flight in the United States owed much to the gospel perspective on the airplane. Indeed, aviation was a kind of crusade for believers. They did whatever they could to foster the public's conversion to the cause: they promoted flying as a means of travel and personal transportation; as a business and professional tool; as a military weapon; as catalyst to municipal growth; and even as a source of inspiration for artists, writers, and students. In gas stations and department stores, in museums and schools, in the media and in the air—everywhere and anywhere, airminded individuals carried the gospel out into society.

This prosyletizing thrust of the winged gospel also recalls secular reform movements in American history. Aviation may, in fact, be understood as a kind of technological reform movement. No less than nineteenth-century advocates of temperance, woman's suffrage, or universal schooling, supporters of the gospel worked to foster beneficial social change. They prescribed the adoption of a new technology rather than a new law, a constitutional amendment, or an institutional change, but their animating impulse, to reform society, was similar. And like many historical reform movements, partisans of the winged gospel also aggrandized the potential of their cause, promising total, extravagent, often utopian results if others became airminded and embraced the airplane with sufficient fervor. The easy assimilation of the airplane to traditional metaphors and symbols regarding heaven and spiritual life aided in recruiting new converts to the gospel, particularly among individuals who otherwise might not have been so euphoric about flying machines. It also, of course, explains the extravagant and utopian expectations which enthusiasts had for the airplane's social and moral impact. The effects of this are hard to judge. Today, we are skeptical of the technological fix and feel too sophisticated to embrace anything like technological messianism. Our awareness of the dire consequences of certain technologies has made us cautious of grand claims for any. Yet if aviation supporters had held more cautious, one might say "realistic," expectations for an aerial future, had they been practitioners of the techniques now popular under the rubric of "technology assessment," it is possible that promotion of aeronautics might have been less fervent. It is certain, however, that without the winged gospel the history of that promotion would be different.

Believing what they did, even though unrealistic or utopian, air-minded men and women left a distinctive mark on American culture. To be sure, many of their hopes—of putting landing facilities atop skyscrapers, incorporating flying into high-school curricula, or aviation into art and literature—did not go far. Yet their embrace of the winged gospel made education, entertainment, family life, and various institutions different from what they would have been without the gospel. The airplane itself did not cause these developments; indeed, to speak of a technology's "impact" on culture and society here is misleading. What happened was that Americans took a tradition of technological messianism, combined it with long-standing symbolic associations of flight with the divine, and blended firmly held values such as individualism, democracy, and privacy into an intellectual and emotional response to the airplane. This response, the winged gospel, "caused" the peculiar historical relationships with the airplane and aviation which we have described in this book. The airplane's impact on American culture, then, is only one side of the story; the other side is the way the culture influenced the technology and its adoption. We see culture shaping technology most clearly in the case of the various aircraft built to implement the dream of an airplane in every garage, but in many other ways the cultural aspirations and values represented by the winged gospel also influenced aeronautical activity.

By about 1950, however, the winged gospel no longer was a significant force in American culture. It had lasted only about

forty years, from 1910 to about 1950, a creature of aviation's beginnings and adolescence. Those were the decades when utopian
optimism regarding the prospects of flying was not only helpful
to the promotion of flight but also the most credible. In the earlier
years, the mere fact of flight supported heady and buoyant expectations. Awed by the miracle of a heavier-than-air-machine leaving
the ground, ignorant of what kept it in the air, and accustomed to
associating flight with the divine, Americans found it easy to imagine the new invention's having some sort of heavenly mission on
earth. In fact the airplane's lack of usefulness in those years paradoxically corroborated this faith, for a machine so miraculous, it
seemed, just had to portend great things in the future. As the
years passed, each dramatic long-distance flight or new flying record fanned the fires of faith in the airplane's limitless promise. Enthusiasts measured aerial progress with mathematical precision,
noting every foot gained in altitude or distance and every mile
per hour added to the airplane's speed. The very rapidity with
which these numbers grew, and their indisputable witness to *material* progress, helped sustain people's faith that social and moral
benefits would eventually follow. When things did not happen as
aviation prophets predicted, however—when even better airplanes
did not end war or find their way into every garage—for a while
believers simply rescheduled their expectations. "Tomorrow," they
would say, the *true* promise of flight would be realized, and then
the *real* air age would finally dawn. Until the Second World War
this looking forward worked and kept alive people's faith in the
gospel's promise.

Dreams deferred too often eventually lose their lustre or are
seen for what they are, dreams with little hope of fulfillment. This
happened to aviation by mid-century. By 1950 few believed any
longer that the airplane pointed to anything like a reordering of
human society. The airplane had ceased to symbolize a future of
unlimited individual mobility, of world peace, of enlightenment
and culture, or of greater democracy and equality. It was simply
a weapon or a vehicle, and as this realization sunk in the winged
gospel faded out. Americans had not lost faith in technical progress, far from it. Indeed, at mid-century one could look backwards
just a few years and see incredible aeronautical developments. And
one could look forward with anticipation to others, such as the
jet revolution in commercial aviation. But the faith in the airplane
as a messiah was definitely moribund as a cultural artifact.

Paradoxically, the airplane's very success helped precipitate this decline in faith. By mid-century the air age had indisputably arrived. One could no longer claim it lay just around the corner. In the United States of 1950, aircraft were already a key component of transportation and the lifeline of a global defense establishment. Executives were already using them for business travel, flying to see far-flung plants and controlling decentralized corporations in ways inconceivable before the air age; professionals of different kinds were attending distant conferences and conventions and finding that the airplane facilitated a new sense of association, not only nationally but also internationally; even ordinary citizens found their lives changed in the air age, as they visited out-of-town relatives or took the kind of foreign vacations which, before the postwar boom in trans-Atlantic air travel, had been a prerogative only of those with the time and money to cross by ocean liner. In short, by 1950 flying already had prompted dramatic alterations in the way many Americans led their lives and how they thought. Observers at the time acknowledged this fact and often singled out the airplane as the most significant mechanical innovation of the century or even of all time, itself a kind of lingering statement of the gospel.[1]

Yet no matter how significant a social force the airplane appeared at mid-century, nobody could deny that it had failed to usher in the millennium or produce anything resembling utopia. The air age obviously had not brought an end to war. Nor had the airplane lessened urban congestion, beautified gritty industrial cities, or relocated the average family in Jeffersonian harmony with nature, just a brief hop in the family plane from city job and marketplace. The collapse of this last tenet of the gospel, once central to popular enthusiasm for flying, contributed greatly to the public's ebbing attachment to aviation. Given the values of most Americans, they simply could never respond to the mid-century airliner reality the way they had to the earlier air-car dream. The giant Douglas, Boeing, and Lockheed transports, no matter how marvelous technically, left little room for the winged gospel. For one thing, whereas anyone could share the dream, only those who could pay the fare rode in the sleek new transports, and at the time only a small minority of the American public could afford to fly. Furthermore, those who could fly obviously did not hop off conveniently from their backyard or community airpark. Instead they struggled by car or bus to reach the airport, now lo-

cated even farther from the centers of population than at the
height of the gospel. Once at the airport, they negotiated the
crowds, hiked to their departure gates, and then squeezed into a
plane with fifty or more strangers. The trip itself resembled nothing so much as riding on a bus or train, notwithstanding the efforts
of advertisers to embroider it with images of luxury. In short, the
mass-transit reality of air travel in the mature air age was undeniable. Those who flew faced the same kind of crowds, endured the
same bureaucratic hassles, and suffered the same personal incon-
veniences common to those old-fashioned and often detested modes
of earthly travel. Even the sensory joys of flying were disappear-
ing by 1950, as aircraft were increasingly pressurized to fly above
the weather, which meant they also flew above the scenery, often
above the clouds, destroying the uniqueness once heralded as a
feature of travel through the heavens.

Although the romance of aviation had ebbed by mid-century
and the promise of wings no longer gripped the popular imagination, a few individuals still retained their faith. In fact, some continue to believe in portions of the gospel long after aviation has
ceased to be a popular religion. In 1978, for instance, Moulton B.
Taylor of Longview, Washington, told an interviewer that his
"flying auto is way ahead of its time," a reference to his "Aerocar," a hybrid airplane-automobile that on the ground pulls its
folded wings and tail section behind it as a trailer. Taylor is not a
recent convert to the gospel, for he built and flew the prototype
for his Aerocar in the late 1940s, as a young veteran driven by the
last great popular enthusiasm for the vision of wings for the
masses. Thirty years later, undaunted by his failure to get his machine into production, Taylor continues to believe in his vision.
He is joined by some latter-day converts to the concept of mass
personal flying, persons not yet born when he first embraced the
vision. Some of these are involved with what are called "ultralights," aircraft resembling a hang-glider crossed with a go-cart.
These machines have frames of aluminum tubing covered with ny-
lon flight surfaces and are powered by engines similar to those in
chain saws or snowmobiles. Ultralights can be lifted by one or two
people and easily disassembled for carrying atop a car or storing in
a garage. Costing only a half or a third the price of a car, they are
relatively affordable and have prompted anew prophecies of widespread aerial commuting and recreational flying. There is no evidence that the general public finds such predictions anything more

than amusing, yet the ardor of the enthusiasts is contagious. Not a few are touting ultralights, along with more sophisticated light planes which fly over 100 miles for every gallon of fuel, as a "solution" to present energy shortages.[2]

One can pick up echoes of the aviation gospel in numerous other quarters, such as the pulpit of the electronic church of evangelist Jimmy "Brother" Swaggert of Baton Rouge, Louisiana. "Will your landing lights be on when you touch down in heaven?" Swaggert asked his national television congregation one Sunday morning in March 1979. He was not preaching about airplanes, of course, but delivering a sermon about preparation for life in the hereafter. The way to get to heaven, Swaggert implied, was by Christian living informed by old-fashioned morality, not through aeronautics or astronautics. Yet his choice of metaphor showed that, at least symbolically, the airplane still could serve the cause of faith.[3]

Moving to the secular realm, to an institution founded as a testament to manned flight, one can pick up much stronger echoes of the gospel. At the Smithsonian Institution's National Air and Space Museum in Washington, D.C., many of the exhibits are in effect hymns to aerial—and astronautical—progress. Here anniversaries such as Kitty Hawk, the Apollo 11 moon landing, and other important firsts are still observed, and the rhetoric still breathes with the older gospel force. Opening a symposium on the seventy-fifth anniversary of the Wright brothers' first flight, for example, the then director admitted in thinking about that flight to seeking "some outstanding revelation that will bring the public to its feet." He could not find words equal to his feelings, however, and so simply told the Kitty Hawk story "that we know so well." On the seventy-seventh anniversary in 1980, a new museum director paid his homage to Kitty Hawk in a ceremony to acknowledge the gift of a relic associated with that miracle, "one of the last remaining pieces of fabric that was on the plane that momentous day."[4]

Beyond celebrations and rhetoric, the very existence of the National Air and Space Museum in a way confirms the survival of the gospel. The Museum, opened in a large and distinctive new building in 1976, is a monumental testament to the belief that the history of flying machines—aircraft and spacecraft—is unique and separate from the history of more earthly technology. For it is only the hardware of aerospace conquest that the Smithsonian has

segregated into a separate museum. One could imagine separate
museums for, say, the technology of communications, railroading,
or agriculture. The artifacts connected with those activities, after
all, were hardly of trifling historical significance. But all the collections dealing with these three areas of endeavor are in a single
Smithsonian museum, the National Museum of American History,
where they compete for gallery space with materials pertaining to
the history of costume, automobiles, maritime commerce, musical
instruments, decorative arts, machine tools, atom smashers, and
much, much more. With this eclectic mélange, however well displayed and interpreted, the National Museum of American History most aptly fits the characterization of the Smithsonian as the
"nation's attic." With its plows and rocking chairs, lathes and
harps, buttons and dresses, the place is as diverse and messy as an
old family attic, as life itself.

Across the Washington Mall in the Air and Space Museum,
however, one finds a collection as conceptually pure and ordered
as American History's is earthy and diffuse. Here one sees only
objects that have been passed through the transforming pale of
flight, things that either have themselves been in the heavens or
which have, like Mrs. Tusch's relics (many of which are in the
Museum), been made sacred so to speak through association with
flying. What is largely missing from the exhibition is a sense of
how aviation and space flight are also ground-based activities. The
building of planes, their use in business, airplane crashes, or airport
design and construction—such earthly subjects are eschewed in fa-
vor of a more airminded treatment that emphasizes flight. What
one finds is a three-dimensional celebration of the uniqueness of
flying and to the airplane's supposedly special role in human affairs, and in that an implicit bow to the winged gospel.

The extent to which visitors to the Air and Space Museum
share this same faith is hard to know. The Museum's record-
breaking attendance reflects many things, including the fact that
it is the Smithsonian's newest museum and the fact that it is on
one of the nation's primary tourist routes. Surely many visitors
come because the Museum has earned a reputation for dramatic,
lively, and entertaining exhibits. For not a few visitors, however,
the Museum still functions as a shrine to flight, a place to pay
homage to the machines that have miraculously broken free of
earth's bondage and entered the heavens. They can see the Kitty
Hawk plane, displayed in the exact center of the Museum, as well

as Amelia Earhart's Lockheed and the one flown by Anne and Charles Lindbergh to China. But today it is not so much the aircraft as the spacecraft which provide the focus of enthusiasm. In the half of the Museum devoted to space flight, where objects such as an original Skylab, satellite models, and various space capsules are exhibited, are the materials beloved of another kind of flight worship.

If there is a latter-day religion of flight, it is to be found in the response of partisans of space flight. Many of their expectations for the space future recall the aviation gospel of the first half of this century. Although the first space flights grew out of the armed competition between cold war superpowers, enthusiasts do not doubt that rocket ships would allow humanity to transcend such petty beginnings. One of the most ardent and respected prophets of the space gospel is Gerard K. O'Neill, a Princeton professor of physics who is the president of the Institute for Space Studies and a leading student of problems connected with space settlement and industrialization. In his most recent book, *2081, A Hopeful View of the Human Future*, O'Neill provides a comprehensive and yet typical statement of beliefs regarding our future in space. He grounds his hopeful view of the future on technologies other than space ships, like the computer, yet it is to the heavens and flying machines that O'Neill ultimately looks for the salvation of the human race. The global population crisis, for example, will be solved by the year 2081, he predicts, thanks to space flight. Within the next century the annual "out-migration" from earth will exceed the yearly increase in population. Space flight will also usher in a period of perpetual plenty, thereby ending earthly shortages of energy and resources as well as most of the social conflict spawned by such conditions. In 2081, aided by robots, human beings will be mining the mineral-rich asteroids and other nearby heavenly bodies and processing the ores into needed products, while space power stations will beam to earth the virtually inexaustible energies of the sun. Space flight will even have triggered an artistic revolution, O'Neill believes. Artists resident in distant space colonies, the locus of most of the human population late in the twenty-first century, will often travel to earth, where they find a ready market for their work. Furthermore, inhabitants of these colonies would finally have found that elusive human goal: perpetual peace. The colonies would be too distant from one another to make war profitable, O'Neill asserts, and in any case the inexhaustible material abundance of the space age will have largely undermined people's greed and their incentive for criminal activity. If one is beginning to feel this is all a little familiar, consider just one more dimension of O'Neill's space age: his predictions regarding personal mobility. In looking at his vision, it is helpful to know that Professor O'Neill for years has been a pilot, flying small planes and gliders.

Because of the benefits from space conquest, O'Neill posits a "social revolution comparable to the revolution in automobile travel brought about by Ford and his Model T" occurring on earth. This revolution would at last put an airplane in every garage, and family planes will become "as common then as is the family car of today." Automatic computer control will have eliminated the dangers associated with pilot error, O'Neill argues, and the fact that "the average family in 2081 will be about twelve times as wealthy, in real, non-inflated currency, as a similar family today" will have eliminated the cost hurdle for personal aircraft. As for families living in the space colonies, most of them would own a "private space yacht," which they would use for astral vacations and travel around the solar system and galaxy.[5]

O'Neill has clearly been inspired not only by his personal flying but also by the space explorations of the 1960s and 1970s. Yet his response, an exuberant replay of the winged gospel, is markedly different from the way so many Americans have reacted to space flight. The first Apollo moon landing can serve as an example. Many writers celebrated the achievement, though not by prophesying. Rather, they hailed the dedication, ingenuity, and prowess represented by the flight. But a significant minority of commentators viewed the space program as a "moon-doggle," as a sign of social callousness rather than a cure for social ills. The giant Saturn boosters pointed for them not toward possible solutions to earthly problems but rather at an irresponsible evasion of those issues. Indeed, the billions spent on the space program meant less funding for social problems here on earth, and not a few Americans therefore watched the Apollo mission and saw only white astronauts nibbling on thousand dollar tubes of exotic snacks in space while black Biafrans starved in Africa. They bemoaned with the editor of *Newsweek* the glaring disparity between American successes in space and failures in "Viet Nam, in the Cities, in the Ghettoes, in the quality of the natural environment, on the campuses, and in the ticky-tacky suburbs." Having experienced the tumult and domestic strife

of the 1960s while pursuing civil rights, social justice, urban better-
ment, and other reforms, many people found it hard to see moon
rockets as socially uplifting phenomena.[6]

Obviously, the social climate in which the space flights occurred
was very different from that which existed in the first half of the
century. During the years when the airplane was adopted, the prevailing popular attitude toward technology generally was extremely positive. If a few intellectuals raised questions regarding its
impact, the vast majority accepted the products of science and
technology uncritically. By the time American astronauts landed
on the moon in 1969, however, things had changed. A gnawing
uneasiness regarding the effects of technology had begun to creep
into American life. Some people were voicing profound opposition
to the directions of contemporary technological developments: the
proliferation of nuclear weapons, the despoiling of the environment, the carnage on the highways, the computer-wrought up-
heaval in the workplace, and the impact on youngsters of growing
up with television. Starting in the sixties these areas of concern
often divided rich and poor, black and white, young and old, lib-
eral and conservative. In a society that had lost whatever earlier
social consensus it had, technology seemed anything but totally
beneficial or even just neutral, and that perspective colored the
popular response to the moon mission.

Beyond the fact that space flight occurred in a very changed
world, two other factors contributed to the more ambivalent response to the Apollo landings and help explain why a gospel of
space has not to date rivaled the earlier winged gospel. One reason
is that we must experience space flight on television. Our feelings
and attitudes toward space flight cannot be wholly disentangled
from the experience with the transmitting medium. Through television we can observe space flight (or portions thereof), but we
get none of the direct sensory experience that watching an airplane,
not to mention going up in one, provided. We must watch the moon
flight on the same little screen that brings us advertisements for
detergents and hemorrhoid preparations or sit-coms and ballgames,
and so this virtually eliminates the possibility of an imaginative and
euphoric response. Finally, what we actually see on the tube seldom gives us any visual sense of flying. Instead of seeing movement, what we see is static, or it is motion in a very prosaic, earthbound sense. We see television commentators, simulation films, or
shots of "mission control," that windowless hall where unidentified

technicians monitor computer terminals and video screens while in effect piloting the space ship.

The image of "mission control" on television points to a second reason why space flight has not generated the same exuberance and expectancy as airplane flight. It is a collective venture, not an individual one. A giant Saturn booster suggests none of the personal promise that an observer of an airplane, whether in 1910 or 1940, could see in the machine overhead. The early airplane was almost graspable, at least in a psychological sense, and one could easily imagine himself at the controls and rising gently from the earth to soar over housetop and countryside. Space flight, by comparison, is a team effort. To put Neil Armstrong and Buzz Aldrin on the moon—even to get them off the ground—required the commitment of thousands of people and a vast panoply of equipment, a kind of social and technical "Megamachine," as a recent scholar has characterized it.[7] The Apollo flight was the culmination of a colossal national effort, measured both in man-years of labor and in treasure expended, and was at essence an organizational and managerial triumph. For the foreseeable future, it appears as if space flight will remain, if not a state monopoly, then clearly a corporate and collective endeavor. Under such conditions, if a prophecy may be suggested, spacecraft will never nurture the kind of individual and personal dreams that airplanes did during the heyday of the winged gospel.

Yet who does not desire to fly, at least in the metaphoric sense of attaining freedom and finding release? That the wish for the wings of a dove, as the Psalmist wrote, was widespread even at the time of the Apollo moon landing can be deduced from a publishing event that followed the year after the landing. The responsive chord which the moon rocket could never strike was struck for many Americans by a sentimental story about a bird, by Richard Bach. The hero of the little work, *Jonathan Livingston Seagull*, and the object of its title, celebrates flying as ecstasy and perfection and as a means to the kind of transcendence once promised by the aviation gospel. Indeed, Jonathan was a most uncommon seagull. He believed his wings were for more than mere transportation. There just had to be more to seagull life, he felt, than simply flying in the pursuit of food. So he rejected the dreary round of the other gulls, whose days passed in cycles of hunting food, eating their fill, and sleeping off satiety on a piling before hunger prompted a repetition. Jonathan had a higher, more noble vision. He engaged in long and systematic practice whereby he taught himself to perform marvelous aerial acrobatics and to fly at unprecedented speeds. Flying soon became his sole reason for living, and in the air he found what had been denied him on the ground: joy, confidence, and peace. Now that he was a real flier, Jonathan no longer required food or sleep. He lived permanently in the air like the Alti-man of Alfred Lawson's early aeronautical vision. In fact, Jonathan came to feel so ethereal and euphoric that he thought he must have died and was living in heaven.[8]

Jonathan Livingston Seagull became a runaway best seller in the early 1970s. It did so in the aftermath of the most publicized and dramatic flight in history, the flight to the moon. Perhaps there was no causal connection between that flight and the popular little seagull story, yet for many readers the book magically evoked the freedom, power, and mastery symbolized by flight in a way that the actual Apollo flight never could. By dedicating the book to "the real Jonathan Seagull, who lives within us all," Bach seemed to acknowledge that no mere machine that flies could satisfy what at root is an existential longing—certainly no machine as cumbersome and complex as the space rocket. Yet as an ardent pilot, a professional writer on aviation topics, and a former editor of *Flying* magazine, Richard Bach may have meant the opposite.[9] Either way his book testifies to the persistence of our habit of linking flight with transcendent hope.

Notes

Chapter I

1. Maximilian Foster, "The Highway of the Air," *Everybody's Magazine*, XX (Jan. 1909), 110; Washington *Post*, Sept. 2-18, 1908.
2. Fred C. Kelly, "They Wouldn't Believe the Wrights Had Flown," *Harper's*, LXXXI (Aug. 1940), 300. On the Wright brothers and their work, see Tom Day Crouch, *A Dream of Wings, Americans and the Airplane, 1875-1905* (New York, 1981), chs. 1, 11-13; Fred C. Kelly, *The Wright Brothers* (New York, 1943).
3. Foster, "Highway of the Air," 105.
4. Charles K. Field, "On the Wings of Today," *Sunset*, XXIV (March 1910), 249. See also Marco R. Newmark, "The Aviation Meet of 1910," in Historical Society of Southern California *Quarterly*, XXVIII (Sept. 1946), 103-8.
5. "Grapho"[J. A. Adams], "The Man Higher Up," *Advance*, LX (Oct. 6, 1910), 12. For popular response to early aviation, see Courtney Gould Brooks, "American Aeronautics as Spectacle and Sport" (Ph.D. diss., Tulane University, 1969); and Roger Bilstein, "The Airplane, the Wrights, and the American Public: Popular Attitudes Toward Aviation, 1900-1925," in Richard P. Hallion (ed.), *The Wright Brothers, Heirs of Prometheus* (Washington, D.C., 1978), 39-51.
6. The witness was John T. Daniels, whose reminiscences are recorded in William O. Saunders, "Then We Quit Laughing," *Collier's*, LXXX (Sept. 17, 1927), 56.
7. Quoted in Fred C. Kelly, "Interview with Orville Wright," St. Louis *Post-Dispatch*, Nov. 7, 1943, reprinted in U.S. Cong., *Congressional Record*, Pt. 12, Appendix A4774-75.
8. Norfolk *Virginian-Pilot*, Dec. 18, 1903, quoted in Mark Sullivan, *Our Times* (5 vols; New York, 1927), V, 593.
9. Kelly, *The Wright Brothers*, 124-26, 134-35, 140-42.
10. Boston *Globe*, June 7, 1908; Monticello (New Jersey) *Republican Watchman*, June 5, 1908. See also memoir by C. Fayette Taylor, who

recalled showing his father an illustrated article about the Wrights
flights in 1908 only to have him reject the possibility out of hand (*Growing Up With the Twentieth Century* (Boston, 1974), 75.

11. *Scientific American*, CV (Oct. 28, 1911), 382. See also George Ethelbert
Walsh, "The Cost of Flying," *Independent*, LXX (May 25, 1911), 1110-
12; "The Man in the Air," *World's Work*, XXI (Dec. 1910), 13, 720-21;
and on the Curtiss flight, see New York *Times*, May 29-30, 1910, and
Clara Studer, *Sky Storming Yankee: The Life of Glenn Curtiss* (New
York, 1937), 218-42.

12. On aviation journalism generally, see Ernest W. Dichman, *This Aviation
Business* (New York, 1929), 124-35. For Elizabeth Hiatt Gregory as
the "dean of aviation reporters," see Los Angeles *Times*, Sept. 8, 1936,
and material in Boxes 1 and 2, Elizabeth Hiatt Gregory Aviation Collection, 1900-1945 (Special Collections Library, University of California,
Los Angeles).

13. Rodgers remark is quoted in the New York *Times*, Nov. 6, 1911; for
his flight generally, see Harry Bruno, *Wings Over America, The Inside
Story of American Aviation* (New York, 1942), 78 and ch. 4; Sherwood
Harris, "Coast to Coast in 12 Crashes," *American Heritage*, XV (Oct.
1964), 46-49, 76-81.

14. "A Courteous Ambush in the Air," *Literary Digest*, LII (May 13, 1916),
1382.

15. "Gallant Feats in the Blue," *ibid.*, LIX (Nov. 16, 1918), 58. See also,
Francis A. Collins, *The Air Man, His Conquests in Peace and War*
(New York, 1917), 169-70, 205, 207, 219.

16. Rickenbacker's mother's advice is quoted in Ezra Bowen, *Knights of the
Air* (Alexandria, Va., 1980), 153.

17. Bill Rhode, "The History of Hollywood in Aviation," American Aviation Historical Society *Journal*, II (Oct.-Dec., 1957), 260-63; Frank
Strnd [*sic*], "Additional Aviation Movies," *ibid.*, III (July-Sept. 1958),
152-57; New York *Times*, Aug. 16, 1930.

18. *Western Flying*, IV (April 1928), 44.

19. The remark was made in the mid-twenties by Ryan's publicity agent,
Tom Mathews, quoted in William Wagner, *Ryan, the Aviator* (New
York, 1971), 53.

20. Charles A. Lindbergh, Jr., *"We"* (New York, 1927), 52-60.

21. *Ibid.*, 60.

22. Charles O. Wagner to Orville Wright, Aug. 8, 1928, Box 72, Wright
Papers (Manuscript Division, Library of Congress).

23. C. R. Schardlandt to Thomas A. Edison, June (?) 9, 1905, "Aerial Navigation File," Edison Papers (Edison National Historic Site, Orange,
N.J.).

24. The definitive account of the flight is Richard K. Smith, *First Across!
The U.S. Navy's Transatlantic Flight of 1919* (Annapolis, Md., 1973).

25. New York *Times*, May 3, 1923.

26. John P. Heinmuller, *Man's Fight To Fly: Famous World-Record
Flights and a Chronology of Aviation* (New York, 1944), 50-56; Joseph

H. Appel, *The Business Biography of John Wanamaker, Founder and Builder* (New York, 1930), 168.

27. New York *Times,* Nov. 23, 1935.

28. For air racing see C. R. Roseberry, *The Challenging Skies, The Colorful Story of Aviation's Most Exciting Years, 1919-1939* (Garden City, N.Y., 1966); Dan Dwiggins, *They Flew the Bendix Race, The History of the Competition for the Bendix Trophy* (Philadelphia, 1965). On the aerial New Deal, see W. B. Courtney, "Wings of the New Deal," *Collier's,* XCIII (Feb. 17, 1934), 12-13, 48-50, and references cited in Chapter 5. For appeal of building and flying model planes in period, see references in Chapter 6.

29. My account of Lindbergh and his public reception relies heavily on Kenneth S. Davis, *The Hero, Charles A. Lindbergh and the American Dream* (Garden City, N.Y., 1959), and Leonard Mosley, *Lindbergh* (New York, 1976). See also Bruno, *Wings Over America,* ch. 3; Lindbergh, *"We";* and John W. Ward, "The Meaning of Lindbergh's Flight," *American Quarterly,* X (1958), 3-16.

30. Daniel F. Guggenheim Fund for Promotion of Aeronautics, press release, Oct. 22, 1927, quoted in R. H. Mayo, "History of the Daniel Guggenheim Fund for the Promotion of Aeronautics," 93-104, unpublished typescript in Guggenheim Fund Papers, Box 20 (Manuscript Division, Library of Congress); Donald E. Keyhoe, "Seeing America with Lindbergh," *National Geographic,* LIII (Jan. 1928), 1-46.

31. Davis, *Hero,* 237; Mosley, *Lindbergh,* 173; U.S. Patents, 74,736, Clock Case, Isadore Greengas, Oct. 12, 1927; 74,011, Combined Reading Lamp and Electric Fan, Daniel Heenan, Dec. 6, 1927; 77,464, Mailbox, Treva M. Cooper, Aug. 6, 1928; 74,832, Box, F. F. Hamilton, June 25, 1927; 73,884, Beverage Container, Isak Weisenfreind, Aug. 29, 1927; 84,304, Filling Station, John L. Smith, Oct. 7, 1930; 77,635, Automobile Body, Gustave Berman, July 13, 1928.

32. Davis, *Hero,* 212-14. For New York City churches, see New York *Times,* May 23, 1927.

33. Davis, *Hero,* 213.

34. Laurence Goldstein, "Lindbergh in 1927: The Response of Poets to the Poem of Fact," *Prospects, An Annual of American Cultural Studies,* V (New York, 1980), 294.

35. Arthur Hobley, writing under the pseudonym, Charles Vale, in an anthology of 100 of the contest poems, including the three prize-winning entries. Vale, *The Spirit of St. Louis* (New York, 1927), iv.

36. *Ibid.,* 161-63.

37. Goldstein, "The Response of Poets," 303.

38. Vale, *Spirit,* 210-11; Ward, "Meaning of Lindbergh's Flight," 15.

39. Ward, "Meaning of Lindbergh's Flight," 9-11.

40. Quoted in *ibid.,* 6.

41. Marquis Childs in the New York *Herald Tribune,* quoted in Dixon Wecter, *The Hero in America* (New York, 1941), 432.

42. Mosley, *Lindbergh,* 165.

43. Charles O. Wagner to Orville Wright, Aug. 8, 1928, Wright Papers. See also C. C. Potter to Orville Wright, Dec. 19, 1927, *ibid.*
44. Roger Q. Williams, *To the Moon and Halfway Back* (Oakland, Calif., 1949), preface (n.p.) and 223.
45. *Western Flying*, II (July 1926), 17.

Chapter II

1. John H. Ledeboer, "The Present and Future of Aerial Navigation," *Living Age*, CCLVIII (Sept. 12, 1908), 670-73; J. Bernard Walker, "The Aeroplane—A Retrospect and a Forecast," *Review of Reviews*, XL (Nov. 1909), 551-59; Waldemar Kaempffert, "Aircraft and the Future," *Outlook*, CIV (June 28, 1913), 452-60; Robert E. Perry, "The Future of the Airplane," *National Geographic Magazine*, XXXIII (Jan. 1918), 107-13; Richard E. Byrd, "The Coming Age in Aviation," *World's Work*, LIV (Oct. 1927), 600-610; Roger Babson, "Air Flivvers and the Future," *Forum*, LXXXI (March 1929); Fitzhugh Green, "Flying in the Future," *Scribner's*, CVXI (Oct. 1938), 665-73; Elizabeth Gordon, "Will You Fly Your Own Plane After the War?" *House Beautiful*, 87 (March 1945), 54-55, 138-40.
2. Mary Moncure Parker, "When the Biplane Flew, as a Woman Saw It," *Advance*, LX (Oct. 6, 1910), 36. See also an assessment of the "look of wonder in the faces of the multitude" by Rev. J. A. Adams, editor of the *Advance*. "The Man Higher Up," *ibid.*
3. "Engineering and Aviation," Aero Club of America *Bulletin* (Jan. 1912), 34; John H. Jouett, "Our Full-Out Aircraft Production," typescript of address to Economic Club of New York, Jan. 27, 1942, in "John H. Jouett" file, Box 53, Am. Inst. of Aeron. Papers (Manuscript Division, Library of Congress).
4. Philadelphia *Press*, Sept. 10, 1909.
5. Henry A. Wise Wood, quoted in New York *Evening Journal*, Aug. 17, 1911.
6. Frank H. Butler, *Fifty Years of Travel by Land, Water, and Air* (London, 1921), 371; *Western Flying*, II (Sept. 1926), 12; Archibald Williams, *Conquering the Air, The Romance of the Development and Use of Aircraft* (New York, rev. ed., 1928), 300; Francis H. Collins, *The Air Man, His Conquests in Peace and War* (New York 1917), 71; *Yale News*, May 20, 1911.
7. *Advance*, LXV (Dec. 1912), 26.
8. Charles Battell Loomis, "The Next Craze," *Century*, LXXIV (July 1907), 347-48.
9. Collins, *The Air Man*, 71.
10. Carthage (N.Y.) *Tribune*, Sept. 29, 1906; Brooklyn *Eagle*, Dec. 25, 1904; Philadelphia *Record*, July 26, 1908.
11. "Unconstitutional—Un-American—Unreasonable," editorial, *Fly*, I (Nov. 1908), 4.
12. Harriet Quimby, quoted in Ralph M. Eastman, "Boston and Aviation," Bostonian Society *Proceedings* (1946), 42; Louise Thaden, quoted in

New York *Times*, Sept. 15, 1929; Margery Brown, "Flying Is Changing Women," *Pictorial Review*, XXXI (June 1930), 30.

13. William J. Powell, *Black Wings* (Los Angeles, 1934); Pittsburgh *Courier*, April 7, 1928; Enoch P. Waters, "Black Wings Over America," unid. clip. in "Aviators and Aviation" file (Schomburg Collection, New York Public Library).

14. Powell, *Craftsmen Aero News* (Los Angeles) 1 (July 1937), 15.

15. S. E. Lasher, "Society," *Airscout*, I (Feb. 1911), 25; Frederick Todd, "The Man in the Air," *World's Work*, XVI (Oct. 1908), 10,810.

16. Stanton Macdonald-Wright, "Influence of Aviation on Art," *Ace*, I (Sept. 1919), 11-12.

17. Waldemar Kaempffert, "The Flying Machine and the Roof," *American Homes and Gardens*, VII (Sept. 1911), 317.

18. "The Age of Aviation," *Independent*, LXVII (July 15, 1909), 155.

19. Quoted in Frederick Todd, "What War Will Be Like with Flying Machines," *World's Work*, XVII (Nov. 1908), 10,912; Hiram Maxim, "The Newest Engine of War," *Collier's*, XLVIII (Sept. 23, 1911), 195.

20. Knox quoted in "The Airship and International Unity," *World's Work*, XIX (Feb. 1910), 12,537; "The New Annus Mirabilis," editorial, *Independent*, LXX (Jan. 5, 1911), 56.

21. Rhoda Hero Dunn, "The Aeronauts," *Atlantic Monthly*, CIII (May 1909), 617; Charlton L. Edhold, "Wings," *Current Literature*, XLVII (Nov. 1909), 572.

22. Henry Woodhouse, "How Aerial Transportation Will Eliminate Within a Generation Factors That Cause Wars," *Flying*, IV (May 1915), 497-500, 503, 505.

23. Charlotte Perkins Gilman, "When We Fly," *Harper's*, LI (Nov. 9, 1907), 1664.

24. F. A. Collins, "How It Feels To Fly," *Review of Reviews*, XL (Nov. 1909), 580; "The Therapeutic Value of Flying, Interesting Cures Found in Upper Air," *Ace*, II (June 1921), 7-8.

25. *Western Flying*, IV (June 1928), 70; Carthage (N.Y.) *Tribune*, Sept. 29, 1906.

26. Cy Q. Faunce, *The Airliner and Its Inventor* (Columbus, Ohio, 1921), 12. For Lawson's biography, see Robert F. Brooks, "The Airliner and Its Inventor—Alfred W. Lawson," Paper Presented at the American Institute of Aeronautics and Astronautics, Annual Meeting Oct. 20, 1969, in Anaheim, Calif., 1; Alfred W. Lawson, *Born Again* (New York, 1904).

27. On Lawsonomy see Lawson, *Lawsonian Religion* (Detroit, 1949); *Lawsonomy* (Detroit, c. 1935); and *Lawson, Aircraft Industry Builder* (Detroit, 1937), 295-304.

28. Lawson's article from *Aircraft*, VI (Oct. 1916), is reprinted in Faunce, *The Airliner*, 195-201.

29. The remark was made by an aeronautical engineer who consulted for Lawson on the Airliner. Vincent J. Burnelli, as told to Booton Herndon, "The Non-Sked Adventure of the First Airliner," *True* (June 1962), 57.

30. For opposition to railroads generally, see Thurman W. Van Metre,

Early Opposition to the Steam Railroad (n.p., n.d.); for environmental based criticism of railroad, see John B. Jervis, "The Hudson River Railroad," *Hunt's Merchants' Magazine,* XXII (March 1850), 283; for early hostility to bicycles, see Richard Harmond, "Progress and Flight: An Interpretation of the American Cycle Craze of the 1890's," *Journal of Social History,* V (Winter 1971-72), 235, 244, and Robert A. Smith, *A Social History of the Bicycle, Its Early Life and Times in America* (New York, 1972), 65, 113.

31. Boston *Transcript,* May 5, 1909; Walker, "The Aeroplane—A Retrospect and a Forecast," 558; New York *Evening Sun,* July 27, 1908.

32. Ledeboer, "The Present and Future of Aerial Navigation," 670; Washington *Sunday Star,* Dec. 16, 1928. For the higher "batting average" of experts in making technological predictions, both as to specific technical developments as well as social consequences, see George Wise, "Predictions of the Future of Technology: 1890-1940," (Ph.D. thesis, Boston University, 1976), 18-22.

33. Curtiss quoted in "Flying in an Aeroplane," *Review of Reviews,* XL (Nov. 1909), 609; Chanute quoted in New York *Herald,* Aug. 30, 1908; Wright is quoted in *Aeronautics,* IV (Feb. 1909), 84. See also New York *Herald,* Sept. 13, 1908.

34. Birmingham (Ala.) *News,* May 26, 1925, clipping from Faurote scrapbook, National Air and Space Museum collection.

35. Wright is quoted in Charles Harvard Gibbs-Smith, *Aviation, An Historical Survey from Its Origins to the End of World War II* (London, 1970), 225; see also New York *Evening Sun,* July 30, 1908.

36. Unidentified London newspaper quoted and criticized in the New York *Sun,* July 30, 1908.

37. W. Joynson Hicks, "The Command of the Air," *Living Age,* LV (May 11, 1912), 414-22; Harold F. Wyatt, "The Wings of War," *Nineteenth Century,* LXVI (Sept. 1909), 450-56; T. G. Tullock, "The Aerial Peril," *ibid.,* LXV (May 1909), 800-809. U.S. journalists and popular writers also saw the "menace of the air," though much less frequently and without the apocalyptic overtones of European commentators. See, for instance, the New York *Herald,* Sept. 5, 1909. See also Wise, "Predictions of the Future of Technology, 1890-1940," 114-15. For a discussion of the optimistic, utopian strain in American fictional writing about the machine, see Howard Segal, "Technological Utopianism in American Culture" (Ph.D. thesis, Princeton University, 1975).

38. Wyatt, "Wings of War," 450-56. *ibid.*

39. Wingrove Bathon, "The Modern War Correspondent," *Airscout,* I, no. 1 (1910), 20.

40. Charles Caldwell, "Thoughts on the Moral and Other Indirect Influences of Rail-Roads," *New England Magazine,* II (April 1832), 291-93, 295-98, 300. For an excellent discussion of pre-twentieth century American attitudes toward technology, see John F. Kasson, *Civilizing the Machine, Technology and Republican Values in America, 1776-1900* (New York, 1976). See also Leo Marx, *The Machine in the Garden: Technology and the Pastoral Ideal in America* (New York, 1964).

41. "Improved Hay Maker," *Scientific American*, n.s., II (March 1860), 216, quoted in Marx, *Machine in the Garden*, 198; John C. Kimball, "Machinery as a Gospel Worker," *Christian Examiner*, LXXXVII (Nov. 1869), 319, 327. See also, "What Are We Going To Make?" *Atlantic Monthly*, II (June 1858), 90, 95.

42. Victor C. Ferkiss employs the phrase, "technological Messianism," in his *Technological Man, The Myth and the Reality* (New York, 1969), while Howard Segal uses the expression, "technological utopianism," in his thesis, "Technological Utopianism in American Culture," *passim*. In England, early nineteenth-century observers also hailed the transforming potential of new technology, particularly the steam engine. But their rhetoric was less explicitly messianic and religious, and it was countered by vocal and rooted comment hostile to machines and their consequences. On the "Gospel of Steam," for example, see Asa Briggs, *The Power of Steam, An Illustrated History of the World's Steam Age* (Chicago, 1982), ch. 3.

43. Winthrop S. Hudson, *Religion in America* (2nd ed.; New York, 1973), chs. 6-7.

44. Berthold Laufer, *The Prehistory of Aviation* (Chicago, 1928), 10.

45. Quoted in Institute of Aeronautical Sciences, *Exhibition of Early American Children's Books of Aeronautical Interest* (New York, 1942), 6.

46. Phillips Brooks, "The Wings of the Seraphim," *The Light of the World and Other Sermons* (New York, 1904), 254; Henry Ward Beecher, "Fact and Fancy," *Sermons in Plymouth Church, Brooklyn* (New York, 1882), 175; for sermons influenced by the airplane, see J. H. Jowett, "The Wing-Life of the Soul," *Advance*, LXV (March 29, 1913), 19, and Clayton D. Russell, "Seeing Things from Above," *Craftsmen Aero News*, I (Sept. 1937), 2, 7-8.

47. Transcript of interview with Gill Robb Wilson, Feb. 9, 1960, Oral History Archive, Columbia University, 1.

48. Louise Thaden, quoted in New York *Times*, Sept. 15, 1929; Larry Rue, *I Fly for News* (New York, 1932), 88.

49. Marcella Holtkamp, "A Bit of Philosophy on Flying," *Air Travel News*, III (Aug. 1929), 21-22.

50. Norman S. Hall, "The New Perspective," *Ace*, I (Jan. 1920), 6; see also Mildred M. Sheffey, "The Thrilling Experience of Learning To Fly," *Southern Aviation*, III (Nov. 1931), 22.

Chapter III

1. *Airway Age*, IX, no. 8 (Aug. 1929), 40; N.Y. *Times*, Feb. 19, 1930.

2. The "holy cause" charge is by Kenneth B. Collings, "Flying Is Still Dangerous," *American Mercury*, XXXII (June 1934), 147; Edward Pearson Warner, Typescript of address, "New England's Future and the Future of Aviation," given to New England Aviation Conference, Sept. 30, 1927; Aero Club of America *Bulletin*, I, No. 1 (Jan. 1912), 38.

3. "Remarks by Milton Wright, On Behalf of the Estate of Orville Wright,

In Presenting the Kitty Hawk Aeroplane to the United States of America," Dec. 17, 1946, Typescript, 2-3, Wright Papers, Box 72, File: "Kitty Hawk Aeroplane, Dedication at Smithsonian Institution," (Manuscript Division, Library of Congress). In 1911 when the U.S. Army intended to modernize "Signal Corps I" the plane acquired from the Wrights after the successful 1908 trials, the brothers recommended against modification and the Army gave the craft to the Smithsonian. Charles D. Chandler and Frank P. Lahm, *How Our Army Grew Wings: Airmen and Aircraft Before 1914* (New York, [1943]), 187.

4. Wright Brothers to Carl Dienstbach. Jan. 9, 1906, Dienstbach to Wrights, Jan. 24, 1906, Wright Papers, Box 22 (Manuscript Division, Library of Congress). The crankshaft and flywheel were never returned; Mabel Beck, "The First Aeroplane—After 1903," *U.S. Air Services*, XXXIX (Dec. 1954), 9-10.

5. Paul Edward Garber, "Report," Typescript of report compiled following trip on behalf of Smithsonian Institution to Mrs. Tusch's home, Jan. 19 to Feb. 12, 1947, NASM Scrapbook Collection, "Mother Tusch."

6. Mary Ogg, "Handwriting on Her Walls," Reprint of *California Monthly*, April 1949; "Wing Talk," *Collier's*, April 6, 1946, both in "Mrs. C. A. Tusch, The Hangar," file, NASM; see also a "Tentative Mockup" of aviation memorial and museum, with Mrs. Tusch's cottage installed, appended to Garber's "Report," NASM Scrapbook Collection.

7. Undated, single sheet flyer in "Airports, 1928-1949" clipping file, District of Columbia Public Library; "Remarks of Hon. Roy O. Woodruff, House of Representatives, Dec. 10, 1928," *ibid.*; Alexandria *Gazette*, Jan. 1, 1930. See also "Henry Woodhouse" file, American Institute of Aeronautics Papers, Box 128 (Manuscript Division, Library of Congress).

8. Newark *Star-Eagle*, Feb. 8, 1930; N.Y. *Times*, Nov. 26, 1929; Newark *Ledger*, Oct. 27, 31, 1929.

9. N.Y. *Times*, Nov. 17, 1929.

10. William L. Waldron, Mesquite, Texas, U.S. Patent 163,837, filed Sept. 24, 1949.

11. N.Y. *Times*, Dec. 25, 1929.

12. Ray Krimm, "Aerial Bridge a Social Innovation," *Air Travel News*, II (Oct. 1928), 22; N.Y. *Daily News*, Dec. 5, 1932.

13. New York *Times*, and Washington *Herald*, July 27, 1929; New York *Herald Tribune*, July 19, 1931; Quote in unidentified, 1929 clipping in Bingham Family Papers, series VI, "HB III War Service and Aviation," folder 73, Box 69 (Yale University Archives). See also, Reuben Maury, "The Flying Senator," *Liberty*, June 29, 1929, 55-56; and "Hiram Bingham" folder in biography files, American Institute of Aeronautics Papers, Box 7 (Manuscript Division, Library of Congress).

14. Harry H. Culver, "The Builder of a City Takes to the Air," *Air Travel News*, II (May 1928), 40. Aeronautical Chamber of Commerce, *Aircraft Year Book, 1930* (Washington, D.C.), 224.

15. New York *Herald Tribune*, July 6, 1945, obituary in biographical files under Clifford B. Harmon, "Newspaper Clippings," American Institute

of Aeronautics, Papers, Box 35 (Manuscript Division, Library of Congress). See also New York *Sun*, Jan. 3, 1929.

16. "The Good Will Fliers in the West Indies," *Tuskegee Messenger*, X (Dec. 1934), 3.

17. Mary J. Washington, "A Race Soars Upward," *Opportunity, A Journal of Negro Life*, XII (Oct. 1934), 301; Pittsburgh *Courier*, July 1, 1933, Sept. 1, Nov. 10, 17, 24, Dec. 22, 1934; Chicago *Defender*, July 29, Aug. 5, 1933; Aug. 4, Sept. 1, 15, 22, Nov. 3, 1934.

18. Smithsonian Institution, *Annual Report, 1910* (Washington, D.C., 1911), 109-10.

19. Unidentified clipping, Dec. 17, 1913, in file, "Kitty Hawk Anniversary," NASM Collections.

20. Editorial, "Let's Celebrate December 17," *National Aeronautics Magazine* (Nov. 1933), 5.

21. "Trip Circular No. 2, Kitty Hawk Trip," Nov. 24, 1928, Typescript in file, "Kitty Hawk Anniversary," NASM Collections.

22. U.S. House of Representatives, 70th Cong. 2d sess., *Twenty-fifth Anniversary of the First Airplane Flight, Proceedings* (Washington, D.C., 1929), 6, 10-13.

23. *Ibid.*, 21, 26, 28.

24. New York *Daily News*, Dec. 18, 1935; New York *Times*, Dec. 17, 1936; Howard Egbert, *The Shop that Became A Shrine* (Dayton, Dec. 17, 1928), pamphlet in NASM Collections.

25. New York *Times*, Dec. 18, 1933.

26. Washington *Herald*, Dec. 18, 1933. Because of a long festering dispute with the Smithsonian Institution over the question of who deserved the accolade of having built the first flyable airplane—the Smithsonian's Langley or the Wrights—in early 1928 Orville Wright sent the original Kitty Hawk Flyer to England for exhibition. The plane remained there until 1948, by which time Orville Wright and all of the other original parties to the controversy were dead. His executor requested the return of the plane to the U.S. and, on the 45th anniversary of flight, Dec. 17, 1948, it was ceremoniously presented to the Smithsonian Institution.

27. New York *Times*, Dec. 16, 18, 1934, New York *Herald Tribune*, Dec. 16, 1934; *National Aeronautics Magazine* (Dec. 1934), 7.

28. New York *Times*, Dec. 17-18, 1936.

29. National Aeronautic Association, *Skylights*, Dec. 8, 1939, p. 2.

30. New York *Herald Tribune*, Dec. 8, 1943; John K. Northrup, "Since Kitty Hawk . . . ," an address delivered before the Aviation Committee of the Los Angeles Junior Chamber of Commerce, Dec. 17, 1943, brochure in "Kitty Hawk" file, NASM Collections.

31. New York *Times*, Nov. 2, 1943; New York *Herald Tribune*, Dec. 18, 1941.

32. New York *Times*, Dec. 17, 1943. See also Russell Owen, "The Dream That Found Wings," New York *Times Magazine*, Dec. 12, 1943.

33. "President Truman's Message Honoring Wright Brothers' Flight at Kitty Hawk To Be Flown 'Round the World,'" Typescript, Dec. 2 [1949],

file, "Kitty Hawk Anniversary"; Air Force Association, "Day-Long Program at Kitty Hawk, N.C., To Mark 46th Anniversary of Wright Brothers' Flight at Kill Devil Hill," News Release (Typescript), Dec. 15, 1943, NASM Collections.

34. Harry S. Truman, "White House Text of Anniversary Message," Typescript, Nov. 23, 1949, file "Kitty Hawk Anniversary," NASM Collections.

35. New York *Times*, Dec. 18, 1949.

Chapter IV

1. New York *Times*, Aug. 30, 1936; Sept. 5, 1936.

2. *Ibid.*, Sept. 5, 1936; Los Angeles *Times*, Sept. 5, 1936.

3. For statistics on women pilots see *Aero Digest*, 20 (May 1932), 74; *ibid.*, 28 (May 1936), 66; U.S. Department of Commerce, Civil Aeronautics Agency, *CAA Statistical Handbook of Civil Aviation* (Washington, D.C., 1958), 73; Elizabeth Jane Burns, "Ladybird, Ladybird, How Do You Fly?" *Sportsman Pilot*, 13 (Feb. 15, 1930), 39. Information regarding professional women pilots and their occupations comes from Roland W. Hoagland, ed., *The Blue Book of Aviation: A Biographical History* (Los Angeles, 1932), 21, 31, 92, 142, 155, 159, 174, 193, 198, 211, 228, 247-48; *Who's Who in Aviation, 1942-43* (Chicago, 1942), 31, 50, 64, 112, 193, 263, 312, 315, 319, 358, 376, 426; Durward Howes, Mary L. Braun, and Rose Garvey, eds., *American Women: The Standard Biographical Dictionary of Notable Women*, 3 (1939; reprint, Teaneck, N.J., 1974), 549, 660, 666, 670, 674, 756, 900; Helena H. Smith, "New Women," *New Yorker* (May 10, 1930), 28-31; Clara Trenckmann, "Women in Aviation," *Curtiss-Wright Review*, 1 (May 1930), 23-24; *ibid.* (July 1930), 22-23; Clara [Trenckmann] Studer, "Bread and Butter and Airwomen," *National Aeronautic Magazine*, 13 (Oct. 1935), 20-21. Biographical information about the better known aviatrixes can be found in Jean Adams and Margaret Kimball, *Heroines of the Sky* (Garden City, 1942); Charles P. May, *Women in Aeronautics* (New York, 1962); and Charles E. Planck, *Women with Wings* (New York, 1942).

4. Elizabeth Hiatt Gregory, "Firsts in Aviation," unpaginated typescript in E. H. Gregory Papers (Special Collections Library, University of California, Los Angeles); Gerald D. Burtnett, "America's First Flying Sportswoman," *Sportsman Pilot*, IV (June 1931), 24-25, 48; May, *Women in Aeronautics*, 76-80; John W. Underwood, *The Stinsons, The Exciting Chronicle of a Flying Family and the Planes That Enhanced Their Fame* (Glendale, Calif., 1974), 5-6.

5. J. P. M'Evoy, "A Woman Who Teaches Men How To Fly," *American Magazine*, LXXXIII (March 1917), 52-53.

6. Bruce Gould, "Milady Takes the Air," *North American Review*, CCXXVIII (Dec. 1929), 691. On development of aviation generally see Lloyd Morris and Kendall Smith, *Ceiling Unlimited: The Story of American Aviation from Kitty Hawk to Supersonics* (New York, 1953); John B. Rae, *Climb to Greatness: The American Aircraft Industry, 1920-*

1960 (Cambridge, Mass., 1968); Henry Ladd Smith, *Airways: The History of Commercial Aviation in the United States* (New York, 1965).

7. Vance Thompson, "The Bird-Men," *Collier's*, 44 (Sept. 25, 1909), 20; George H. Guy, "Real Navigation of the Air," *Review of Reviews*, 38 (Sept. 1908), 319; Boston *Post*, Nov. 14, 1909; Clarence D. Chamberlin, *Record Flights* (Philadelphia, 1928), 13; Ford Ashman Carpenter, *The Aviator and the Weather Bureau* (San Diego, 1917), 9; Frank W. Wiley, *Montana and the Sky* (Helena, Mont., 1966), 86. For characterizations of Lindbergh as a birdman see Richard J. Probert, "Odysseys of the Air," *Western Flying*, 4 (March 1928), 21-22; and John W. Ward, The Meaning of Lindbergh's Flight," *American Quarterly*, 10 (Spring 1958), 8.

8. "Uncle Sam's Trump Card, Will the American 'Ace' Win the Final Trick in the Great War Game? *Sunset*, 41 (July 1918), 33-34.

9. "The Physique of the Flyer," *Western Flying*, 4 (May 1928), 8, 8-9; Robert J. Pritchard, "Ten Thousand Airplanes at $700?" *ibid.*, 12 (Dec. 1933), 809; W. B. Courtney, "Wings of the New Deal," *Collier's*, 93 (Feb. 17, 1934), 50.

10. Thaden quoted in W. E. Debnam, "Women's Place in Aviation as Seen by Endurance Fliers," *Southern Aviation*, 4 (Dec. 1932), 11; Davis quoted in unidentified, undated clipping in Manila Davis Talley scrapbook, NASM Collections; Nichols quoted in New York *Times*, Jan. 18, 1931. See also Ruth Nichols, "You Must Fly," *Pictorial Review*, 34 (Aug. 1933), 48; "All God's Chillun Gettin' Wings," *Literary Digest*, 109 (May 2, 1931), 29; Burns, "Ladybird, Ladybird," *Sportsman Pilot*, 13, 10. For male version of stereotype, Gould, "Milady Takes the Air," 691. See also Louise M. Thaden, "Training Women Pilots," *Western Flying*, 9 (Feb. 1931), 22.

11. Figures computed from Hoagland, ed., *Blue Book of Aviation;* Trenckmann, "Women in Aviation," *Curtiss-Wright Review* (July 1930), 22.

12. Frank T. Copeland, "The Women's Air Derby and Why," *Aeronautics*, 6 (May 1930), 412. For discussion of air-car vision, see Clarence D. Chamberlin, "Shall We All Fly Soon?" *North American Review*, 207 (Oct. 1928), 409-15; Alexander Klemin, "An Airplane in Every Garage?" *Scribner's*, 51 (Sept. 1935), 179-82; Roger Babson, "Air Flivvers and the Future," *Forum*, 81 (March 1929), 157-63.

13. Aeronautical Chamber of Commerce of America, *Aircraft Year Book, 1931* (Washington, D.C., 1931), 229; Louise Thaden, *High, Wide and Frightened* (New York, 1938), 187-88.

14. Thaden, *High, Wide and Frightened*, 167, 170; Richard S. Allen, *Revolution in the Sky: Those Fabulous Lockheeds and the Pilots Who Flew Them* (Brattleboro, Vt., rev. ed., 1967), 91, 93-94; John W. Underwood, *Of Monocoupes and Men: The Don Luscombe, Clayton Folkerts Story* (Glendale, Ca., 1973), 12, 14-15, 29-30.

15. Ruth Nichols, "Behind the Ballyhoo," *American Magazine*, 113 (March 1932), 82; Amelia Earhart, *The Fun of It: Random Records of My Own Flying and of Women in Aviation* (New York, 1932), 137. See also Earhart, "Flying the Atlantic—and Selling Sausages Have a Lot of

Things in Common," *American Magazine*, 114 (Aug. 1932), 17; Ruth Nichols, *Wings for Life: The Life Story of the First Lady of the Air* (Philadelphia, 1957), 134; Thaden, *High, Wide and Frightened*, 76-77.

16. Nichols, "You Must Fly," *Pictorial Review*, 34:48; Typescript interview with Blanche Noyes, March 1960, Archives of Oral History, Columbia University, 36.

17. Noyes interview, *ibid.*, 18, 36, 41-43.

18. Los Angeles *Times, Aug.* 20-22, 1929. See also Earhart, *Fun of It*, 138.

19. Thaden quoted in Debnam, "Women's Place in Aviation," *Southern Aviation*, 4, 11. For Richey's experiences, see New York *Times*, Jan. 1, Nov. 8, 1935 *Newsweek* (Nov. 16, 1935), 22; W. B. Courtney, "Ladybird: Pilot Helen Richey," *Collier's*, 93 (March 30, 1935), 16, 40, 43; May, *Women in Aeronautics*, 137; Planck, *Women with Wings*, 91-92.

20. Nichols, "You Must Fly," *Pictorial Review*, 34:48; Helen K. Schunck, "Is There a Place for Women in Aviation?" *Aeronautic Review*, 7 (Dec. 1929), 39; Burns, "Ladybird, Ladybird," *Sportsman Pilot*, 13:39; Nichols, unidentified and undated clipping, American Institute of Aeronautics Papers, Library of Congress; Barbara Southgate, "Not in Competition with Men," *Airwoman*, 2 (Nov. 1934), 4; Mary C. Alexander, "Why Do Women Fly?" *Southern Aviation*, 3 (April 1932), 16; Amelia Earhart, "Women's Influence on Aviation," *Sportsman Pilot*, 3 (April 1930), 15; Janet Mabie, "Amelia Earhart's New Flight: Expedition into the Realm of Academics To Show Women the Pathway to a New Career," *Christian Science Monitor Magazine*, April 29, 1936, 5.

21. J. C. Johnson, "Betsy Ross Goes Modern," Cincinnati *Enquirer*, June 11, 1933.

22. Clara [Trenckmann] Studer, "Women on the Wing," *Independent Women*, 14 (April 1935), 121; "Husband and Wife Teams in the Aviation Game," *Literary Digest*, 105 (April 12, 1930), 39; Burns, "Ladybird, Ladybird," *Sportsman Pilot*, 13:11; "Mr. and Mrs. Pilot," *99'er*, pt. 1, 1 (April 1934), 6-7; pt. 2 (May 1934), 8-9, 13. For biographies of Omlie and O'Donnell see Hoagland, ed., *Blue Book of Aviation*, 21, 228; Howes, Braun, Garvey, eds., *American Women*, 670, 674; *Who's Who in Aviation*, 319; Adams and Kimball, *Heroines of the Sky*, 69-84, 257.

23. Leonard Mosley, *Lindbergh* (New York, 1977), 191-92, 199-200, 212-13, 231.

24. "Husband and Wife Teams," *Literary Digest*, 105:39; Anne Morrow Lindbergh, *North to the Orient* (New York, 1935), 17; and Kenneth S. Davis, *The Hero: Charles A. Lindbergh and the American Dream* (Garden City, N.Y., 1959), 279, 282; George P. Putnam, *Soaring Wings: A Biography of Amelia Earhart* (New York, 1939), 186.

25. Earhart, *Fun of It*, 165, 168-69; New York *Times*, April 16, 1930; *Popular Aviation*, 14 (May 1934), 304. See also Elizabeth H. Gregory, "Flying Costumes Worn by the Early Women Pilots," *U.S. Air Services*, 20 (Nov. 1935), 26-27.

26. Frances Drewry McMullen, "The First Women's Air Derby, An Interview with Amelia Earhart," *Woman's Journal*, 14 (Oct. 1929), 38.

27. Roy Cross, *Great Aircraft and their Pilots* (Greenwich, Conn., 1971), 115; Don Dwiggens, *They Flew the Bendix Race* (Philadelphia, 1965), 105; New York *Times*, Sept. 4, 1938.

28. Jacqueline Cochran, *The Stars at Noon* (Boston, 1954), 65; Frederick Graham, "First Lady of the Air Lanes," New York *Times Magazine*, Sept. 25, 1938, 23.

29. Typescript of interview with Ruth Nichols, June 1960, Archives of Oral History, Columbia University, 7. See generally William H. Chafe, *Women and Equality: Changing Patterns in American Culture* (New York, 1977), 29, 33-41; Jill Conway, "Women Reformers and American Culture," *Journal of Social History*, 5 (Winter 1971-72), 164.

30. Graham, "First Lady of the Air Lanes," New York *Times Magazine*; Thaden, *High, Wide and Frightened*, 138; Nichols, *Wings for Life*, 24. New York *Times*, Sept. 15, 1929. See also Margery Brown, "Flying Is Changing Women," *Pictorial Review*, 31 (June 1930), 30, 108-9; Amelia Earhart, quoted in Putnam, *Soaring Wings*, 205; Marcella Holtkamp, "A Bit of Philosophy on Flying," *Air Travel News*, 3 (Aug. 1929), 21.

31. Lindbergh, *North to the Orient*, 17; Nichols in New York *Herald Tribune*, July 14, 1933; Thaden, *High, Wide and Frightened*, 229-54.

32. Nichols, *Wings for Life*, 93-98; Viola Gentry, *Hangar Flying* (Chelmsford, Mass., 1975), 104-5.

33. Planck, *Women with Wings*, 91-92; Louise Thaden, "The Ninety-Nines," *Western Flying*, 12 (Sept. 1932), 28; Miss Spectator [pseud.], "The Ladies Launch Their Own National Air Meet," *Sportsman Pilot*, 12 (Sept. 15, 1934), 21, 44; *99'er*, 1 (Dec. 2, 1933), 8; 2 (March 1935), 11.

34. *99'er*, 4 (Jan. 2, 1934); and *ibid.* (March 1935), 14.

35. The quotation appears in the dedication of Jacqueline Walker, *Equator South, Equator North* (San Francisco, 1939). On the era's ideas about feminism and femininity, see generally, William L. O'Neill, *Everyone Was Brave: A History of Feminism in America* (Chicago, 1971), 313; Putnam, *Soaring Wings*, 138, 145; Peter G. Filene, *Him/Her/Self: Sex Roles in Modern America* (New York, 1975), 140-41.

36. Frances Vivian Drake, "Air Stewardess," *Atlantic Monthly*, 151 (Feb. 1933), 185-93; the quotation is from Courtney, "High Flying Ladies," *Collier's*, Aug. 20, 1932, 30. See also Kenneth Hudson, *Air Travel: A Social History* (Totowa, N.J., 1972), 46.

Chapter V

1. Thomas E. Stimson, Jr., "Here's Your Helicopter Coupe," *Popular Mechanics*, February 1951, 268.

2. Clarence D. Chamberlin, "Shall We All Fly Soon?" *North American Review*, CCVI (Oct. 1928), 409-15; Alexander Klemin, "An Airplane in Every Garage?" *Scribner's*, LXLVIII (Sept. 1935), 179-82; Harold S. Kahm, "Coming—The Helicopter Land Boom," *Barron's*, XXIII (Oct. 18, 1943), 3; Roger Babson, "Air Flivvers and the Future," *Forum*, LXXXI (March 1929), 161; S. C. Frazier, "John Doe's Flying Carpet,"

Aircraft Age, II (Dec. 1943), 20-21, 56-59; R. R. Blythe, "Building Our Cities in the Country," *Aerial Age,* XVI (Sept. 1922), 443; the Cessna advertisement is from *Collier's,* June 5, 1943, 63. The earliest article prophesying a flying car is A. M. Herring, "The Horseless Carriage of the Next Generation," *Horseless Age,* II (May 1897), 1.

3. For architects' response to problem of home design for the air age, see Stuart E. Cohen and Stanley Tigerman, *Chicago Architects* (Chicago, 1976), plates 66, 68, and 68.5; and "The Future American Country House," *Architectural Record,* CXIV (Nov. 1928), 417-20. For promotion of small airports and airparks, see Esso Oil Company, *Community Airports and Airparks* (n.p., 1945); Aeronautical Chamber of Commerce of America, Personal Aircraft Council, *Put Your Town on the Air Map* (n.p., 1944); U.S. Department of Commerce, CAA, *Small Airports* (Washington, D.C., 1945). For federal government's subsidy of "poor man's" airplane and educational reforms connected to aviation, see notes below and for Chapter 6.

4. Philadelphia *Press,* Sept. 10, 1909. For biographical information about Lawson, see Robert F. Brooks, "The Airliner and Its Inventor—Alfred W. Lawson," Paper presented at the American Institute of Aeronautics and Astronautics Annual Meeting, Oct. 20, 1969, Anaheim, Calif., copy in NASM file, "Alfred W. Lawson; Cy Faunce, *The Airliner and Its Inventor, Alfred W. Lawson* (Columbus, Ohio, 1921), 10, 12, 15; "New York's First Airboat Commuter!" *The World Magazine,* Nov. 16, 1913; and the New York *Tribune,* Oct. 11, 1913; for McCormick's air commuting, see Glenn F. Curtiss, "The Popularity of Water Flying in America," *Flying,* II (May 1913), 15; and *Some Pictures and a Few Words about the Curtiss Flying Boat* (Hammondsport, N.Y., n.d.), pamphlet in collection of NASM, file "Curtiss; Early Flying Boats," 4.

5. F. Trubee Davison, quoted in *U.S. Daily,* Dec. 4, 1930.

6. On Ford's aeronautics work, see generally Douglas J. Ingells, *Tin Goose, The Fabulous Ford Trimotor* (Fallbrook, Calif., 1968), 13-17, 21, 23.

7. Johnstown (Pa.) *Leader,* no date, in Alan Hawley Aeronautical Scrapbook, 1917-18, New-York Historical Society Collection; Chamberlin, "Shall We All Fly Soon?" 410.

8. New York *Times,* July 31, 1926; New Bedford (Mass.) *Times,* Feb. 8, 1928; New York *American,* July 29, 1926; Detroit *Times,* Feb. 5 and 22, 1928; Detroit *News,* Aug. 8, 1926.

9. New York *Evening Sun,* Aug. 7, 1926.

10. Ironwood (Mich.) *Globe,* July 7, 1926; Ethel Bennett to Henry Ford, Jan. 1, 1928, Ford Fair Lane Papers, Box 783 (Ford Archives, Dearborn).

11. Ingells, *Tin Goose,* 33-34.

12. For efforts to make planes safer, see Richard P. Hallion, *Legacy of Flight, The Guggenheim Contribution to American Aviation* (Seattle, 1977), ch. 8; Alexander Klemin, "Notes on the Guggenheim Safety Competition," *Aviation,* XXIV (Jan. 30, 1928), 247-49; "Looking for Safer Aircraft," *ibid.,* XXVII (Oct. 19, 1929), 795-96; Otto C. Koppen, "Happier Landings," *ibid.,* (Sept. 1934), 275-77; John S. Hammond, "Six New Ships," *Western Flying,* XV (April 1935), 19-20; Alexander

Klemin, "Possibility of Two-Control Operation of the Airplane," *Aeronautical Digest,* XXVI (April 1935), 30.

13. Fred E. Weick, "Development of the Ercoupe, an Airplane for Simplified Private Flying," *SAE Journal* [*Transactions*], XLIX (Dec. 1941), 520-31.

14. I am indebted for these observations to conversations with staff at the National Air and Space Museum.

15. W. B. Courtney, "Wings of the New Deal," *Collier's* (Feb. 17, 1934), 50; Hallion, *Legacy of Flight,* ch. 8.

16. *New York Times,* May 25, 1934; "Plan for Widespread Development of Private Flying," Typescript, Nov. 8, 1933, Aeronautics Branch, General Records Department of Commerce (National Archives), Box 570; Robert J. Pritchard, "Ten Thousand Airplanes at $700?" *Western Flying,* XIII (Dec. 1933), 8-9; Eugene L. Vidal, "Low-Priced Airplane," *Aviation,* XXXIII (Feb. 1934), 40, 50.

17. For negative opinions of Vidal's proposal, see Clara Gilbert, "Are Air Flivvers Possible?" *99er* (March 2, 1934), 6; Cy Caldwell, "Boners of a Bureau Bungler," *Aeronautical Digest,* XXVI (Sept. 1935), 17, 33.

18. Henry T. Hunt, General Counsel, to Vidal, Dec. 9, 1933, Public Works Administration Records, Record Group 135, Records Relating to the Justification of Projects, file "Commerce—Aeronautics, Rescind" (National Archives); Harold L. Ickes, *The Secret Diary of Harold L. Ickes* (New York, 1953), 142-43.

19. *New York Times,* March 8, 1934; Caldwell, "Boners," 17.

20. For safety plane competition, see U.S. Secretary of Commerce, *Twenty-third Annual Report of the Secretary of Commerce, 1935* (Washington, D.C., 1935), 14; *New York Times,* May 25, 1934; "Department of Commerce Light Plane Specifications," *Aviation,* XXXIII (July 1934), 3.

21. *New York Times,* Aug. 28, 1934; *Newsweek,* Sept. 8, 1934; and Secretary of Commerce, *Twenty-third Annual Report,* 15.

22. William B. Stout, "A Few Fallacies Concerning the 'Cheap Airplane' Idea," *Aeronautical Digest,* XXVII (Sept. 1935), 15.

23. "Air Commerce Bureau's Development Section Chief Says Tailless Airplane Is Very Close to Being Fool-Proof," Typescript Press Release, Department of Commerce, Bureau of Air Commerce, Aug. 12, 1935, in NASM file "Waterman Arrowbile"; "Comments of the Press," a printed summary of press comment on Waterman plane, in Elizabeth Hiatt Gregory Papers, Box 6 (Special Collections Library, University of California, Los Angeles); Max Karant, "The Unbelievable Truth About Hammond's Experimental Plane," *Popular Aviation,* XIX (Oct. 1936), 56.

24. See generally, Donald J. Bush, *The Streamlined Decade* (New York, 1975), especially ch. 6.

25. Willis L. Nye, "Pusher vs. Tractor Planes," *Popular Aviation,* XII (July 1933), 23-24, 72; "Waterman 'Arrowbile,'" *Historical Aviation Album,* III (1966), 132-38.

26. Secretary of Commerce, *Twenty-third Annual Report,* 15; John H. Geisse, "Material for Annual Report," Memorandum, Aug. 14, 1937,

File No. 820, "Aeronautics Development by Civil Aeronautics Administration," CAA Records (National Archives).

27. Fred D. Fagg, Jr., Memorandum on Status of "Monocoupes," July 6, 1937, File no. 820, "Aeronautical Development by Civil Aeronautics Administration," CAA Records (National Archives).

28. *Ace*, IV (Nov. 1920), 28; *Western Flying*, III (April 1927), 19; U.S. Dept. of Commerce, Aeronautics Branch, Air Information Division, *Information Bulletin, No. 9* (3rd ed.; March 31, 1928), 2.

29. Beaux-Arts Institute of Design, *Bulletin*, I (July 1925), 5; Harry B. Brainerd, "An Aeroplane Landing in a Metropolis," *American City Magazine*, XXXIV (Feb. 1926), 187-90. For similar designs, see also [H. Wiley Corbett?] "Building the Modern Airport," unidentified article from an aeronautical monthly for Nov. 1929 in "Airports, Planning" File, NASM Collections; "Sky Harbors of the Future," *Popular Mechanics*, LII (Dec. 1929), 970-75; Norman Bel Geddes, *Horizons* (New York, 1932, 1977), ch. 5, "By Air Tomorrow," including plan for floating rotary airport, pp. 100-108.

30. Vidal's obituary is in New York *Times*, Feb. 21, 1969; for Vidal's work with heat-molded plywood, see Paul Christian and David G. Wittels, "Airplanes and Bathtubs: Cooked to Order," *Saturday Evening Post* (July 18, 1942), 12-13, 36, 39; U.S. Dept. of Commerce, Civil Aeronautics Administration, *CAA Statistical Handbook of Civil Aviation*, 1958 (Washington, D.C., 1958), 77; U.S. Dept. of Commerce, Bureau of Census, *Historical Statistics of the United States*, Part 2 (Washington, D.C., 1975), 716.

31. The question about Mr. and Mrs. John Q. Public comes from Air-Age Education Research, *Wings Over One World* (New York, 1945), 20; for the Airways to Peace Exhibition, see *Cue Magazine*, Oct. 9, 1943.

32. Various wartime polls and surveys are reviewed in U.S. Dept. of Commerce, Civil Aeronautics Administration, *Civil Aviation and the National Economy* (Washington, D.C., 1945), 42-43.

33. *Saturday Evening Post Aviation Survey* (Philadelphia 1946), 52-53; Civil Aeronautics Administration, *Civil Aviation and the National Economy*, vii, 37, 99.

34. Study cited by W. A. Mara, "Marketing Methods for Private Airplanes," in *Proceedings*, Second National Clinic for Domestic Aviation Planning, Oklahoma City, 1944, 97.

35. John M. Blum, "The G.I. in the Culture of the Second World War," *Ventures*, VIII, No. 1 (1968), 51-56.

36. John W. Studebaker, "Air Youth's Place in the Schools," *Air Youth Horizons*, I (Jan. 1940), 3.

37. Aeronautical Chamber of Commerce of America, *Aircraft Yearbook, 1948* (Washington, D.C., 1948), xxvi; and *Time*, Oct. 29, 1945, 81-82; Civil Aeronautics Administration, *CAA Statistical Handbook, 1958* (Washington, D.C., 1958), 36, 116; New York *Times*, Sept. 23, Oct. 9 and 10, 1945; "Cars That Fly, Swing High, Sweet Chariot!" *Special-Interest Autos* (April-May 1972), 36-41, 54-55.

38. *Aircraft Yearbook, 1949*, 449.

Chapter VI

1. The Monarch advertisement appears in *Saturday Evening Post* (New York), CCI (Feb. 2, 1929), 114; World Congress on Air Age Education, *Proceedings and Abstracts of Speeches* (New York, 1946), 10; Betty Peckham, *Women in Aviation* (New York, 1945), 155.

2. U.S. Office of Education, *Aviation in the Public Schools* (Washington, D.C., 1936), cover; the Rivera mural is illustrated, though erroneously attributed to Edwin Rosskam, in William Stott, *Documentary Expression and Thirties America* (New York, 1973), plates following p. 144; magazine cover, *Saturday Evening Post*, April 6, 1940; for a calendar painting by Harold Anderson, see *Air Youth Horizons*, Jan. 1941, cover.

3. Aero Club of America *Bulletin*, I (Jan. 1912), 38; Mary E. Burt, "Aeronautics Will Develop a Broader Vision," *Flying* (New York), IV (Oct. 1915), 697. Typical of articles promoting model airplane building in the period is Cecil Peoli, "How To Make a Model Aeroplane," *Scientific American* (New York), CV (Oct. 14, 1911), 334; see also *Time Magazine*, XXXIV (Aug. 7, 1939), 56.

4. On explosion of interest in model making and the systematic cultivation of youthful aeronautics by adults, see: "Teaching the Young Idea How To Fly," *Literary Digest* (New York), XCVIII (June 9, 1928), 41; "Young America Builds Airplanes," *Playground* (New York), XXI (Aug. 1927), 244-45; Albert Lewis, "Nation's Newest Hobby," *National Aeronautic Magazine* (Washington, D.C.), XVII (Sept. 1939), 32; E. L. Hughes, "Miniature Airplane Developments," *Aircraft Age*, III (March 1932), 11; "A Survey of Junior Aviation in Groups and Schools," *Air Youth Horizons* (New York), I (Jan. 1940), 6-7; Aero Club of Pennsylvania, Minute Book, Dec. 1933–Oct. 1940, p. 2 (Aero Club of Pennsylvania Papers, Pennsylvania Historical Society, Philadelphia); *Playground*, XXI (Nov. 1927), 397; Chicago Park District, Recreation Division, *Indoor Model Airplanes* ([Chicago], 1938); Bernard C. Friedman, for South Park Commissioners, Chicago Recreation Department, *Model Airplanes* ([Chicago], 1934); John C. Henderson and L. A. Orsatti, *Official Miniature Aircraft Instruction Manual, Written for Los Angeles Times–Playground Aircraft League* (Los Angeles, 1931).

5. Detroit's experience is described in Clarence E. Brewer, "How One City Took to Models," *Air Youth Horizons*, I (Jan. 1940), 8; and William F. Durand, *Aeronautics Education* (New York, [1928?]), 33.

6. Willis C. Brown, "Model Builders Are Sportsmen," *National Aeronautic Magazine*, XIII (Oct. 1935), 37; Stern Brothers' Department Store to Augustus Post, Feb. 9, 1931, Augustus Post Papers (New York Public Library); "A Layman Business Leader Becomes an Aviation Sponsor," *Air Travel News* (Detroit), II (May 1928), 50.

7. "A Survey of Junior Aviation," *Air Youth Horizons*, I (Jan. 1940), 6-7.

8. See, for example, columns by Major Burdette A. Palmer, Junior Birdmen Field Director, in San Francisco *Examiner* (1937); William R. Hearst to Orville Wright, Oct. 22, 1936, Wright Papers, Box 30 (Manuscript Division, Library of Congress).

9. *Jimmie Allen Club News* [1935?-1936?], nos. 1, 2, 8, 22, 23, 26, 27, un-paginated and undated newspaper in Elizabeth Hiatt Gregory Papers, file "Models, Jimmie Allen Club" (Special Collections Library, University of California, Los Angeles).

10. *99er* (New York), I (July 1934), 4; *Jimmie Allen Club News*, vol. 1, no. 2, 3, 17.

11. *Jimmie Allen Club News*, nos. 17, 23, 25; Jacqueline Cochran, "Girls Are Model-Plane Fans, Too," *Air Youth Horizons* (Feb. 1940), 3; San Francisco *Examiner*, July 11, 1935, August 8, 1937; *99er*, II (March 1935), 14.

12. *Jimmie Allen Club News*, nos. 11, 16.

13. Roland H. Spaulding [for Daniel Guggenheim Fund for the Promotion of Aeronautics], *Some Present Practices in Secondary Aeronautics Education* (n.p., 1929), 33.

14. Interview with Irwin Polk, founder of Polk's Hobby Shop in New York City, one of the earliest, March 10, 1980; interview with Frank Ehling of Academy of Model Aeronautics, Washington, D.C., Jan. 9, 1980.

15. For detailed history of the model airplane from antiquity through World War I, see Louis H. Hertz, *The Complete Book of Model Aircraft, Spacecraft, and Rockets* (New York, 1967).

16. Charles Hampson Grant, "Gas Models Are Here To Stay," *National Aeronautics Magazine*, XIV (Sept. 1937), 39-40; Gurney Williams, "Small Fry," *Collier's*, CIV (July 15, 1939), 38; [Paul Edward Garber ?], "The Sport of Building and Flying Aircraft Models as Developed in Washington, D.C.," typescript in NASM Collection, 4-5.

17. Durand quoted in Harry F. Guggenheim, *The Seven Skies* (New York, 1930), 117-18; Durand, *Aeronautics Education*, 9-10.

18. Spaulding, *Some Present Practices in Secondary Aeronautics Education*, 1-2, 37.

19. *Ibid.*, 41; "A Public School Course in Flying," *Western Flying* (Los Angeles), IV (June 1928), 38.

20. Dr. Wolfgang Klemperer, "Soaring Flight," *Commercial Aeronautics* [numbered pamphlets 3, 11, 17] (Chicago, 1929), CAA, *Education for the Air Age*, 3; Lucien Zacharoff, "War Threats Speed Air Education," *National Aeroneutics Magazine*, XVI (Feb. 1938), 16-17; 73 Cong. 2d Sess., *Congressional Record*, April 6, 1934, p. 6168; 74 Cong. 2d Sess., "Aviation Instruction Courses for Public Schools," *Senate Reports*, Report no. 1724, Feb. 24, 1936, pp. 1-2.

21. "Legionnaires Sponsor Air Cadets of America," *Speed* (Los Angeles), IV (June 1933), 7; E. A. Hough, "The Falcon's Civilian Air Corps," *Aircraft Age*, IV (July 1933), 7; A. C. "Gus" Haller, "Since We Are Spending Money Anyway," *National Aeronautic Magazine*, XIV (Jan. 1936), 14-15, 31; *ibid.* (March 1936), 14; *ibid.* XVII (Jan. 1939), 17.

22. "Air Youth of America," Typescript in "Winthrop Rockefeller" file, American Institute of Aeronautics Papers, Box 107 (Manuscript Division, Library of Congress); New York *Times*, Oct. 24, 1938; Sept. 21, 1939; Aug. 6-7, 1940.

23. Robert H. Hinckley, *Air Conditioning American Youth* (Washington, D.C., 1942).

24. CAA, *A Question and Answer Discussion Relating to the Introduction of Pre-Flight Aeronautics in High Schools* (Washington, D.C., 1942), 7.

25. Office of Education, Press Release, March 20, 1942; John W. Studebaker, "Proposed Organization and Procedures for Development of Aviation Education," *Typescript notes,* March 10, 1942, Overall Defense Correspondence, Central Records Commissioner of Education (National Archives); Edgar Fuller, "Educational Services of the Civil Aeronautics Administration," in Claremont Colleges, *Education for the Air Age, A Compilation of Papers and Reports* (Claremont, Calif., 1945), 5; George T. Renner, *Human Geography in the Air Age* (New York, 1942); Rose N. Cohen, *Flying High, An Anthology of Aviation Literature for Junior High Students* (New York, 1942). See also CAA, Aviation Education Research Project, *Education for the Air Age, A Preliminary Statement for Teachers and School Administrators* (New York, May 1, 1942), 6-14; Stanford University, School of Education, *Aviation Education Source Book* (New York, 1946).

26. Aviation Education Research Group, Teachers College, University of Nebraska, *Elements of Pre-Flight Aeronautics for High Schools* (New York, 1942); George W. Frasier, "Elementary Schools," *Air Affairs* (Washington, D.C.), II (Winter 1948), 189-91; Howard W. Sinclair, "Aviation's Contribution to Education," *Education* (Boston), LXVIII (Jan. 1948), 269.

27. Frank Knox to John Studebaker, Dec. 3, 1941, Overall Defense Correspondence, Box 2, Central Records Commissioner of Education, Record Group 12 (National Archives); "History of National Model Building Program," Typescript (Nov., 1944), in file "Model Airplanes for World War II" (National Air and Space Museum, Washington, D.C.); David C. Cooke and Jesse Davidson, eds., *The Model Plane Annual, 1943* (New York, 1943), 144-45; "Once They Were Only Toys," *New York Times Magazine,* April 5, 1942, 16-17.

28. Harry A. Sullivan, "Airline Aids to the Schools," *Air Affairs,* II (Winter 1948), 245; Fuller, "Educational Services," *Education for the Air Age,* 7; Second National Clinic for Domestic Aviation Planning, *Proceedings* (Oklahoma City, 1944), 301; Fuller, "Educational Services," *Education for the Air Age,* 6-7; M. K. Fahnestock, "Aviation Education in Colleges and Universities," in Second National Clinic, *Proceedings,* 280.

29. William E. Givens, "Air Lanes and Education," *Education,* LXIV (June 1944), 594; *Air-Age Education News* (New York), II (Nov. 1944), 11; Frank M. Williams, "Pre-Flight Aviation in the Small High Schools," *California Journal of Secondary Education,* XIX (Oct. 1944), 297; Ralph Haefner, *Teaching Aeronautics in High Schools, A Study of Methods, Principles and Measurements* (New York, 1947), 59-60.

30. John H. Furbay, "This Shrinking World," American Association of School Administrators, *Official Report, 1946* (Washington, D.C., 1946), 223-25.

31. American Association of School Administrators, Air Age Education Committee, *The Waging of Peace; A Program for the Air Age* (Washington, D.C., 1944), 6.
32. *National Aeronautic Magazine*, XXVI (March 1947), p. 2; Wendell Willkie, *One World* (Urbana, Ill., 1966); Gill Robb Wilson, "Man—The Major Problem," Address quoted in *Air-Age Education News*, IV (Sept. 1946), 1; I. James Quillen, "Education, Aviation and Society," *Air Affairs*, II (Winter 1948), 165; John H. Furbay, "Global Minds for a Global World," American Association of School Administrators, *Official Report, 76th Annual Convention, 1950*.
33. CAA, *Report of the Aviation Education Committee of the American Association of Colleges for Teacher Education* (Washington, D.C., Sept. 1, 1949), 9, appendix A; Howard W. Sinclair and H. E. Mehrens, "Current Efforts To Solve Aviation Education Problems," *National Elementary Principal* (XXVIII (Dec. 1948), 8; "Aviation Education Meetings," *Air-Age Education News*, IV (Dec. 1946), 3-4.
34. Blanche G. Bobbitt, "2 Aviation Programs in Los Angeles," *Clearing House* (New York), XXV (April 1951), 483; Englehardt, "Teacher Education," *Teacher-Educational Journal*, V, 159; Englehardt, "Education for This Age," *Education*, LXVIII (Jan. 1948), 265; "Aviation Education in California Public Schools," California State Department of Education, *Bulletin* (Sacramento), XIII (Sept. 1944), 22-23; Marian C. Wagstaff, "Aviation Education in California," *California Journal of Secondary Education*, XXII (Feb. 1947), 82; *CAA Journal* (Washington, D.C.), VII (Aug. 15, 1947), 182.
35. "Air Globe," *Air-Age Education News*, (Sept. 1944), 3, 9; Lilly Lindquist, "Language in the Air," *ibid.*, 18.
36. [Four Airline Educators], "Airline Aids to the Schools," *Air Affairs*, II (Winter 1948), 233-46.
37. Air-Age Education Research, *Proceedings and Abstracts of Speeches, World Congress on Air Age Education* (New York, 1946), 2, 5-9, 80-97; *Air-Age Education News*, III (March-April 1946), 3-4.
38. George Gardner, "Pan American World Airways Educational Program," *Education*, LXVIII (Jan. 1948), 279.
39. "Who Controls the People's Air," *Air-Age Education News*, I (Sept. 1944), 10; "International Airlines—One or Many," *ibid.* (May 1945), 10-11; "Your Neighbors—India and Pakistan," *ibid.*, V (Oct. 1947), 10-13; Enrique Porter, "An Air View of Brazil Today," *Classroom Clipper* IV (Oct. 1947), 3-7, 11.
40. "Classrooms in the Air," *ibid.*, V (Oct. 1947), 4-5; "News of the Air World," *ibid.* (Feb. 1948), 16; "A Word from Youth," *ibid.*, V (Sept. 1947), 1; Stanton Leggett, "Global Air School Urged by Educators," *ibid.*, II (Jan. 1945), 3; Herbert C. Clish, "How Can the Use of Air Contribute to Better Human Relationships and Peace?" in Air-Age Education Research, *Wings Over One World* (New York, 1945), 50-51; *ibid.* (Jan. 1945), 1. Cherrington is quoted in the New York *Times*, May 18, 1945.
41. Wagstaff, "Aviation Education in California," *California Journal of*

Secondary Education, XXII, 182-83; *Education Index,* VI-VIII (New York, 1947-53).

42. Nickolaus Louis Engelhardt, Jr., *Who's Who in America* (38th ed.; Chicago, 1974), 921; *Union List of Serials* (3d ed.; New York, 1965), I, 95.

Chapter VII

1. Roger Burlingame, *Engines of Democracy* (New York, 1949), 113; Frederick G. Kilgour, "Technological Innovation in the United States," *Cahiers d'Histoire Mondiale,* VIII, no. 4 (1965), 742.
2. Taylor is quoted in the New York *Times,* April 30, 1978.
3. Television broadcast, New Orleans, March 2, 1980.
4. Acting Director Melvin Zisfein's remarks are in "Foreword," *The Wright Brothers, Heirs of Prometheus,* Richard P. Hallion (ed.), (Washington, D.C., 1978), ix; Director Noel Hinners received the gift .of fabric from the original Kitty Hawk plane in 1980. My observations about the National Air and Space Museum and the Smithsonian Institution are based on personal observation during two years at NASM as a postdoctoral fellow. For a review of NASM exhibits from a different but complementary perspective, see Michael McMahon, "The Romance of Technological Progress: A Critical Review of the National Air and Space Museum," *Technology and Culture,* XXII (April 1981), 281-96.
5. Gerard K. O'Neill, *2081, A Hopeful View of the Human Future* (New York, 1982), especially 188-95, 224. See also his *The High Frontier: Human Colonies in Space* (New York, 1976).
6. "Moon Watching," *Commentary* (New York), XXXXVIII (October 1969), 84-86; Ralph E. Lapp, "Send Computers, Not Men, into Space," *New York Times Magazine* (Feb. 2, 1969), 40; Norman Cousins, "Moon Over Owerri," *Saturday Review of Literature,* Aug. 2, 1969, 16; 38; and "Giant Leap for Mankind?" *Ebony,* XXIV (Sept. 1969), 58; and Amitai Etzioni, *The Moon-Doggle, Domestic and International Implications of the Space Race* (Garden City, N.Y., 1964), particularly ch. 8; *Newsweek* (July 7, 1969), 40.
7. Lloyd S. Swenson, Jr., "The 'Megamachine' Behind the Mercury Spacecraft," *American Quarterly,* XXI (Summer 1969), 210.
8. Richard Bach, *Jonathan Livingston Seagull* (New York, 1970). See also his *Illusions: The Adventures of a Reluctant Messiah* (New York, 1977).
9. Richard Bach, *Nothing By Chance, A Gypsy Pilot's Adventures in Modern America* (New York, 1969); *Biplane* (New York, 1966); *Stranger to the Ground* (New York, 1963); *A Gift of Wings* (New York, 1974).

Index

A-frame pusher (model airplane), 119, 120
Aces, 11, 74-75
Addams, Jane, 85
"Aerial healing," 39-40
Aerial League of America, 54-55
Aero Club of America, 114
"Aerocar" (prototype), 109-10, 140
Air-Age Education, 113-15, 125, 127-33; airlines and, 129-33
"Air-Age Education" (textbook series), 125
Air-Age Education News (periodical), 130-31
Air-Age Education Research, Inc., 130, 132
Air cars, 102-4, 106, 107, 109-10
Air Cadets of America, 123
Air Commerce Department (Bureau of Air Commerce), U.S., 75, 80, 87, 98-104, 106-7
"Air Globe," 129, 130, 132
Air stewardesses, 89-90
Air Youth of America, 123-24
Air Youth Horizons (periodical), 124
Air World Education Program, 130
Air Circus (motion picture), 12
Aircraft (periodical), 40-41
"Airliner" (airplane), 40
"Airphibian" (prototype), 109-10
Airships, *see* Dirigibles
"Airways for Peace" exhibition, 107
Albany Flyer (airplane), 8
Albatross Model Aero Supply Shop (Newark, N.J.), 119

Aldrin, Buzz, 146
"Alti-man," 41, 147
America (airplane), 19
American Airlines: and aviation education, 129-32
American Association of School Administrators, 128
American Legion, 123
Amundsen, Roald, 15
Anderson, C. Alfred, 59-60
Apollo space missions, 141, 144, 146, 147
Armstrong, Neil, 146
Arnold, Henry H., 14
"Arrowbile," 102, 103
"Arrowplane," 101-2
Associated Press, 101
Atlantic (periodical), 38
Atlantic Ocean: first air crossing of, 14, 17, 54; Lindbergh's crossing of, 17-21
Atom bomb, *see* Nuclear weapons
Autogiros, 58, 102-4, 106
Aviation Education Research Group, 125

Babson Statistical Organization, 104
Bach, Richard, 146-47
Balkan War of 1912, 11, 38
Bamberger's department store (Newark, N.J.), 115
Barnstormers, 12-13, 16, 75
Battle of Britain, 124
Beck, Martin, 105-6

Beech Aircraft Corporation, 77, 96
Beechcraft (airplane), 71
Beecher, Henry Ward, 49
Bell, Alexander Graham, 32
Bendix Trophy air race, 71-72, 77,
    84-85
Bennett, Floyd, 15
Betsy Barton Cloud Club, 87-88
Betsy Ross Corps, 81
Bingham, Hiram, 57-58, 60-62, 69
"Birdmen" and "birdwomen," 9
Bishop, William (Billy), 11, 54
Black pilots, 35-36; "Good Will
    Flight" (1934), 59-60
Black Wings (Powell), 36
Blériot, Louis, 44
Boeing transports, 139
Bonner, Herbert C., 67, 68
Booker T. Washington (airplane),
    59-60
Born Again (Lawson), 40
Boswell, Florence H., 72
Brooks, Harry, 95
Brooks, Phillips, 49
Brown, Margery, 35
Bureau of Air Commerce, *see* Air
    Commerce Department, U.S.
Byrd, Richard E., 15, 17

Caldwell, Charles, 46, 47
Central Airlines, 80, 87
Century magazine, 33
Chamberlin, Clarence, 17, 19
Chanute, Octave, 5, 43
Cherrington, Ben, 131
China, Lindberghs' flight to, 82,
    142-43;
China Clipper, first flight of, 15-16,
    29
Christianity, 47-50, 52, 61, 136, 141
Civil(ian) Aeronautics Administra-
    tion, (CAA), U.S., 108, 123, 125,
    126
Civilian Defense, 126
Civilian Pilot Training Program
    (CPTP), 123
Clark, Bennett C., 66
Classroom Clipper (periodical),
    130-32
"Clipper" flying-boat, 15-16, 29
Cloud Rider (motion picture), 12
Cochran, Jacqueline, 82, 84-85; on

liberating aspect of flying, 85; and
    model airplane hobbyists, 114
Coli, François, 19
Collier's magazine, 75
Columbia University, 125
Commerce Department, *see* Air Com-
    merce Department, U.S.
Congress, U.S., aerial reserves bill in,
    123
"ConvAircar" (prototype), 109-10
Coolidge, Calvin, 21
Crosson, Muriel, 79-80, 83
Cue magazine, 108
Culver, Harry H., 58
Curtiss, Glenn H., 8-9; on future of
    flying, 43
Curtiss-Wright Aeronautical
    Corporation, 67, 86
Curtiss-Wright "Baby Bunting"
    (airplane), 118

Daniel Guggenheim Fund for the
    Promotion of Aeronautics, 22, 97-
    98, 121
Darwinism, 74
Davis, Dwight D., 61, 62
Davis, Manila, 75
Davis, Noel, 17, 19
Dawn to Dusk transcontinental flight,
    54
Dawn Patrol (motion picture), 12
Dayton (Ohio), Wilbur Wright's
    gravesite at, 63
deMille, Cecil B., 11-12
Detroit, model-making programs in,
    115, 117, 118
Dewey, John, 121
Dirigibles, 7-8, 15, 25
Doherty, Henry L., 71
Douglas transports, 139
Dunn, Rhoda Hero, 38
Durand, William F., 120

Earhart, Amelia, 61, 73, 74, 76, 82, 89,
    120, 122, 142-43; anti-female preju-
    dice and, 78; on aviation, 63-64; in
    Bendix Trophy race (1936), 71;
    career of, 72; dress habits of, 83; as
    feminist, 77-78 ,86-88; and model
    airplane hobbyists, 114, 118; tests
    Waterman "Arrowplane," 101; on

women as fliers, 81, 84; work in aircraft sales, 72, 76-78
Edhold, Charlton L., 38
Edison, Thomas A., 13
Education, *see* Air-Age Education; Model plane building; Schools, aviation education in
Elliott, Edward C., 122
Engalls, Laura, 71
Englehardt, Nikolaus, Jr., 130-32
England: attitudes toward flight in, 44-46; reactions to technology in, 155
English Channel: Blériot's crossing, 44; Quimby's crossing, 72
Ercoupe (airplane), 96-97, 110
Evans, Mrs. T. W., 56

Falcon's Civilian Air Corps, 123
Federal government: and aviation education, 125, 126; *see also specific agencies*
Flight (motion picture), 12
"Flight experience," 129, 132
Florence H. Boswell Flying Service, 72
Flyer, *see* Wright Flyer(s)
Flying (periodical), 38
Flying High (Aviation Education Research Group), 125
"Flying Is Changing Women" (Brown), 35
Flying Laboratory (airplane), 71
Flying magazine, 147
Fokker T-2, first non-stop cross-U.S. flight by, 14-15
Fonck, René, 11, 17, 19
Ford, Edsel, 94
Ford, Grace, 39
Ford, Henry, 15, 63, 94-96, 115
Forsyth, Albert, 59-60
Franklin Institute (Philadelphia), 63
Ft. Myer, Wrights' 1908 flights at, 3-4, 7-8, 21, 60
Furbay, John H., 130

Galt (California) High School, 122
Garvey, Marcus, 36
Geddes, Norman Bel, 105, 106
Geisse, Fred, 101
"General language" courses, 129

"George Washington Air Junction," 54-55
Germany, 122, 123
Gilbert, Clara, 87
Gilman, Charlotte Perkins, 39
Gimbel's department store (New York), 115
Gliders, Wright brothers and, 4-5
"Good Will Flight" (1934), 59-60
Gregory, Elizabeth Hiatt, 9-10
Guggenheim, Daniel C., 22
Guggenheim, Harry, 22
Guggenheim Fund for the Promotion of Aeronautics, 22, 97-98, 121

Hall, Norman, 50
Hambrook, Robert W., 124
Hammond Y-1 (prototype), 101-2
Harding, Warren, 14
Harmon, Clifford, 39, 58-60
Harper's magazine, 39
Harvard University, 122
Hearst, William Randolph, 10, 116
Helicopters, 91, 107-8, 110
Hell's Angels (motion picture), 12
Herrick, Myron T., 21
Hiller, Stanley, 91
Hinckley, Robert H., 124
Hobby shops, 119
Howard, Bennie, 71
Hoxsey, Arch, 9
Hughes, Howard, 12
Hughes, Raymond P., 105
Huffman's Prairie (Ohio), Wrights' flights at, 7
Human Geography for the Air Age (Aviation Education Research Group), 125

Ickes, Harold, 99
Immelman, Max, 11
"Influence of Aviation on Art" (MacDonald-Wright), 36-37
Institute for Space Studies, 143

"Jimmie Allen Club" (radio program), 116-17
Jimmie Allen Club News (periodical), 117, 118
Jimmie Allen Clubs, 117, 118

Johnstone, Ralph, 9
Jonathan Livingston Seagull (Bach),
146-47
Jordan Marsh department store
(Boston), 115
Josephine Ford (airplane), 15
Junior Aviation League (Newark,
N.J.), 118
Junior Birdmen of America, 116, 120,
122

Kaempffert, Waldemar, 37
Kelley, Florence, 85
Kelly, Oakley G., 14-15
Knox, Philander C., 37
Kresge's department store (Newark,
N.J.), 115, 118
Kitty Hawk flights, 5-8, 26; commem-
oration of, 52-53, 60-69, 141
Kitty Hawk Flyer, *see* Wright
Flyer(s)
Klingensmith, Florence, 78

Lafayette (Elizabeth, N.J.) Junior
High School Air Cadets, 121
Langley, Samuel P., 60, 157
Laufer, Berthold, 48
Law, Ruth, 73
Lawson, Alfred W., 35, 40-43, 147; as
"aerial commuter," 92, 93
"Lawsonomy," 40
League of Nations, 59
Lebaudy brothers, 7
Lehigh Portland Cement Company,
105
Lilac Time (motion picture), 12
Lilienthal, Otto, 4-5
Lindbergh, Anne Morrow, 82-83, 86,
143
Lindberg, Charles A., 12, 17-27, 42,
59-60, 75, 93, 97, 113, 119, 120, 127;
as barnstormer, 13; California to
St. Louis flight, 18; China flight, 82,
142-43; early life and career, 17-18;
marriage, 82-83; and model airplane
hobbyists, 114; New York to Paris
flight, 17-21, 73-74; reactions to feat
of, 21-27, 36
Listen, the Wind! (Anne Morrow
Lindbergh), 82
Lockheed Aircraft Company, 77

Lockheed airplanes: Earhart's and
Lindbergh's, 142-43; transports, 139
Loomis, Charles B., 33-34
Los Angeles: "Junior Airport" of,
115; plans for rooftop landing facil-
ities in, 104
Lynn, Dorothy, 81

McCormick, Harold F., 92-93, 100
MacDonald-Wright, Stanton, 36-37
McMahan, Harold, 57
Macready, John H., 14-15
Macy's department store (New
York), 110
Mannock, Edward, 11
Manufacturer's Aircraft Association,
63
Maughhan, Russell, 54
Maynard, Belvin M., 57
Model Airplane Club of the Air, 116
Model plane building, 16, 17, 113-20,
126; department stores and, 115-16;
girls and, 117-18; hobby shops and,
119; media promotion of, 116-18;
in schools, 114-15, 118; techniques
of, 119-20
Monocoupe (airplane), 77-78
Mono(coupe) Aircraft Company,
77-78, 96
Moore, Colleen, 11-12
Morrow, Dwight D., 82
Motion pictures, 11-12, 75

National Air and Space Museum,
141-43
National Aviation Day, 60; *see also*
Kitty Hawk flights–commemoration
of
National Museum of American His-
tory, 142
National Playground Miniature Air-
craft Tournament, 118
National Woman's Party, 87
National Women's Air Derby, 79, 83-
84
"Natural Prophecies" (Lawson), 40-
41, 92
NBC Model Airplane Club of the
Air, 116
NC-4, first cross-Atlantic flight by,
14, 17, 54

Nebraska, University of, 125
Nebraska Aircraft Company, 18
New York Aero Club, 53
New York Aeronautical Society, 72
New York Beaux Arts Institute of
    Design, 105-6
New York City: airport plans for,
    104; first flights in, 8; Lindbergh's
    welcome in, 22
New York *Evening Sun*, 95
New York *Herald Tribune*, 25-26, 49
New York *Times*, 8, 16, 51, 56, 64, 71;
    on Lindbergh, 24
New York *World*, 8, 9
New York *World Telegram*, 101
Newsweek magazine, 144
Nichols, Ruth, 75-76, 85, 86; dress
    habits of, 83; on liberating aspect
    of flying, 85-86; on women and
    aviation, 80-81, 86
99'er (periodical), 87-88
Ninety-Nines, 87-88
"Noble Experiment" (Thaden), 86
North American Review, 76
North to the Orient (Anne Morrow
    Lindbergh), 82
North Pole, first flight over, 15
Northrup, John K., 66
Noyes, Blanche, 72, 82, 89; and anti-
    female prejudice, 78-79; wins
    Bendix Trophy, 71; work in air-
    craft sales, 76
Nuclear weapons, 65, 69, 128, 132, 145
Nungesser, Charles, 17, 19

O'Donnell, Gladys, 82; and Jimmie
    Allen Club, 117
O'Donnell, James, 82
Office of Education (OE), U.S.,
    124-26
Omlie, Phoebe, 78, 82
Omlie, Vernon, 82
One World (Willkie), 128
O'Neill, Gerard K., 143-44
"Open skies" policy, 131
"Operations Institutes," 126
Orteig, Raymond, 17
Orteig prize, 17-19

Pacific Ocean, first commercial flight
    across, 15-16, 29

Pan American Airways: and aviation
    education, 129-31; first commercial
    flight to China, 15-16, 29; Good
    Will Flight (1926), 54
Parker, Mary M., 30-31, 42, 50
Phantom Flyer (motion picture),
    11-12
Phillips, Wendell C., 43
Physical Sciences in the Air Age
    (Aviation Education Research
    Group), 125
"Plymacoupe" (prototype), 100
Popular Mechanics (periodical), 91,
    110
Powell, William, 36
Public Works Administration
    (PWA), U.S., 99
Pulitzer Trophy, 16
Purdue University, 71, 122

Quimby, Harriet, 9, 35, 72-73

Raiche, Bessica, 72, 73
Ray, John, 102-3
"Red Baron" (Manfred von
    Richthofen), 11
Richey, Helen, 71, 80, 87, 89
Richfield Oil Company, 116-17, 122
Richthofen, Manfred von, 11
Rickenbacker, Eddie, 11, 26, 120
Rivera, Diego, 114
"Roadable" aircraft, 102-4, 106, 107,
    109-10
Rockefeller, John D., 35
Rockefeller, Laurence S., 123
Rockefeller, Winthrop, 123
Rodgers, Calbraith P., 10-11, 14, 29
Rooney, Mickey, 117
Roosevelt, Eleanor, 57, 85
Roosevelt, Franklin D., 16-17, 57, 64,
    98; and National Aviation Day, 60;
    and "open skies" policy, 131
Roosevelt, Theodore, 34, 35
Roosevelt, Theodore, Jr., 4
Roper, Daniel, 100
Russell, Frank H., 63
Ryan, Claude, 12-13

"Safety-plane" program, 99-104, 106
Saint Exupéry, Antoine de, 82

Samuel P. Langley medal, 60
San Diego *Union*, 14-15
San Francisco, plans for landing facilities in, 104
Santos-Dumont, Alberto, 7
Saturday Evening Post (magazine), 113, 114; survey of private plane ownership by, 108
Schneider Cup, 16
Schools, aviation education in, 114-15, 120-21, 124-33
Science of Pre-Flight Aeronautics for High Schools (Aviation Education Research Group), 125
Scientific American (magazine), 9
Scott, Blanche, 9
Seversky, Alexander, 66
Seversky Aircraft Company, 84
"Signal Corps I" (airplane), 156
Sikorsky Helicopter Company, 107-8
"Silver Wings of Peace," 58-59
"Skycar" (prototype), 109-10
Sky Parade (motion picture), 117
Sky Skidder (motion picture), 12
Smithsonian Institution, 60, 64, 65, 155-57; National Air and Space Museum of, 141-43; National Museum of American History of, 142
Southgate, Barbara, 81
Space flight, 141, 143-46
Spirit of St. Louis (airplane), 18-23
Squire, G. O., 37
Standard Oil of Ohio, 78-79
Stanford University, 122
Steel, Dudley, 116-17, 122
Stern Brothers department store (New York), 115
Stinson, Eddie, 73
Stinson, Katherine, 73
Stinson, Margaret, 73
Stix, Baer and Fuller department store (St. Louis), 115
Studebaker, John D., 109
Swaggert, Jimmy ("Brother"), 141

T-2 (airplane), 16
Taft, William Howard, 34, 37
Taylor, Moulton B., 140
Teachers: and Air-Age Education, 126-27
"Technological messianism," 46-47, 137, 155

"Technological utopianism," 46-47, 155
Temple, Shirley, 117
Thaden, Louise, 35, 72, 82, 89; dress habits of, 83; wins Bendix Trophy, 71, 77; on women and flying, 75, 80, 86, 87; work in aircraft sales, 76, 77
"Therapeutic Value of Flying, The" (article), 39-40
Time magazine, 130
Town and Country (magazine), 9-10
Travel Air Corporation, 77
Truman, Harry S., 67-68; and "open skies" policy, 131
Turner, Roscoe, 71
Tusch, Mary ("Mother"), 53-54, 142
TWA: and aviation education, 129-30
2081, A Hopeful View of the Human Future (O'Neill), 143-44

Ultralights, 140-41
United Airlines, 89-90
U.S. Air Force Association: and Kitty Hawk commemorations, 67-69
U.S. Army, 16, 156; first non-stop cross-U.S. flights, 14-15; and Wright brothers, 3-4, 6-8
U.S. Navy: first cross-Atlantic flight, 14, 17, 54; and model-building program in schools, 126

Vidal, Eugene L., 64, 75, 98-104, 106-7, 110
Vin Fiz (airplane), 10

Walker, James ("Jimmy"), 22
War in the Air, The (Wells), 44
Waterman, Waldo, 102-4
Waterman "Arrowbile," 102, 103
Waterman "Arrowplane" (prototype), 101-2
Weick, Fred, 96, 97, 101
Wells, H. G., 44
Western Flying (periodical), 121
"When We Fly" (Gilman), 39
White Bird (airplane), 19
William and Mary, College of, 122

Williams, Roger Q., 26
Willkie, Wendell, 128
Wilson, Gill Robb, 49
Wilson, Woodrow, 34, 94
"Wings" (Edhold), 38
"Wings of War, The" (Wyatt), 44-45
Women's Home Companion (magazine), 108
Women Air Service Pilots (WASPS), 89
Women pilots, 35, 71-90, 108; "aerial domesticity" doctrine and, 81, 84; dress of, 83-85; in earliest exhibitions, 9; and feminism, 76-78, 86-88; jobs available to, 76-78; marital status of, 81-83; number of, 72; stereotyping of, 76, 78-80, 83-85; and World War I, 73; and World War II, 88-89
Women's Air Derby, 79, 83-84
Women's National Aeronautic Association, 64
Won on the Clouds (motion picture), 12
Woodhouse, Henry, 38, 54-55
World Congress on Air Age Education, 130

World War I, 11, 38; women pilots and, 73
World War II, 124; effect of, on "winged gospel," 65-68; women pilots and, 88-89
Wright, Orville, 3-5, 7-8, 13, 21, 157; on future of flight, 43-44; and Kitty Hawk commemorations, 61, 63, 64; on World War II, 66; *see also* Wright brothers
Wright, Wilbur, 3, 5-8; death of, 63, 68; *see also* Wright brothers
Wright brothers, 3-9, 26, 29, 43, 72, 114, 127, 155-56; commemorations of Kitty Hawk flights, 52-53, 60-69, 141; Ft. Myer flight trials (1908), 3-4, 7-8, 21, 60; Kitty Hawk flights, 5-8, 26, 157
Wright Exhibition Company, 9
Wright Flyer(s) (*including* Kitty Hawk Flyer), 3-8, 52-53, 64, 142-43, 155-57
Wyatt, Harold F., 45

Yale *News*, 33
"Youth and Aviation" conference (1930), 124